Spinoza: Then a

Antonio Negri

Spinoza: Then and Now

Essays Volume 3

Translated by Ed Emery

polity

Polity Press
65 Bridge Street
Cambridge CB2 1UR, UK

Polity Press
101 Station Landing
Suite 300
Medford, MA 02155, USA

ISBN-13: 978-1-5095-0350-6
ISBN-13: 978-1-5095-0351-3 (pb)

A catalogue record for this book is available from the British Library.

Library of Congress Cataloging-in-Publication Data

Names: Negri, Antonio, 1933- author.
Title: Spinoza : then and now / Antonio Negri.
Description: Cambridge, UK ; Medford, MA : Polity, [2019] | Series: Essays
  ; volume 3 | Summary: "In this book, renowned theorist Antonio Negri
  examines how Spinoza's thought constitutes a radical break with past
  ideas and a key tool for envisaging a form of politics beyond
  capitalism. His philosophy gives us new ways of looking critically at
  our present, revealing that power must always be seen as a question of
  antagonism and class struggle"-- Provided by publisher.
Identifiers: LCCN 2019011789 (print) | LCCN 2019980272 (ebook) | ISBN
  9781509503506 (hardback) | ISBN 9781509503513 (paperback) | ISBN
  9781509503544 (epub)
Subjects: LCSH: Spinoza, Benedictus de, 1632-1677. | Spinoza, Benedictus
  de, 1632-1677--Political and social views. | Power (Philosophy)
Classification: LCC B3999.P68 N4445 2019   (print) | LCC B3999.P68   (ebook)
  | DDC 199/.492--dc23
LC record available at https://lccn.loc.gov/2019011789
LC ebook record available at https://lccn.loc.gov/2019980272

Typeset in 10.5 on 12pt Plantin by
Servis Filmsetting Ltd, Stockport, Cheshire
Printed and bound in Great Britain by TJ International Ltd

For further information on Polity, visit our website: politybooks.com

Contents

Author's preface: Two histories for Spinoza   vii

Part I   Spinoza in 1968

1   Starting from Masaniello ... Deleuze and Spinoza, a
    political becoming   3

2   Spinoza and Deleuze: The good moment   16

3   Joyous Spinozists   25

Part II   Spinoza Today

4   Spinoza: *Another* power of action   35

5   Concerning the concept of multitude   47

6   Reflections on the immaterial: Spinoza, Marx ... and
    today   59

7   Spinoza, necessity and freedom: Some interpretational
    alternatives   72

8   Justice: Spinoza and others   88

9   A small note on fear in Spinoza   103

10   Hatred as a passion   114

Part III   Spinoza in the Seventeenth Century

11   Politics of immanence, politics of transcendence: A
    people's essay   127

12 Rereading Hegel, the philosopher of right   138
13 Problems of the historiography of the modern state:
    France 1610–1650   154
14 Considerations on Macpherson   194
15 Reflections on Grossmann and Borkenau   203
16 Notes on the history of politics in Tronti   221

Bibliography   228

Author's preface

Two histories for Spinoza

This is my fourth book of writings devoted to Baruch Spinoza (1632–77). The previous volumes were *L'anomalia selvaggia* (originally published in 1981; see Negri 2006a), *Spinoza sovversivo* (1992), and *Spinoza et nous* (2010). This is a body of work that, in a nutshell, seeks to relate Spinoza to two historical episodes: the period around 1968 (and up to the present), when the recovery of Spinoza's thought made it possible to re-establish the idea of democracy and the common; and a second history, that of Spinoza in the seventeenth century, where the Spinozist break with the liberal political paradigm immediately became a sign of freedom and indicated a path towards constructing democratic order in the modern period – a path that differed from the bourgeois and capitalist path.

In Part 1 I bring together three essays in which, through a critical reading of a number of authors, I suggest that we might see '68 as a 'good moment', propitious to the operation – conducted by a number of 'joyous Spinozans', thanks to Spinoza's thought – of affirming democratic thought and of encouraging struggles open to the desire for happiness. The studies by Matheron, Deleuze and Gueroult, followed shortly by those of Macherey, Balibar and Moreau as well as by my own, were fundamental to that moment. This is true in particular of Matheron's work, which opens three new strands in Spinozist research: one of time, duration and eternity; another of *potenza* [power] and action; and yet another of the relationship between the body and the mind (as suggested by Chantal Jacquet). It would be possible to produce an extensive commentary on each of these themes and to follow their development by Matheron and his students. But here I need only emphasise how materialism, seen through the epistemological and ontological lens of Spinozism, was able to abandon its traditional foundation in dialectic and to embark on a project that was simultaneously constitutive and subjective. Thus Spinozism corresponds to a call for insurrection and to the new figure of class struggle that, from 1968 on, was no longer willing to squeeze through metaphysical straits towards teleological destinations.

It is interesting that Matheron's analysis achieves these political objectives through extreme philological rigour. It is not by chance that Matheron is mentioned as a student of Gueroult's, a distinguished example of philological prowess. But he was nobody's pupil: his philology has an autonomous soul and renders political the bifurcation that Spinoza introduced into modern philosophy. This same bifurcation was also present in the philosophy of 1968, where Spinozism was reborn in opposition to Heideggerism, implementing political realism in the face of the mysticism that had been the end point of the metaphysics of modernism and of Schmittian cynicism in political thought. Here I wish to stress the importance of the rediscovery of Spinoza in the 1960s and 1970s: in the exit from traditional Marxism, it was Spinozism that rejected all the variants, strong or soft, of *Krisis* thinking. Instead of celebrating, with a modicum of angst, the need to return to order and to submit to the crude exercise of the economic weapons of capitalism, instead of accepting a conception of being in which the memory of a time of struggle could be erased, one could begin to reconstruct a revolutionary perspective on the terrain of Spinozism, because – as Matheron and his pupils taught – being is a *dispositif* for the destruction of sadness, desire is a *dispositif* of collective construction of freedom and joy, and absolute democracy (in other words, the democracy of struggles) is the only conceivable form of freedom and equality.

Thus I have outlined the general horizon in which my work on Spinoza took shape. In the first part of the present collection I retrace the elements of this general perspective, examining in particular the relationship between Spinoza and Deleuze. I emphasise that this relationship was fundamental in creating the fabric on which Deleuze and Guattari enacted (between *Anti-Oedipus* and *A Thousand Plateaus*) the critique of contemporaneous capitalism; in their reading of Spinoza we find a verification of his rupture with the historical and philosophical tradition. On the one hand, the Deleuzian reading had the merit of asserting the *potenza* of singularities against the ethics of individualism and against the totalitarianism of commodities consubstantial with bourgeois culture. This is what the spirit of May 1968 (and of the following years) sought to abolish, and the work of Deleuze and Guattari represented a weapon to that end. On the other hand, in the context of the new readings made at the time, the malicious definition of Spinoza's ontology contrived by Hegel and designed to normalise the subversive power of Spinoza's work was set aside. Spinoza's world was supposedly acosmic, and characterised by temporal immobility. Actually Spinoza seems to ignore the word 'time': the fact is that he transforms the traditional metaphysical definition, according to which time is a measure. He opts for time-life [*tempovita*]; he fixes this concept between lived reality and the imagination. For Spinoza, time does not exist except as liberation. And the liberated time is 'productive imagination' rooted in ethics as a capacity to create being. Liberated time is neither becoming nor dialectics nor mediation – it is being that is constructed, dynamic creation, imagination realised. Time is not measure but ethical action. Thus imagination discloses hidden dimensions of Spinozist being – that ethical being that liberates new production. There is, then, no utopia in Spinoza, just as there is no teleology. *There is the world as it is.* I propose here to speak of disutopia, by which I mean the capacity to derive, from within contingency, the relation between the difficulty of living and the dynamic of emancipation, and yet also – and above all – the passion to follow the traces of the *potenza* of being and to carry out the never-ending project of organising the infinite.

In Part 2 ('Spinoza Today'), I address problems related to a number of Spinozist concepts that have found a new life in our contemporary world: concepts such as 'the *potenza* to act', 'multitude', 'necessity' and 'freedom', 'immateriality', as well as other, more familiar concepts such as justice, love and hate. The rereading of these concepts in a Spinozist light opens new possibilities for understanding the present, which began and was defined after 1968, then developed in postmodernity. The Spinozist lexicon and ontology give us access to novelties that the end of modernity presents, and also to the often equivocal figures of postmodernity. To those who are interested, I hope to offer here new critical openings to complement the effort to understand the present that I attempted to develop in my more recent books – especially those written together with Michael Hardt (*Empire*, published in 2000, *Multitude* in 2005, *Commonwealth* in 2011 and *Assembly* in 2017).

Part 3 of the book ('Spinoza in the Seventeenth Century') gives us another history, no longer in the present but in the past: the seventeenth century. The materials I offer to the reader represent the historiographical presuppositions of my work on seventeenth-century political philosophy, on the birth of political modernity, and on Spinoza and Descartes. Here I focus on the historical assumption of a 'bifurcation' that governs the political philosophy of the modern age. My research from the 1960s onwards started from the realisation that, already in the moment of primitive accumulation (typical precisely of the seventeenth century), nascent capitalism was traversed by powerful contradictions. After the crisis of Renaissance culture, which had reached its peak at the end of the sixteenth century, the anxious desire for liberation, born in humanism and nourished by the reformed and Protestant sects, would soon be crushed by the reborn dogmatism of the churches and by the affirmation of the absolute monarchical state. The Netherlands in the seventeenth century (that period known as the 'golden age') was in the midst of a dramatic confrontation between democratic movements and the aristocratic elites who wanted to transform the republic into a monarchy. Resistance was harsh, and the transition to absolute monarchy that took place in the rest of Europe clashed here with an efficient force of opposition. The people's passion, the capacity for economic success and the spirit of solidarity, freedom and equality were firmly rooted in the Netherlands. And Spinoza's political thought (powerfully expressed in his metaphysics) was produced and lived in that libertarian anomaly. For Spinoza, freedom is wild, indomitable, and as luminous as Rembrandt's light. I republish in this volume an article written in 1966, 'Problems of the historiography of the modern state: France 1610–1650', which analyses the birth of the modern state. In this article I show how the humanist Renaissance had expressed a radical revolution in values and how, in the first half of the seventeenth century, the emergence of the modern individual, the emergence of productive singularities and the first images of their collective essence came up against insurmountable obstacles. In countries such as France, where absolute monarchy imposed its order, the bourgeoisie restructured itself through crisis, through a negative dialectic that opposed it to the state – to that monarchical state that it certainly supported and developed, defending it against those who wanted to destroy it (for instance the never-ending popular uprisings of the time), but that it failed to appropriate to itself. In the Netherlands and, later, in England during the Glorious Revolution, it was, on the contrary, the resistance and the republican alternative that were on the front lines of the struggle to define the form of the state. Spinoza should be read in the context of this history, because he is an expression of it.

About ten years before my book on Spinoza, I had written a book on Descartes (*Descartes politico o della ragionevole ideologia*, originally published in 1970; see Negri 2006b). But the historical framework I

evoked at that time was the same: the Thirty Years War, the peasant
jacqueries, the economic and political crisis and, throughout all this, the
growth of the bourgeoisie and the consolidation of royal absolutism.
The historians whom I referenced in that text were Boris Porshnev,
Lucien Febvre and Roland Mousnier. In the appendix to the English
translation of this piece (2006b, pp. 317–38), I substantially updated
the historical references. In this context, Descartes represents an
acceptance of the present, the tormented internalisation of the defeat
of the Renaissance and of the hopes of the bourgeoisie; he represents
it by constructing an indefinite horizon, a relative mediation with the
absolute, on the certainty of truth proved by doubt. He knows that
free inquiry has been annihilated: Galileo was the latest victim of this
process. Descartes was thus left with only the hope of freedom. His
doubt expresses the *potenza* of a consciousness ready to enter into
a relationship of mediation with the world – *if the world opens up*.
With Descartes we enter into the time of interiority, of consciousness
defeated, of recourse to a God who is transcendent and solitary – and
of a 'rational' compromise with the absolute power of the monarch.
Descartes represents the ideology of a bourgeoisie nostalgic for the
potenza of its own humanist genesis, a bourgeoisie that had sought
power and, with a realistic awareness of having been defeated, was
now willing to negotiate with the absolute state. Spinoza, by contrast,
embodies the historical anomaly of a resistant freedom.

It seems to me that I have deepened the analysis of the bifurcation between the absolute state and republican democracy that has
dominated modernity and from which we still suffer. Now Spinoza
(together with Machiavelli and Marx) represents a line of political
immanentism that opposes critically the line of political transcendence represented by Hobbes–Rousseau–Hegel. This is *potenza* versus
potere [power], immanence versus political transcendence: 'For a free
multitude is guided by hope more than by fear, whereas a multitude
which has been subjugated is guided more by fear than by hope.
The first want to cultivate life; the second care only to avoid death'
(Spinoza, *Political Treatise*, ch. 5: 6). *Potenza* thus asserts itself here
against the religion of a sovereignty founded on fear – as would be
the case in Hobbes – but also, implicitly, against the illusion of an
abstract and transcendent political representation of the multitude –
as will be the case in Rousseau; and against any dialectical apology,
à la Hegel, for a civil society that is individuated as a moment of
the absolute. The great clash between these two lines, represented
at its peak by the opposition between Spinoza and Hobbes, is to be
found in the debate on contractualism, that is, on the hypothesis of

a contract-based genesis that lays the basis of political association
and thus pushes humanity out of the state of nature. The Hobbesian
contract hands over to the sovereign a relationship of domination
that takes away all rights – save the preservation of life – from the citizens who adjudicate the contract. In Spinoza, on the other hand, the
contract is conceivable only as an abstract hypothesis – on the contrary, the fact of association is itself what produces the government,
or rather the engine of the development of a democratic government, defined as *omnino absolutum imperium* [power absolute in every
respect]. Democracy is the absolute expression of the political, and
the multitude organises itself spontaneously into a democracy.

> No, the object of government is not to change men from rational
> beings into beasts or puppets, but to enable them to develop their
> minds and bodies in security, and to employ their reason unshackled;
> neither showing hatred, anger, or deceit, nor watched with the eyes of
> jealousy and injustice. In fact, the true aim of government is liberty.
> (*Theological–Political Treaty*, ch. 20: 6)

Against the social contract of the liberals, which expropriates the
autonomy of the citizen with the value of labour, Spinoza – like
Machiavelli before and Marx after him – conceives of the democratic
multitude as the base and the motor of free political life. In opposing
the Machiavelli–Spinoza–Marx line to the Hobbes–Rousseau–Hegel
line, I feel that I have not done much more than renew the secular proposal, dear to the Enlightenment, of the value of political knowledge
– a proposal that affirms democratic radicalness, presents itself as
an open temporality undoing identities, individualism and private
property, and therefore asserts a republican and democratic passion.

A small parenthesis regarding Hegel. I should explain why, at this
point in the collection, I have inserted the essay 'Rereading Hegel,
the philosopher of right'. This is an article written in 1967 in which
I distanced myself from Hegel, although he had been a major focus
of my studies during my first years of philosophical research. Indeed,
my PhD thesis (published in Italian in Padova, in 1958) bore a title
translatable as 'State and law in the young Hegel'. The research for
it was accompanied by an Italian translation of two early writings by
Hegel, which I published under the title 'Le maniere di trattare sci-
entificamente il diritto naturale' ('The scientific modalities of treating
natural right') and 'Sistema dell'eticità' ('The system of ethics') in
the volume G. W. F. Hegel, *Scritti di filosofia del diritto* (Laterza:
Bari, 1962). I thought it would be appropriate to document in the

present volume, in chapters 12 and 13, my rethinking of Hegel in the decade that followed, as an indication of the intensity of my break with metaphysical idealism and bourgeois political cynicism. Indeed, distancing myself from Hegel meant placing myself in a philosophical *Kampfplatz* [place of struggle] in which Spinoza was to be my support in the discovery of the concept of absolute democracy.

The essays gathered in Part 3, in addition to illustrating the historical antecedents of Spinoza's thinking about the state, open the way to a series of comparisons with theoretical positions in Marxism that have accompanied my researches into the seventeenth century. The chapters on Macpherson, on Borkenau and Grossmann, and on Tronti belonged originally in the Italian edition of my *L'anomalia selvaggia* (Negri 1981), as appendix material. The appendix did not appear in the 1991 English translation (published under the title *The Savage Anomaly*) and was not subsequently reprinted. But these writings mark important polemical moments along my Spinozist path. They say 'no' to any transcendental, mechanist, or transcendent conception of power – respectively as in Hobbes, as in Grossmann (i.e. according to the dictates of economic determinism), or as in Tronti's later writings (i.e. expressed in terms of 'the autonomy of the political'). Power can be neither analysed nor defined in these terms; the history of power is always that of an antagonism, its nature is a nature determined by class struggle. All unitary conceptions of power are pure metaphysics, and every metaphysical idea is always invented or constructed for the purpose of founding and exalting power. 'Politics of immanence, politics of transcendence', the chapter that opens Part 3, provides an introduction to the great bifurcation of the seventeenth century, summarises it and projects it forward to the present day. From that point on, one is compelled to take sides.

Paris, December 2017

Part I

Spinoza in 1968

1
Starting from Masaniello ...

Deleuze and Spinoza, a political becoming

On being revolutionaries

Other than here, I have written about Deleuze's relationship with Spinoza in 'Gilles Felix' (published in *Marx and Foucault*, Polity, 2018) and in 'Spinoza and Deleuze: The good moment' (chapter 2 in this volume). It was a relationship that exploded in political form in 1968, when Deleuze took Spinoza on board as a symbol of the revolution of desire. Now, as we know, 1968 is the year in which Deleuze also met Félix [Guattari]. It was the right moment for making a break with structuralism by developing a radical critique of psychoanalysis. From there began a journey characterised by the desire to go beyond working on concepts only, but also to base his analysis on a theoretical and practical conception of the unconscious as a machine. What was the reason for this radical reorientation of his philosophical efforts? Deleuze replies: it's the fact that we are in a state of revolution. *Anti-Oedipus* and *A Thousand Plateaus* are the books in which Spinoza becomes a political revolutionary. Let us reread this famous passage in *A Thousand Plateaus*:

> After all, is not Spinoza's *Ethics* the great book of the BwO [body without organs = *CsO, corps sans organes*]? The attributes are types or genuses of BwO's substances, powers, zero intensities as matrices of production. The modes are everything that comes to pass: waves and vibrations, migrations, thresholds and gradients, intensities produced in a given type of substance starting from a given matrix. [...] It is a problem not of the One or the Multiple but of a fusional multiplicity that effectively goes beyond any opposition between the one and the multiple. [...] The BwO is the *field of immanence* of desire, the *plane of*

consistency specific to desire (with desire defined as a process of production without reference to any exterior agency, whether it be a lack that hollows it out or a pleasure that fills it). (Deleuze and Guattari 2004, pp. 170–1)

For ten years, the actor of this revolution of desire 'is Spinoza in the garb of a Neapolitan revolutionary' (Deleuze and Guattari 1982, p. 28 = 1999, p. 37): Spinoza = Masaniello.

How does this symbolic typology come to be established? We will not understand it if we stay glued to the letter of the text and generally fail to raise the matter of the context of these statements. How is the life in which they are inscribed? What does 'being revolutionaries' mean in 1968? It means bringing about what the 'resistance' against fascism and the military victory of 1944 had promised but had not achieved: liberating the passion for freedom and joining it with the passion for what is common; dismantling all the repressive and fascistoid structures of society and building new 'forms of life'; getting one's hands on the capitalist machine and submitting it to the desire for human happiness. 'The real problem of revolution, a revolution without bureaucracy, would be the problem of new social relations where singularities come into play, active minorities, in a nomad space without property or enclosure' (Deleuze 2004, p. 145 = 2002, p. 201).

We need to make the concepts materialise and to understand how they were proclaimed among militants in the course of struggle. This is because, for Deleuze and Guattari's interlocutors, the liberation of desire meant the construction of a new democracy, the end of capitalism, the renewed development of social life, and the invention of a new system of production. Deleuze and Guattari are militants. They don't care about Marcuse, or about Freudian Marxism – they want to talk in the movement and to the movement. Deleuze's preface to Guattari's *Psychanalyse et transversalité* is a discourse on this going 'beyond' Freudian Marxism, beyond Reich, to a place where the *libido* does not empty itself into the negative but is constructed in the social:

It is indeed a question of libido as such, as the essence of desire and sexuality: but now it invests and disinvests flows of every kind as they trickle through the social field, and it effects cuts in these flows, stoppages, leaks and retentions. To be sure, it does not operate in a manifest manner, as do the objective interests of consciousness or the chains of historical causality. It deploys a latent desire coextensive with the social field, entailing ruptures in causality and the emergences of singularities, sticking points as well as leaks. The year 1936 is not only an event in historical consciousness, it is also a complex of the unconscious. Our love affairs, our sexual choices, are less the by-products of a mythical Mommy-Daddy, than the excesses of a social reality, the interferences and effects of flows invested by the libido. (Deleuze 2004, p. 194 = 2002, pp. 271–2)

Deleuze and Guattari's interlocutors are the young people of the Mouvement du 22 Mars [Movement of 22 March 1968], anarcho-communists, or the organisations and groups that break with the French Communist Party and with Trotskyism on libertarian terms. It is towards these groups and their militant experience that the dis-course of Deleuze and Guattari reaches; but it also delves deeply into those experiences and behaviours. The *Anti-Oedipus* continuously forges togther the intensity of the militant groups, the experiences of liberation, and critical work. Intensity and compositional differences, organisational slogans, analysis of the dynamics of nomadism, of micropolitics, of sexual liberation, and so on are concepts and prac-tices pulled out from the life of groups. The idea was to build a toolkit [*boîte à outils*], and to build it *for them*.

What does Spinoza offer for the preparation of this toolkit? It seems to me that he offers the concept of revolutionary institution. This proposal is the unique mechanism [*dispositivo*] that Deleuze and Guattari offer to the movements of '68. It is an 'abstract machine' that allows one to imagine, and eventually to cause to function together, both insurrection and institution and that unites them in representing a demand for power and a transformation of life. In this figure there come together the immediacy of *conatus* [striving] and the all-encompassing dynamic of *cupiditas* [passion], the corporeal mater-iality of *appetitus* [longing] and the tension of *amor* [love] – these are passion-related modes that do not designate processes but con-stitute mechanisms and promote the ontological consistency of the advancement of passions. For revolution is not only an uninterrupted continuity, but a repository of institutions and the development of freedom. Deleuze and Guattari draw from the Spinozist geometry the design of a continuous movement of affects and of their consistency in bodily intercrossings. Spinoza or the 'revolutionary institution' – therefore Deleuze and Guattari are not anarchists, they are commu-nists who want to describe and organise the movement of liberation. Here the constructive phylum of the 'abstract machine' recovers and organises the wealth of the desiring world and puts it into pro-duction. As in Spinoza, the theory of passions becomes a course of action. Thus *Anti-Oedipus* is within the great rhizome that was built by 1968. This helps us to understand that Spinoza in the uniform of a Neapolitan revolutionary is not a caricature and that he must be understood in this light, as producer of a revolutionary institution of desire.

The revolutionary institution of desire

Spinoza has a commanding position in the development of the *Anti-Oedipus*. First of all, in the struggle against the mystification that Oedipus imposes – the situation where the productivity of desire is shut within a development that downgrades desire to a 'need due to lack' and considers it dominated by a 'miraculous' force, which expropriates its productivity. 'Refuge of ignorance', as Spinoza would say, '[c]apital is indeed the body without organs of the capitalist, or rather of the capitalist being' (Deleuze and Guattari 1982, p. 10). 'The body without organs now falls back on [*se rabat sur*] desiring-production, attracts it, and appropriates it for its own' (ibid., p. 11); it reduces it to a production of ghosts – precisely the point of triumph of the idealist principle that defines desire as a lack and not as a production. But desire resists and produces reality. The pages in *Anti-Oedipus* that surround the sentence about 'Spinoza in the garb of a Neapolitan revolutionary' – of Masaniello – build the factory, *l'usine du désir* ['the worshop of desire']. They are a summary of Books III and IV of Spinoza's *Ethics*. And, as in *Ethics*, the appearance of an act of social repression of the expression of desire does not interrupt it but stimulates its production. What is being proposed here, in Spinozist form, is a real process of ontological constitution. Desiring machines organise themselves as technical social machines; the desiring production transforms itself into social production; in short, desiring machines are both technical and social (ibid., pp. 36–7). This is where their principle and the beginning of their 'becoming institution' lie, because they are not given only as sparks of becoming but also as tendencies, continuities of their self-making. Here Spinoza is represented as the revolutionary intellectual rather than as Masaniello; he plays the Marxist, toys with the law of the falling rate of profit (ibid., p. 33), and moves within the social institution of revolutionary desire. If the reason for the collapse of capitalist development is in this development itself, then Spinozist *cupiditas* can operate savagely on the destruction of the capitalist order, when we look at its destiny from the point of view of desire.

And yet desire emerges from the fray, proposing itself as an institution regulated in freedom, through an infinite process of liberation – as construction of being.

Two observations. The first one starts from an objection raised by Serge Leclaire. He says: 'In my opinion, you yourselves have disarmed your desiring machine, which should work only by breaking down, through its failures and backfires: whereas thanks to this "positive" object and the absence of any duality, as well as any lack, it is going to work like... a Swiss clock!' (Deleuze 2004, p. 222 = 2002, p. 309).

Is this not a paradoxical accusation of 'Spinozism' (when Spinoza is read in the Hegelian way) raised against the revolutionary institutionality of desire? The answer comes from the new figure that Spinoza acquired in Deleuze's reading – which is here claimed not simply as a product of the ethical Spinoza, but as an ontological effect. Deleuze and Guattari are faithful Spinozists on the ontological terrain, while Leclaire's objection brings us back to that classical image of a God-Nature (irreducible multiplicity of attributes – infinity of ways), which was brusquely overturned in the 'Neapolitan' reference to the whole BwO. Not without reason, Deleuze reminds us of a proposition by Gueroult that he cited when rejecting Leclaire's objection: 'On two occasions, moreover, Gueroult uses the term "motley" [*bigarré*]: God is simple insofar as he is not composed of parts, but no less complex insofar as he is constituted by *prima elementa*, which alone are absolutely simple; God is thus a motley *ens realissimum*, not a pure, ineffable and unqualifiable *ens simplicissimum* in which all differences would disappear'; 'God is motley, but unfragmentable, constituted of heterogeneous but inseparable attributes' (Deleuze 2004, p. 150 = 2002, p. 209). Here is another observation, this time by François Châtelet – who, in the fabulous discussion of the *Anti-Oedipus* organised by Maurice Nadeau, recognising the Lucretian stamp of the book's materialism, exclaimed: 'Anyway, if I call it a materialist eruption, I'm thinking primarily of Lucretius' (Deleuze 2004, p. 220). Not only Lucretius, not only Nietzsche, not only Marx: it is the whole revolutionary tension of modernity, summarised in Spinoza and projected onto 1968, that is found here in the work of Deleuze and Guattari.

'After all, is not Spinoza's *Ethics* the great book of the BwO?'

What we have seen developing in the *Anti-Oedipus* so far is proof enough. However, even at the time, [in 1972,] the problem was shifting. In *A Thousand Plateaus* we are no longer looking to relate every attribute to substance. The problem is no longer that of the one and the multiple, but that – as we have seen – of the multiplicity of singularities that fuse, overcoming every opposition of the one and the multiple. This is the point at which the comparison of Deleuze to Spinoza – and the revival, among his militant writings, of *Spinoza et le problème de l'expression* (and now also of *Spinoza: Philosophie pratique* – and it matters little that it was published a while later) – is more direct. However, at that moment Deleuze and Guattari had not yet shed the dress of Masaniello, of the Neapolitan revolutionary; indeed, a rather extremist breeze was blowing. And here are the drug addicts, masochists, schizophrenics and lovers, all invited to pay tribute to Spinoza. Spinoza dominates the passage in which the BwO that capital has invested and voided of substance, has turned from full to empty, revolts and recognises the greatest *potenza* [power] in its own rest. A classic dialectical gesture, a Kojève moment? Absolutely not; rather an absolutely Spinozist moment. I give an example that I draw from the thinking and practice of 'workerism' [*'operaismo'*]. Here we have the worker, completely drained by his work at the Taylorist machine, crushed by the weight of an unbearable working day, frustrated by low wages and the impoverishment of desire. The worker revolts, and this revolt has the fullness of a very radical rejection, which cannot be absorbed by a new mediation: it is labour's 'refusal of work'. The same *potenza* is expressed by the revolt of the BwO. It is the BwO in revolt that reveals the field of immanence – or rather the plane of consistency proper to desire – that organises itself here as a process of production.

A new revolutionary event:

> a rereading of *Héliogabale* and *Les Tarahumaras*. For Heliogabalus is Spinoza, and Spinoza is Heliogabalus revived. And the Tarahumaras are experimentation, peyote. Spinoza, Heliogabalus, and experimentation have the same formula: anarchy and unity are one and the same thing, not the unity of the One, but a much stranger unity that applies only to the multiple. (Deleuze and Guattari 2004, p. 175)

This is because, in order to constitute itself, the 'field of immanence = plane of consistency' has to traverse a chaotic terrain, which is itself traversed by confused and contradictory agents. A fierce, perpetual and violent battle is in progress to free the BwOs from the organism, from the signifier [*dal Significante*] and from subjectivation – to make it into a place, a plane, a collective in which desire resides. It asks for a solution. We shall return to this passage.

But let me try to answer the question raised in this paragraph: what does Spinoza actually have to do with the *machines désirantes* – the desiring machines? One can answer that, first of all, the *Ethics* is grounded in the same ontological fabric. The characteristics of this foundation are: a full univocality of being, a positive ontology of immanence, degrees of intensity, and *potenze* that structure attributes and modalities along their continuous conversion. Equally, in *Anti-Oedipus* and in *A Thousand Plateaus* this ontological background has priority. In a movement that resembles the game of the BwO, the attribute is revealed at zero intensity in order to express fully the productive matrix that is proper to it. And here, on these matrices, scroll the infinite modes, or 'everything that happens'. It is no longer the one and the multiple, but a fusion that overflows them both. And, secondly, that ontology is traversed by the logic of imagination. It, too, overspills the chaos of reality and moves across a conceptual vegetation that the 'common notions' describe and put in motion. True information, effective communication and common virtuality give wings to the mental *conatus* so that it may orient desire and lead it to practise an affirmative ethic of *potenza* in a world of singular and active bodies. With a third and final movement, we enter that field where the simultaneity of actions of the body and passions of the mind is finally given: *idem natura et mens* [mind and nature are one]. This is a human horizon where the modes find, in self-regulation, the cooperation of individual things and of affects, and that opens itself to the politics of the common – of the multitude and of democracy. Here the 'unconscious as machine' of *Anti-Oedipus* and the 'revolutionary institution' of *A Thousand Plateaus* are the presupposition – the 'abstract machine' – that opens to history the movement of desire.

Between ethics and ethology

Hence Spinozist ontology pervades the entire space in which capitalism, or the world of capital, is crossed by schizoanalytic critique.

This does not change the fact that, when we arrive at the conclusion of this analysis, we perceive that the overlap between Spinoza and the positions of Deleuze and Guattari is incomplete and that a touch of bitterness, not to mention a certain anguish, follows this realisation.

BwO is the egg, the zero intensity as the principle of production. But this principle is undifferentiated.

> The BwO is desire: it is that which one desires and by which one desires. And not only because it is the plane of consistency or the field of immanence of desire. Even when it falls into the void of too sudden destratification, or into the proliferation of a cancerous stratum, it is still desire. Desire stretches that far: desiring one's own annihilation, or desiring the power to annihilate. Money, army, police, and State desire, fascists desire, even fascism is desire. (Deleuze and Guattari 2004, p. 183)

Furthermore, the aporia had already been announced in the *Anti-Oedipus*: 'This is why the fundamental problem of political philosophy is still precisely the one that Spinoza saw so clearly, and that Wilhelm Reich rediscovered: "Why do men fight *for* their servitude as stubbornly as though it were their salvation?"' (Deleuze and Guattari 1982, p. 29 = 1999, p. 38). The anxiety is evident when one tries to go beyond the drift to non-differentiation. And the salvation that follows, again, from the appeal to the great 'abstract machine' seems entirely precarious:

> the identity of effects, the continuity of genera, the totality of all BwO's, can be obtained on the plane of consistency only by means of an abstract machine capable of covering and even creating it, by assemblages capable of plugging into desire, of effectively taking charge of desires, of assuring their continuous connections and transversal tie-ins. Otherwise, the BwO's of the plane will remain separated by genus, marginalised, reduced to means of bordering, while on the 'other plane' the emptied or cancerous doubles will triumph. (Deleuze and Guattari 2004, p. 184)

It is therefore imagined that the 'abstract machine' is, under these conditions, still capable of developing its own *potenza*. This is a problematic passage, to which I shall return.

Take note: when Deleuze and Guattari say 'machine', they do not speak metaphorically ('We do not start from a metaphorical usage of the word machine, but from a (confused) hypothesis concerning origins: the way in which heterogeneous elements are determined to constitute a machine through recurrence and communications; the existence of a "machinic phylum"', Guattari 2008, pp. 91–2). The machine consists of recurring and communicating elements. The tools and the human are linked, in the constitution of the machine, by a machinic phylum. This phylum, this machinic dimension is, in the definition of the machine, more important than any instrument (*outil*, tool) that composes it. The machine always precedes the tool. All this is to conclude that '[d]esiring-machines are not in our heads, in our imagination, they are *inside the social and technical machines themselves*' (Guattari 2008, p. 106).

The final pages of the *Anti-Oedipus* (Guattari 2008, pp. 109–15 = Deleuze and Guattari 1999, pp. 484–8) summarise, from four different points of view, the definition of the desiring machine and conclude its design by fully integrating the desire with the machine. It is in maintaining this interiority of the machine that, according to the *Anti-Oedipus*, modernity is defined. To the exaltation of machinism in Italian futurism, to the insistence on the collective force of machines in Soviet constructivism, to humanist anti-machinism, Deleuze and Guattari then oppose the 'Dadaist molecular machinery, which, for its part, brings about a reversal in the form of a revolution of desire, because it submits the relations of production to the trial of the parts of the desiring machine, and elicits from the latter joyous movements of deterritorialization that overcome all the territorialities of nation and party' (Guattari 2008, pp. 114–15). This is how the political proposal of the *Anti-Oedipus* concludes – a formidable request for freedom of desire that get nevertheless blocked, in the absence of any definitive constructive capacity.

In the passage from the *Anti-Oedipus* to *A Thousand Plateaus* this lack becomes more acute: the insufficiencies or the absence of the 'great machine' will follow the opening of the horizon of the war. And the non-pacified indeterminacy of the desiring machine will be followed, always anew, by the ironic and distressing parable of the Dadaist.

Yet two consequences follow, and they are not insubstantial. In the first place, in this crisis of the desiring machine, one has to grasp the ability to narrate the transformation of the capitalist mode of production that occurred in the decade 1970–80 – the same decade that saw the publication of *Anti-Oedipus* and *A Thousand Plateaus*. The work of Deleuze and Guattari perceives that transformation and makes it internal to philosophical research – a profound transforma-tion, which, when one seeks to analyse it with precision, prevents one for example from keeping the 'forces of production' divided from the 'production relations' the way Marx did:

> For man and the tool are already components of a machine constituted
> by a full body acting as an engineering agency, and by men and tools
> that are engineered (machines) insofar as they are distributed on this
> body. (Guattari 2008, p. 110 = Deleuze and Guattari 1999, p. 483)

The influence of Foucault is clear here. The forces of production,
the working classes, are thus inside the machine; they constitute
its parts and are transformed along with the transformation of the
machinery. Deleuze and Guattari read the transformation of labour
in the 1970s and follow its further development and entry into the era
of general intellect.

Secondly, while they read Spinoza, Deleuze and Guattari proceed
as trackers of what was changing in life, in work, and in the human
sciences for those who had critical experience of them. Trackers of
the *post-*, the postmodern as much as the postindustrial. What opens
to their understanding is a world of precarious networks and connections, of communicative uncertainty and expressive richness – a
world where the construction of the existent undergoes the assault
of an irresistible multiplicity. Here, however, the mobility of affects
seems to turn upside down, into a confusion of affects, and it seems
that the surplus, the excess that in Spinoza characterised the progression from *appetitus* to *amor*, can no longer be grasped.

So, between *Anti-Oedipus* and *A Thousand Plateaus*, Deleuze and
Guattari do not complete their reading of Spinoza but seem to exhaust
his trail, the ontological phylum, opening the *Ethics* to ethology:

> Affects are becomings. Spinoza asks: What can a body do? We call the
> *latitude* of a body the affects of which it is capable at a given degree of
> power, or rather within the limits of that degree. *Latitude is made up
> of intensive parts falling under a capacity, and longitude of extensive parts
> falling under a relation.* In the same way that we avoided defining a
> body by its organs and functions, we will avoid defining it by Species
> or Genus characteristics; instead we will seek to count its affects. This
> kind of study is called ethology, and this is the sense in which Spinoza
> wrote a true *Ethics*. (Deleuze and Guattari 2004, p. 283)

Ethologie = naturalisation?

But is this transition to ethology conclusive?

Let me return to those two points in Deleuze and Guattari's discourse that seemed to be problematic – if not aporetic – in their
encounter with Spinoza. The first is when, revealing themselves to

be impossible to synthesise, anarchy and unity form an uncertain network of the multiple, on whose ground takes place the struggle for the reterritorialisation of desire. In other words insurrection and institution are made to merge into a single ontological perspective, which does not produce univocal compositions (as in Spinoza's *Ethics*) but accentuates their scattered nature. The second point is when the 'abstract machine' is given the task of making up for the presence, or rather hegemony, of elements of undifferentiation: and here the reference to Spinoza no longer really holds, because in Spinoza, whether the abstract machine exists or not, the ontological fabric is such that every way of being is qualified and different, singular and powerful. The immanence of the singularity is the infinite, an infinite that is actual, ordered, real in the highest degree [*realissimum*].

Now, it is claimed (for example in Sharp 2011) that, in order to solve these difficulties, Deleuze renews his reading of Spinoza, admitting that the problem of undifferentiated multiplicity is impossible to solve by reference to the abstract machine, unless one goes back, from the hypothesis of the dynamism of the (abstract) machine, to the position of a generic foundation, static and easily differentiated according to gradients of being – instead of assuming, like before, that its *potenza* is constitutive of new adventures of being. Here is where nature can reappear. It is called in aid: a horizontal and flat machine, a surface of modal substitutions, flows of human and animal bodies.

This important modification of Deleuze's reading of Spinoza would have taken place in *Spinoza: Practical Philosophy* (Deleuze 1988b = 1981). Let us then follow in this matter Hasana Sharp, who considers the notion of an 'ethological' ethics to be useful for underlining a genuine alternative that Spinoza might offer to Deleuze's difficulties, through a renaturalisation of human existence. Here is how Sharp explains this transition:

> Ethology demands a patient and tentative prudence that entails experimentations and 'the construction of a plane of immanence or consistency'. Rather than internalising an apparatus of principles that will be valid on every occasion and in every situation, ethology constructs and organises a plane, a flat horizon of action and passion. As obscure as this may sound, with the notion of the 'plane of immanence', Deleuze suggests that there is only one order of being. Thus, there is no superior aspect of the self, or realm of being, that might order the other part. There is no rational principle that ought to command the 'natural', corporeal, affective, or sensuous aspect of oneself or the world. The plane of immanence expresses an ontology with a 'flat geography'. The plane of immanence, what he sometimes calls the

'univocity of being', names a horizontal field of powers and counter-powers that can be arranged from within in more or less enabling ways from the perspective of distinct agents, or 'degrees of power', but that cannot be directed from without to reflect an external or higher principle. (Sharp 2011, p. 214)

And she concludes: 'As Spinoza's *Ethics* progresses, God "disappears" into nature and we are left with an infinitely complex but flat horizon of being' (ibid., p. 215).

Can this solution hold, if we reconsider the political becoming of Deleuze and Spinoza? I do not think so. If indeed it is correct to argue, with Deleuze, that ethics has nothing to do with morality and that Spinoza 'conceives it as an ethology, that is, as a composition of fast and slow speeds, of capacities for affecting and being affected on this plane of immanence' (Deleuze 1988b, p. 125); if this definition relieves us from the worry of having to solve the problem of undifferentiation; and if we must in consequence accept Deleuze's conclusions – namely:

> In short, if we are Spinozists we will not define a thing by its form, nor by its organs, nor as a substance or a subject. Borrowing terms from the Middle Ages, or from geography, we will define it by *longitude* and *latitude*. A body can be anything. It can be an animal, a body of sounds, a mind or an idea; it can be a linguistic corpus, a social body, a collectivity. We call longitude of a body the set of relations of speed and slowness, of motion and rest, between particles that compose it from this point of view, that is, between *unformed elements*. We call latitude the set of affects that occupy a body at each moment, that is, the intensive states of an *anonymous force* (force for existing, capacity for being affected). In this way we constitute the map of a body. The longitudes and latitudes together constitute Nature, the plane of immanence or consistency, which is always variable and is constantly being altered, composed and recomposed, by individuals and collectivities. (Ibid., p. 171)

– then we cannot stop here. For Deleuze goes on to clarify that there are two opposite conceptions of production and of plane. The first:

> Any organization that comes from above and refers to a transendence, be it a hidden one, can be called a theological plane: a design in the mind of a god, but also an evolution in the supposed depths of nature, or a society's organization of power. [...] It always has an additional dimension; it always implies a dimension supplementary to the dimensions of the given. (Ibid., p. 128)

[The second:]

> On the contrary, a plane of immanence has no supplementary dimension; the process of composition must be apprehended for itself, through that which it gives, in that which it gives. It is a plane of composition, not a plane of organization or development. (Ibid.)

Now, this last plane is exactly the one that the *machines désirantes* built and that the BwO released. There is no 'extra dimension' to it, but only *potenza*.

In Deleuze's interpretation of Spinoza there is no 'ethological' way out that could remove the machinic and artificial character nature has retained from divine essence. Neither can nature be reduced to an 'ethological flatness' without holding (and expressing) ethical power. One has to 'renaturalise' the world of Spinoza, as Hasana Sharp and others have done: the resonant political urgency that Spinoza's voice expresses on this terrain is compelling and very strong, freeing us from the tiresome catastrophisms that we hear all around – but without forgetting that renaturalising Spinoza's world will always reposition nature in continuity with divine action, and hence with human activity. Ethology does not remove the *Ethics*. The machine – the great desiring machine – recomposes in a dynamic and creative way the one and the multiple, the effect and the doing, insurrection and institution. Renaturalising the world will not be something different from 'remechanising' it.

What is certain is that Spinoza (in Deleuze's reading) is never abandoned to an ethological drift – if ethics is not a morality, it is nevertheless always a constitutive ontology. The decade of revolt was followed by the winter of restoration; Masaniello was laid to rest (killed, as is customary in real revolutionary events). And yet the abstract machine remains, and the virtuality of the desire for revolution is always there – and of the 'virtual' it will not be said that it is 'possible', but simply that 'it is'. 'We will say of pure immanence that it is A LIFE, and nothing else. It is not immanence to life, but the immanent that is in nothing is itself a life. A life is the immanence of immanence, absolute immanence: it is complete power, complete bliss' (Deleuze 2001, p. 27). Spinoza and Deleuze raise this virtuality as a challenge to all of us. So Masaniello never disappears: he may be less coarse and violent – but he is still there. And he is that unconscious and insurrectional machine of desire that is always standing up against the father, the good and power [*Potere*].

2

Spinoza and Deleuze

The good moment

It was a good moment when, with '68 in the offing, Deleuze began to write about Spinoza. At that time, as we know, Deleuze was working on *Difference and Repetition*. He had arrived there influenced by Bergsonism, by trying to discover, in the flow, a prospective opening, a determination in movement, and thus to show the productive force of difference. It has been said that at this point his philosophy defined itself as 'an ontology of the virtual' – where 'the virtual is not actual, but possesses, as such, an ontological reality that contests and exceeds every logic of the possible' (Alliez 2004, p. 106). So, to demolish the logic of the possible (of *dunamis*, and of the act, and of the cause that connects them), was it sufficient to focus on the Bergsonian principle that time is not space and work around that?

At first glance, it seems that Deleuze simply wants to multiply the Bergsonian effect. In fact the conclusion of his piece *Le Bergsonisme* (originally published in 1966) ends as follows:

> at the outset we asked: What is the relationship between the three fundamental concepts of Duration, Memory and the *Élan vital*? [...] It seemed to us that Duration essentially defines a virtual multiplicity. [...] Memory then appears as the coexistence of all the *degrees of difference* in this multiplicity, in this virtuality. The *élan vital*, finally, designates the actualization of this virtual according to the *lines of differentiation* that correspond to the degrees. (Deleuze 1988a, p. 112)

But it is not that simple, and for Deleuze it is not enough. He then discovers himself as a philosopher of the concrete, of ontological determination. He asks: How realistically does one harden virtuality, maintaining its imaginative power but stripping it of any categorial fixity? And any function or idea of simulacrum or of representation? Before 1968, Bergsonism might well have served to weaken the solid scaffolding that structuralism had offered to the organisation of philosophical thought in the period after the Second World War. However, it was no longer sufficient for obtaining the effects that Deleuze now proposed, in the earthquake that he sensed approaching. Structuralism, as Deleuze reminds us, had set in place a project to neutralise *potenza* [power], which consisted in fixing static relations with the real and rigid topologies of conceptual space and in describing a differential relationship of symbolic functions and serial movement of the structure, and which then presented itself in the colouring of the structural relationship as 'unconscious'. How to break with all of this? How to break with that attempt to neutralise *potenza* and to exorcise difference? If a new reading of Bergson had introduced us onto this terrain, there still remained much to do – first of all, guarantee the immanence of the ontological ripping [*strappo*] that the virtual marks out.

It is here that the presence of Spinoza imposes itself overwhelmingly, alongside that of Duns Scotus and Nietzsche. Whereas in Duns Scotus – as Deleuze tells us – being and its univocity are thought of neutrally, without paying heed to the finite or the infinite, and in Nietzsche difference manifests itself as an unfinished paradox of a principle in the process of becoming, it is only in Spinoza that univocal being is the object of a pure affirmation – and substance is an expressive *potenza* – whose degrees are intensities of being and whose modes are singular entities. What had been said of duration, memory and vital impetus (*élan vital*) as concepts can and must now be recovered 'from below', where the aporias of the subject and the object are overcome and where the field of immanence presents itself as life.

Deleuze takes on Spinoza as a 'ferryman' who could get him out of structuralism and as an architect of that vitalistic fabric inherited from Bergson – or rather, to which Deleuze had found himself to be destined by Bergson. Now, the project was accomplished because, following Spinoza, vitalism is ordered – and this works to replace the rigidification of the structuralist universe – and expressive – and this means that the potentialities [*potenze$_2$*], expressing themselves as desiring singularities, remove the residual metaphysical conditions of Bergsonism. Deleuze thinks that Spinoza's ontology is self-expressive. It is possible to grasp it, not in the manner of an objective order, but in the form of an active, living thought, in movement. Whether or not inspired by Gueroult (as Deleuze himself declares in his reflection on Gueroult's Spinozist work), this approach moves from the interpretation of the first eight propositions of Part I of the *Ethics* to show how substance is not and cannot be transcendent to itself, since, by being made up of an infinity of attributes, it constitutes production of itself, a genealogy that is continually renewed, a consistency that the modes describe in actuality. The duplication of origin, when it is maintained in a causal relationship, is removed; what remains is expression, self-expression. Therefore onto-theology, be it pantheist or panenteist, and both the alternatives that traverse it and the consequences that are drawn from it, no longer have any subsistence here.

This is also a good moment for Spinoza. At the edges of '68, Spinoza's immanentism ceases to be related back to theological definitions (pantheist or panentist: this is how the historical–philosophical tradition had neutralised it and modernity's critique had exorcised it). It should be noted immediately that the expressive univocality that Deleuze rediscovers in Spinoza is not an interpretative exploit; rather it is verified by a new generation of readers – Gueroult, Matheron, Macherey, and so on. What is Deleuzian in this going beyond structuralism? There is the fact that, where pantheism and structuralism were determinist, Deleuze stresses how little Spinoza's ontology is determinist; and this in the name of the univocity of being, which – considered radically – diffuses substance in the intensity of the modes. Thus any residual, Cartesian distinction within substance is abolished, so that the attributes themselves are unspoken and the modes (expressing themselves as if they were God expressing himself) display the freedom that characterises and fills the univocal activity of being.

From this derive effects that are entirely remarkable. Ontologically, the univocity of being overflows substance, transforms it into a transcendental field, into a plane of absolute immanence, on which – from an epistemological point of view – the idea, or rather the mode, in which thought expresses itself adequately through its own determinations must not subject itself to any external order. The 'common notion' should be defined as fusion of true information and effective communication, fusion of an act of knowledge and of common virtuality. And, finally, here is an anthropological level: the world of finite modes, where the self-regulation of modes, of singular things, is situated on a par with the organisation of human affects.

Thus a new materialist conception of the body takes shape in Spinozist anthropology. Spinoza says: 'no one has yet determined what the Body can do' (Spinoza 1985: *Ethics* III, Proposition 2). But let us begin to discover it – against the pre-eminence of the Mind that Descartes had proposed – given that 'the order of actions and passions of our body is, by nature, at one with the actions and passions of the mind' (*Ethics* III, Proposition 2, Note). Deleuze comments: 'the order of actions and passions of our body is, by nature, at one with the order of actions and passions of the mind' (Deleuze 2010, p. 200, citing *Ethics* III, Proposition 2, Note). But here there is a new detachment, because this simultaneity of passions and actions demolishes, in the very ambit of experience, every isolation of thought, and the self-affirmation of being does not even refer to the determination of attributes any more, but is given directly in the unique modalities of existence. The logic of expression thus reveals itself as 'practical philosophy'. Expression is the immanence of thought (of experience and of affect) in nature, and the path of expression immerses itself into nature, building an act, forms of life, and an ethos that are concrete. This process is desiring; 'practical philosophy' is not a reflexive withdrawal of thought into action but the very machine that gives organisation to the development of action. Reason is not a separate *potenza*, it is born as an emotional cell of every action: desire is an action implanted on the simultaneity of thought and affect.

This is how Deleuze was able to get out of that 'structure without structure' into which he feared that *Difference and Repetition* had locked him. To succeed, thought had to be productive again. But it could only be productive when body and mind held each other tightly.

At this point Deleuze meets Félix Guattari: 'I was working only in concepts, and still very timidly. Félix talked with me about what he was already calling desiring machines: a theoretical and practical conception of the machine unconscious, the schizophrenic unconscious. So I felt that he was ahead of me' (Deleuze 1972, p. 47). But his work on Spinoza was also moving ahead, and it was only on that ground that advances could now be made: a place where the body and the mind are absolutely assimilated, where being is no longer order but production of order, multiplicity of ways, fusion of events, in other words *potenza*.

'Body without organs!' Deleuze wonders aloud: 'After all, is not Spinoza's *Ethics* the great book of the BwO?' (Deleuze and Guattari 2004, p. 170). And he answers:

> The attributes are types or genuses of BwO's substances, powers, zero intensities as matrices of production. The modes are everything that comes to pass: waves and vibrations, migrations, thresholds and gradients, intensities produced in a given type of substance starting from a given matrix. [...] It is a problem not of the One or the Multiple but of a fusional multiplicity that effectively goes beyond any opposition between the one and the multiple. [...] The BwO is the *field of*

immanence of desire, the *plane of consistency* specific to desire (with
desire defined as a process of production without reference to any exterior agency, whether it be a lack that hollows it out or a pleasure that
fills it). (Deleuze and Guattari 2004, pp. 170–1)

This is where immanence and infinity become a life.

But let us return to Spinoza. That broadening of the anthropology of freedom – from ontology to the movement of the passions
– brings about a further opening: an opening towards politics. Here
too, through Deleuze and through many others (but with Deleuze in
a fundamental way), one discovers the extent to which, in Spinoza,
sovereign absolutism is fought against or, better, annihilated through
philosophical – and democratic – polemic. From this perspective,
Hobbes' metaphysical utilitarianism – which the standard interpretation assimilates to that of Spinoza – is instead swept away by
Deleuze's critique: if 'Hobbes and Spinoza both conceive the act
of reason as a process of addition, as the formation of a whole; for
Hobbes it is a calculation, for Spinoza it is rather a composition of
relationships that is an object of intuition' (Deleuze 2010, p. 206).
Intuition: when Deleuze recovers this function of intelligence from
Bergson, he immediately recognises its productive power. Intuition is
a method. When we resort to it, we recognise that 'the real is not only
that which is cut out [*se découpe*] according to natural articulations or
differences in kind; it is also that which intersects again [*se récoupe*]
along paths converging toward the same or ideal point' (Deleuze
1988a, p. 29). And then, to affirm that for Spinoza the act of knowledge is intuitive implies that the political act does not determine a
renunciation of natural law; on the contrary, it produces a powerful
development of it.

Let me underline that, whenever we say 'natural law' in Spinoza,
we should immediately add that here 'natural law' does not mean
production of norms, as it does for Hobbes, but rather production
of 'forms of life'. In Spinoza as in Machiavelli, norms are part of, are
included in, the forms and are expressed in the experiences of life; so
it is not as in Hobbes, where the forms of life are always produced
by norms.

When, in Part IV of the *Ethics*, Spinoza (1985) builds the concept
of a *cupiditas* that 'cannot have excess' (Proposition 61; a really
bizarre way of reading the law of nature!) and places this desire in a
certain dimension of eternity (Proposition 62, Demonstration), we
find in the crescendo of the subsequent Propositions, from there up
to the conclusion of Part IV, how this '*cupiditas* that has no excess' is

pushed towards the refoundation of a 'common life' in the state. It is a concept of the state (*civitas*) viewed as rejection of solitude and as estalishment of a life based on common decision, *ex communi decreto*. The definition of democracy as collective free life under the rule of reason is therefore looked at from some kind of 'eternal' [*sc.* objective] perspective, *sub quadam aeternitatis specie*. But eternity, *species aeterna*, is itself productive; it is a motor and a multiplier that are productive. Deleuze comments:

> if two individuals make up their relationships in their entirety, they naturally form a twice as large individual who has a right of nature twice as large: the state of reason does not exaggerate and does not limit the state of nature, leads it to a power without which it would remain unreal and abstract. (Deleuze 2010, p. 207)

In defining productive cooperation and the consequent multiplication of the value of labour, Marx uses almost the same words that Deleuze finds in Spinoza when he defines the surplus value of political association. But we can proceed even further – because in Spinoza the 'common' is not simply *civitas*, the state, in other words an expansion of sovereignty (of public law) – it is that process that grows on the desiring *potenze₂*, from the self-valorisation of singularities, from singular claims, up to that right of the common that is absolute; politically, it expresses itself as an 'other' of and from sovereignty, and thus as a product of the 'absolute democracy' of the multitude.

A non-sovereign democracy? The ambiguities of this reading can be numerous. However, here 'democracy' is no longer that third specific form of government management – equivalent to monarchy or aristocracy or both – that the classical tradition has handed down to us. Thus we can read in a completely different light what Spinoza constructs as a conclusion at the end of his political thinking:

> To man, then, there is nothing more useful than man. Man, I say, can wish for nothing more helpful to the preservation of his being than that all should so agree in all things that the Minds and Bodies of all would compose, as it were, one Mind and one Body; that all should strive together, as far as they can, to preserve their being; and that all, together, should seek for themselves, the common advantage of all. From this it follows that men who are governed by reason – i.e., men who, from the guidance of reason, seek their own advantage – want nothing for themselves that they do not desire for other men. Hence, they are just, honest, and honorable. (Spinoza 1985: *Ethics* IV, Proposition 18, Note)

So then: Deleuze's reading represents a favourable moment for the integration of Spinoza into contemporary philosophical and political debate. With it all the repetitions of the 'theological–political' refrain in the definition of power are eliminated – both in the sense of justification of sovereignty (of its legitimacy, of its admittance of exception) and in the opposite sense, when the demythologising critique inspired by Weberian *Entzauberung* [disenchantment], albeit sacrificing those justifications, in the final instance retains them implicitly, as an object of analysis.

This last tendency is as perverse as the former was at one time, because, in the post-Weberian critique of the secularisation of power or in the apology of its desacralisation, it nevertheless repeats and alludes to the hypothesis of a foundation [*fundamentum*] to sovereignty that is not visible as a theory and not solvable, and thus *numinosum* [numinous], as a problem. But this is still the 'theological–political' that Spinoza's *Tractatus* tries to destroy, thereby constituting a definition of democracy that is irreducible to sovereignty.

I would therefore say that in Spinoza the constituent theme of the passions, the Machiavellian realism implicit in treating history and antagonism as the essence of the political, and the 'absolute' character of democracy constitute a synthesis that projects its vision of the political in a perspective that, today, can be considered essentially *biopolitical*. By biopolitical I mean – following here the indications of Michel Foucault – the manner in which power relations invest life and at the same time make it the object and the *enjeu* [stakes] of their application; and the manner in which this very life – the ways of life, the types of existence, the form of cooperation (in short, life in its material and historical determinations) – responds to the power that assumes it as an object, affirming its productive *potenza*, its excedence, its irreducibility. To this radical conception of democracy is added, as I have already mentioned, the overstepping of every individualistic conception of the social bond. The multitude lies in fact at the base of absolute democracy; and the multitude is the opposite of solitude. In the modern tradition, the individual should move from solitude to social plurality through a supposed contractual process whose conceptual grain is woven into the most fantastical connections and into the most illusory ideological *dispositifs* to be found in modernity. Spinoza rejects the contractual hypothesis – he could not do otherwise, because that thinking is negative. He conceives of the contract as a renunciation of *potenza* and as a flight from the fullness of life, as an experience of deathly neutralisation. Now, on the contrary, Spinozist individuals do not think of death. Their tension in relation to the other, towards social constitution, is not based on fear of death but on a will for joy.

Deleuze has grasped with great force this positive constitution of singularity, this naturalist and antagonist conception of *conatus* [striving]. It determines an affirmative process (a common increase in the *potenza* to act and in the common development of joyful passions) as a tendency of the real – and this means persevering in existing and acting under the guidance of reason in the common constitution of the city.

Once, while I was interviewing Deleuze, he told me: 'I think Félix Guattari and I have remained Marxists' (Deleuze 1995, p. 171). I always doubted the truth of this and suspected that *La Grandeur de Marx*, supposedly his last work, was a myth. I believe that what Deleuze meant was, we have always remained communists. But it is clear that their communism was precisely the construction of a common that went beyond the categorial simulacrum or the fetishism of natural common goods; it rather interpreted the self-valorisation of singularity within the multitude and the composition of the common as an 'eternal' project of production and of life.

One last point. I have talked quite a bit about a 'good moment' for both Spinoza and Deleuze, and I have interpreted this event as the making of a common name for oneself: the affirmation of a desire that cannot know excess and the constitution of the common – an encounter with ontological effects. Let us therefore ask ourselves whether there cannot be, in the meeting of great philosophical authors, a moment in which the common names, generated and ascertained in the theoretical project, represent an expression of *kairos* [the right time]. Here an arrow, shot by Spinoza, reaches Deleuze. This *kairos*, when that encounter is defined and when a name becomes common [between the two], unveils an increase in being. The common name gathers and promotes new singularities, new *potenze*; and at this interpretative intersection the common notion then finds a new thickness.

The *potenza* of the 'good moment' has found here full expression, and imagination supports its expression: a constructive projection of being towards the future. In this case, in the relationship between Baruch Spinoza and Gilles Deleuze, that common notion of democracy is shifted from the community of the episteme to the ontological common. The common name of democracy is thus a powerful trace that unites interpretative events in the construction of a community to come. Insisting again on the *potenza* of interpretation that has determined this opportune moment, we may perhaps also be introduced to a further modality of being, when the intersection of reasonable passions builds what we call praxis.

30 April 2011

3

Joyous Spinozists[*]

In Italy this book is anomalous. In schools and universities the old schemas of idealist and pantheistic interpretation continue to be churned out. The work of deprovincialising Spinozism energetically pursued by Emilia Giancotti remained limited in its reach, although many young people are now in favour of renewing it. By contrast, in France (and also in Germany, England, and Spain, not to mention the United States) things are moving in a different direction. There this book would not be anomalous; it is part of the best writing there is on the subject of Spinoza's philosophy. To explain this situation without going further into the profound backwardness of Italian Spinoza studies, I shall examine the following two points: first, the refoundation of Spinoza studies in the period around 1968; and, second, an illustration of how much and in what way Laurent Bove's book is inserted into and completes a new hermeneutic tradition of joyous Spinozists.

Spinoza was reborn in France in the years around 1968 as a reference point for a number of responses to the crisis of structuralism. In 1968, Deleuze and Matheron published their fundamental contributions. Writing through and against structuralism, they find in Spinoza the affirmation of a radical plan of immanence and a launchpoint for the reconstruction of the acting singularity. When we speak of the crisis of structuralism, we speak about something that involves, to various degrees, all the philosophers of Rue d'Ulm. The figures most

* SOURCE: Originally published as preface to Laurent Bove, *La Stratégie du conatus: affirmation et résistance chez Spinoza* (see Bove 1996). The preface was then published in French in 2004, in *Multitudes* 17, under the Italian title 'Spinozisti gioiosi' (visit http://www.multitudes.net/Spinozisti-gioiosi).

strongly engaged in the critique of structuralism, albeit on opposing fronts, are Althusser and Foucault, but behind them can be seen Lacan and Canguilhem. They are all united in their criticism of that secular figure of Marxism, structural methodology, in their exposure of its ready-made interpretation of history. In short, the analytical *dispositif* of 'base–superstructure' was radically called into question, and words and things had to be understood as relating to each other without reference to the vulgar notion of reflection. Structuralism was perhaps the last form of dialectic, and it was presented as a perverse game in which knowledge, ethics and politics were always referred back to another explanation, which was in turn referred back to another. Structuralism had constructed an inverted figure of dialectic and had proclaimed its extinction, but was in fact one of its latest instantiations. Spinoza was the opposite. The philosopher was rediscovered as an author of absolute immanence, of the impossibility of separating what life has united, of the recognition that the real knows neither sublimation nor teleology of any kind. Philosophy had to restart from here, from Spinoza, from the plane of immanence.

But how does one move inside immanence? How can ontology be articulated? Could Spinoza give a helping hand to defining not only the plane of immanence, but the new movements and the original pulsations of being? The generation that followed the rupture of 1968 – a generation that included Deleuze and Matheron but developed more than anything from the side of a critique of Marxism put forth by people who nevertheless considered it an achievement of thought – this second generation (that of the likes of Balibar, Macherey and Moreau) raised questions about the movement of immanence. The experience of being became a fundamental theme. It appeared to be the old spiritualist pathway: but what a difference in their analyses between, say, Moreau and Alquié! In Moreau's Spinoza, experience is lived precisely inside, from within – any transcendence is definitively cancelled; it is an experience that is material, alive. And Alquié's old Sorbonne philosophy, with its metaphors, its profundities, its inspirations, is swept away. In the poststructuralist experience of being, the forms of ontology will be rather those configured by the movement of ontology itself, the devices of immanence, the *dispositifs*, the concatenations [*agencements*], the active articulations of ontology. With Moreau's (1994) book on the experience of being in Spinoza, the plane of immanence is completely rearticulated as an ontological fabric of singularity or, better, of the subjective *potenze* [powers] that recompose life. Eternity becomes an experience that produces and constructs a *telos* [end] on every mode of being.

In the continuity between the first and a second generation of new Spinoza scholars, there thus emerged a new image of Spinoza, as a *hero of immanence* and as an *artisan of the movement of immanent being.* Accordingly, readings of Spinoza began specifically to raise a series of new themes and new lines of interpretation. I may list some of these as follows:

(a) An ontological deepening of the line *conatus–appetitus–cupiditas–amor* [striving–longing–passion–love]: the steps of the composition of being are now interpreted as different and continuous forms of a *potenza* that invests the world, constructing it and articulating it.

(b) Another fundamental point in the new foundation of Spinozism is that which presents imagination as a *filum* [thread] that integrates the different forms of power into knowledge. Imagination is no longer simply tied to sensible knowledge; it is recognised in rational knowledge and exalted in the divine intellect. Beyond the overcoming of idealist dialectic, we see here the overcoming of the dialectic of forms of knowledge. Imagine what this might have meant in the seventeenth century, when the whole of classical philosophy was exercising itself around forms of knowledge that were epistemologically limited!

(c) Then the relationship between attributes and modes in Spinozist metaphysics comes once more into play on this basis. Attributes begin to seem like empty forms in an ontology that makes itself increasingly into a world of bodies and singularities, where the modes become the true subjects of the real drama. It is on this terrain that Balibar grasped the familiarity of 'singularity' in Spinoza and of the dynamics of Simondon's 'transindividual' – an experiment that shows the complete blurring of attributes in the hybrid modes of singularity.

(d) And it is in this way that the contemporaneity of Spinoza comes to the fore. He constructs for the ontological machine an imagination formed on the expressivity of being, an ethical common organised by the convergence between passions and intelligence, an immanence moved by the eternal multiplicity of modes… and one could continue at length in describing the radical novelty that the new Spinozist interpretation has introduced into the reading of Spinoza, shaping his impact on the literature of contemporary thought.

Thus far I have discussed the metaphysical themes that the new critique has introduced. Now I need to list the themes of political

philosophy that found a place in the new readings of Spinoza, in line
with the first point. Spinoza innovates in the conception of natural
law and refuses the bourgeois proposal to found the passage from
natural law to positive law on elements of transcendence. On the
contrary, he affirms that between natural law and positive law there is
a constructive sequence of *potenze*. With this we are on a terrain that,
as well as standing radically against modern and Hobbesian conceptions of the absolutist state, constructs an alternative that remains
valid for the contemporary world. Against the state of dominion
there arises in fact absolute democracy, a democracy without representation, democracy as an expression of the multitude. This is
how much Spinoza innervates the political questions of the contemporary world! Here, in this reference to the *potenza*$_2$ [potentiality]
of political thought and to the radical nature of the experiment in
theoretical revolution, he represents a rational tendency implanted in
the future. (Spinoza also represents the centre of a philosophical line
that traverses modernity, contesting the hegemony that the thought
of transcendence and sovereignty had enjoyed in it: he closes the
virtuous circle that runs from Machiavelli to Marx; he builds an alternative to the perverse movement of modernity that runs from Hobbes
to Hegel – and here we have another way of reading Spinoza.)

To sum up and round off this first point, I can therefore say that
today Spinoza presents us with a philosophical position that is articulated by (a) a positive ontology of immanence; (b) a constructive logic
of the imagination; and (c) an affirmative ethic of *potenza*$_2$. Having
said this, I can now integrate the position, by saying that (d) this
positive ontology of immanence of which I have spoken is in reality a
theory of the constitution of bodies, an active phenomenology of the
embodiment of the mind – and also (e) a theory, or an ontological
and political praxis of cooperation of bodies and singularities; and (f)
a politics of the multitude is born on these presuppositions, where
metaphysics therefore finds itself uncovering an ontological *thread*
that stands at the base of the resistances that constitute the surface of
the political world.

The rediscovery of Spinoza since the late sixties thus opens a
series of fundamental problems, all concentrated around the theme
of defining materialism today. But it is a materialism renewed by
those radical determinations of ontology, ethics and politics that we
have listed above. Spinoza is the philosopher of materialism, where
by materialism we mean a radical *dispositif* of free constitution of the
world.

De te fabula narratur ['The story is about you']: Laurent Bove's

book is one of the more mature fruits of this new interpretation of
Spinoza. Its thematic centre is Spinoza's political philosophy. We
may consider it a central track for the reorientation of Spinoza's
thought as a whole. The book follows the 'strategy of the *conatus*',
interpreting it as a projection of the infinite *potenza*$_2$ of the existing
being. The whole is contained within a well-defined metaphysical
arc, which one could describe as circular. In fact the Spinozist undertaking develops within this circle, as it goes from experience to the
infinite, and to a strategy that reconstructs the infinite. From that
perspective, the Spinozist system is an open system, a machine of
essences and eternities in movement. We can take this openness as
the starting point for looking at the book as a whole. The first three
chapters follow the process of the formation of subjectivity through
the schema of a constitutive strategy. Now, the constitution of a
strategic subject is not given simply in relation to the singular body,
but especially in relation to the collective body. Thus we see a continuous advance that goes from the constitutive predisposition of the
subject, according to the principle of pleasure, to the determination
of a teleological structure of the subject, 'in habit' [*nell'abitudine*].
The subject thus constituted is essentially amorous and hence effec-
tually strategic. As for the *conatus*, in its own movement it becomes
imagination, and on this effort is redefined an active, free and constitutive 'human nature'. Strategic subject and human nature are thus
one and the same thing, namely a desiring activity that tends towards
joy. It is from this trace that Bove draws the political determination
of Spinozist being. Thus far we have been on the terrain of infinity
as a strategy, of the formation of subjectivity as a motor of collective
constitution. From Chapter 4 onwards the *potenza*$_2$ of being subjec-
tivises itself; and the subjective strategy of the infinite begins. One
chapter here, namely Chapter 4, is a small and bizarre masterpiece of
moral philosophy and critical ontology. It is dedicated to *hilaritas* – to
joy, or being cheerful – as a key to perceiving a dynamic of joy that
leads to the collective body. *Hilaritas* is fleeting, but it has the great
ability to make us pass from passive to active affects, and thus to open
human subjectivity to the *potenza*$_2$ of a full experience. Chapters 5,
6 and 7 provide the analysis of the definitive making of Spinoza's
politics. The subject is defined as resistance, that is, as an amorous
and joyful essence that opposes and resists hatred and sadness. Here,
through the *Theological Political Treatise*, Spinoza's politics argues its
linear, constructive path. But a theoretical and political antinomy
that pits determinism against subjectification can also be observed
here. This theme is analysed through the study of 'superstitious

mediation', in other words of that sort of positive effect that comes
from the negativity of the falsification of being. How can one overcome this political antinomy? According to Bove, the passage from
the *Theological Political Treatise* to the *Political Treatise* characterises
and qualifies the act of overcoming the antinomy. In fact the strategy
of political *conatus* is conceived of here as a movement, both free and
necessary, of the self-constitution of society as a body. Finally, in the
last chapter, theory returns to us, in subjectivity, resistance – as a
sovereign and eternal right.

The most original element of Bove's research is its focus on the
concept of resistance. Resistance is not a generic figure. Of course,
it constructs itself as a modality of *conatus*, when the subject proves
itself against sadness: gradually it constructs itself as a stage of high
complexity in the development of *conatus*, between singular and
common gesture. Resistance, within this development, is enriched
by expressive modalities: even when it presents itself as reaction, it
extends into loving desire. Resistance is never passive, it organises
positive passions. Thus we arrive at the heart of the political problem,
where the ethics of resistance, or the strategy of the *conatus*, becomes
a political weapon – that is, an instrument of political autonomy.
Forming the subject, resistance transforms it from a subjected being
into an actor of liberation. The definition of absolute democracy as a
product of *potentia multitudinis* [the power of the multitude] assumes
the strategy of resistance as its motor. It is resistance that makes the
citizen, within a political project of autonomy that the *potenza* of the
multitude develops.

Once the force of this argument has been appreciated, it is still
worth stressing the breadth and the interpretive richness, not to
mention the elegance, of Bove's work. It invites reading not only in
its general outline but also on many particular aspects of conceptual
and thematic analysis of Spinoza's political thought. I have already
mentioned *hilaritas*, but there are other analyses of partial themes
that deserve attention, in particular those of obedience and prudence;
and then again the concept of 'resistance', in all its range. After this
thesis, Bove also produced a series of wide-ranging studies that trace
the history of French moral philosophy between the sixteenth and
the eighteenth centuries. To him we owe the definition of a precise
relationship between Spinoza's thought and the civic and resistant
ethics that developed in the French classical age against the absolutist perversion of knowledge and ethics. In his recently published
edition of the *Political Treaty*, Bove provides a commentary in which
many of these themes are addressed. I recommend it to his readers,

because in this way, through this wonderful book, we can all grasp
the thinking of Spinoza – his political thought in particular – as a text
that relaunches our own ethics. What, from Bove's point of view,
Spinoza perpetuates is the combative inspiration of Machiavelli and
La Boétie. His is a mass point of view: it leads from the resistance
of an individual, the true crucible of the self-organisation of the collective body, to the liberation of all... Breaking with the imagery of
natural law and of contract, Spinoza makes the concept of resistance
the very concept of the possibility of a history of the multitude.

Part II

Spinoza Today

4

Spinoza

Another power of action

Spinoza's thought is a reflection on *potenza* [power]. However, when one delves deeply into the Spinozist conception of being from the point of view of political philosophy, one often comes up against different interpretations of the development of that being–power [*essere–potenza*] in relation to the definition of *potere* [power]. There are different assessments of the ontological intensity of *potenza* and different descriptions of its political productivity. For my part, considering that the identity between being and *potenza* creates no problem in Spinoza, I would argue that his political thought developed around a proposition that is 'constituent' in relation to the concept and reality of *potenza* – that is, starting from the fact that the fundamental political figure in Spinoza is that of ontological monism and democratic immanence. I believe that I have sustained this premise continuously and centrally in my interpretation: an ontological (i.e. constituent) *potenza*, a political (i.e. democratic) immanence, and a strategic (i.e. programmatic) monism of *cupiditas* [desire, passion] and of the resulting *praxis communis* [common practice].

The subtitle of my presentation is 'an*other*' power of action in Spinoza. Why do I stress the 'other'? I do so for various reasons.

In the first place, I stress the 'other' because the Spinozist concept of *potenza* is not properly defined by Aristotelian, late scholastic, or neo-Stoic traditions. Of course, you will probably find such influences reflected in it. But we can be sure that, if these existed around the start of the seventeenth century, in Spinoza they were mixed (and deeply fused) with a concept of divine *potenza* (as love) that derived rather from Leone Ebreo and the Neoplatonic tradition, as received and transformed in Renaissance thought. Besides, in various forms, this influence permeated the conception of being in Spanish and

Dutch thought of the period, which was Spinoza's immediate source (as has been correctly observed by Ansaldi 2001 and others). In this context, the definition of *potentia* in Spinoza is in no way reducible to the concept of the 'individual' or of an individual *potenza* to act: it would be if the concept of *potenza* had Aristotelian origins, if it had adapted itself to the scholastic dynamic of individuation, and if it were exclusively implanted in that tradition. But it was not. On the contrary, the thought of '*potenza* as constitution' insists not so much on the stamp of individuality as on that of modal singularity, of the continuous expansion of *potenza* and of the epistemological and ontological tension towards the composition of the common. And it is not true, either, that social *potenza* is structured and activated in the direction of individuals and through them (as some interpreters think). Nor is it enough, to avoid this error, to exclude from Spinoza's method the methodological individualism (of Hobbesian origin) that we find in certain schools of sociology today. If the dynamic of *potenza* is reliably differential, relational and horizontal and if it is never definable or subject to instrumental use, this is because it is constitutive in social terms (exactly), innovative on the terrain of simple interaction, and always more turned, tendentially, towards the common. Thus Spinozist *potenza* is *other* in the first place because it is a modal *potenza*, and for this reason collective, common.

Second and consequently, we should not confuse *potentia* with *vis* [force]. *Vis* will never be common, but *potentia* becomes so: the genesis and the structure of institutions form in Spinoza a continuum that transforms precisely the interaction of forces into institutions of *potenza*. If we were to assume that *potentia* is *vis individua* [indivisible force], we would approach a mystified genealogy of institutions and would imagine the relationship between *potenze* as a flat, neutral and mechanical relationship, a temporary and provisional relationship, transindividual: nothing but a horizontal, geometric *relationship*. But if this were the case, how would we explain the historicity of the Jewish institutions in the *Theological–Political Treatise*? How would we grasp the formation of *summa potestas* [supreme power] in the *Ethics* and in the *Political Treatise*? To give an answer, those who write about 'transindividual relationship' speak of the process of *potenza* as an 'accumulation' – and this point is of course very important: indeed, it makes it possible to maintain a radically critical position in relation to all transcendental conceptions of power, typical of the modern Hobbesian tradition in political philosophy. The accumulation of the products or effects of social *potenze* in fact presents a *monistic* perspective, if there ever was one. It constructs the strongest idea of the immanentist refusal of any state–society 'contract', and therefore removes any possibility of a transcendental transfer of *potenza* in the direction of power. To put it even more eloquently: in this way, on this point, working on the idea of accumulation of *potenze*, we remove all those political theologies that accompany the postmodern restoration of the concept of sovereignty, more or less in the manner of Schmitt or Agamben, from right and left.

But what are the modalities of this accumulation? In general, they are delimited by the tendential unification of constitutive *potenza* and legal positivity. This is right in some respects: the tendential unity of *potentia* and *ius* is repeatedly affirmed in Spinoza. But at this point the tendendential unity should be compared with the statement in the *Political Treatise* (2.13, getting back to the *Ethics*) that *potenza* increases with the expansion of association. There cannot be a zero sum through the association of singularities and the accumulation of *potenze*: *they produce.* But, then, how can one simultaneously affirm the flat neutrality of the relationship between individuals, or of social cooperation? In short, we are faced here with a contradictory argument, because the *positive* identification of *potenza* and *ius* cannot be flattened in a *positivist* manner. In the second place, then, Spinozist *potentia* is 'other' because it is a productive *potenza*.

It is worth mentioning that I consider important in this regard the three chapters of the second part and the introduction to the third part of Pascal Severac's *Spinoza* (Severac 2011), precisely where the productive characterisation of the relationship between bodies in Spinoza's rational physics is demonstrated according to the criterion of 'simultaneous multiplicity' and where the concept that derives from it, far from being defined in passive terms, 'seems to express an action of the Mind' (Spinoza 1985: *Ethics* II, Proposition 2, Definition 3) – or, even better, presents itself as a finite part of divine *potenza*.

There is a third reason for considering the *potentia* of Spinoza as 'other'. It consists in modulating the rejection of any finalistic determination in Spinoza's theory. It is obvious that, in Spinoza's ontology, nothing is teleological; but the defence of liberty is certainly a value in Spinoza, and this defence assuredly represents the *telos* of his thought and political activity. How can one avoid calling this *praxis* teleological? And how can one give a material basis to, and qualify from the point of view of ontology (but also from that of a Spinozist 'sociology of affects'), this discovery that seeks to make the social process anything but a zero-sum process, also from the point of view of the intentionality of the *potenze* themselves? In fact, here the *potenza* is presented within a real and proper strategy of singular resistances which develops towards the collective, or rather, as a process that leads from the singularity to the social whole, and which modifies, transforms and moulds collective institutions. The Spinozist immanence of the collective (modal, common) is constituent through the conflicts of singularities. Laurent Bove (1996) has shown this very effectively. And Filippo Del Lucchese (2004) has shown how Spinoza's appropriation of Machiavelli never takes place in the form of 'Machiavellianism' (that is, in a neutralising political science, in a positivist formalism, in an apology for violence, and in the philistinism of a *raison d'état*), but rather represents an inexhaustible instance of freedom that is built in and through struggle.

In the third place, therefore, Spinozist *potenza* is 'other' because, far from being teleological, it is traversed by a *telos* that is formed through the resistances and confluences of *praxis*, through the conflicts of singularities. A strategy of the collective reveals the absolute desire for freedom as intransitive, and thus opens the way to the dynamic of love.

In the fourth place, we now find ourselves addressing another essential point of the discussion on the concept of *potentia*. As we know, the constitutive process of *potentia* develops, through successive integrations and institutional constructions, from *conatus* to *cupiditas*, through to the rational expression of *amor*. At the central point of this process lies *cupiditas*. This, in fact, is the moment at which the physicality of *appetitus* and the corporality of *conatus*, organising themselves in social experience, produce *imagination*. Imagination is an anticipation of the constitution of institutions, it is a *potenza* that approaches rationality and structures its path; *it expresses it*. Deleuze was right to call Spinoza's thought a 'philosophy of expression'. Imagination is what carries singularities from resistance to the common. And it is precisely here that *cupiditas* acts and, in its acting, '[a] desire which arises from reason cannot be excessive' (Spinoza 1985: *Ethics* IV, Proposition 61). So it is here that immanence is affirmed in the most fundamental way and where the strategy of *cupiditas* reveals the *asymmetry* between *potentia* and *potestas*, in other words the irreducibility of the development of constituent desire (social, collective) to the (albeit necessary) production of the rules of organisation and command. Now, it is this positive asymmetry, this abundance, this excess of *potentia* that the theories that seek to neutralise the transformative radicality of Spinoza's thought must cancel out: the perpetual excess of that liberatory reason that, through imagination, constructs itself between the action of *cupiditas* and the tension of *amor* – on the edge of being, constructing eternity.

There we have yet another attempt to remove that 'otherness' that radically characterises Spinozist opposition in the face of the ontotheology of modernity.

Note that a strange attitude emerges here. Those who seek to neutralise the ethical excess of *cupiditas* in Spinoza often base their analysis of his political thought on Spinoza's *political* texts rather than on the *Ethics*. But I should recall here that, on the contrary, Spinoza's political thought is located in the most authoritative fashion in his ontology, and thus in the *Ethics*, more than in any other parallel or subsequent work. In any case, this effort ends in a contradictory way: it is on the matter of the relationship between *cupiditas* and *amor* that all those who want to isolate political *potentia* seem to fail – because, in discarding the *Ethics*, they forget the excessive specificity of the relationship *cupiditas–amor*, and thus forget that what *cupiditas* constructs as *summa potestas*, *amor* exceeds as *res pubblica*, as commonwealth. The asymmetry between *potentia* and *potestas*, entirely in favour of *potentia*, is therefore grasped with the same intensity, no matter whether we look at it from above – in the efficiency of the nexus *cupiditas–amor*, which exalts its productivity – or from below – indeed when *potentia* is formed and acts with a view to an infinite opening.

In the fourth place, then, I conclude that *potentia* is imagined and expressed on the basis of an excess that breaks the symmetry between *potentia* and *potestas*, and does so in favour of *potenza*. The ontology of *potenza* will thus be marked by the force of love.

Let me now close with the characteristics of 'otherness' – or 'difference' – of *potentia*. In the fifth place, against the detractors of Spinoza's *potenza*, we can conclusively retort that the political in Spinoza is not a transversal medium, an *ubique* ['everywhere'] of the social, and therefore it cannot be defined either as a simple element of action or as a simple property of structure. In Spinoza the political is not a *medium* of the social but is its permanent source and its continuous constitutive rupture, a *potenza* that is excessive in relation to any measurement, and this excess constitutes an ontological asymmetry in relation to *potestas*. If this were not so, we would truly be condemned to acosmism – not only of the pantheistic conception of being, as Hegel would have it, but also of that of the political. And if the political in Spinoza can never be instrumental, this is because it is marked by the force of the ethical; if it builds up in the relationship and in the dialectic between individuals and groups, in this dialectic (which is not a dialectic) there is always a surplus of the constitutive process: a surplus that works to establish and communicate, and hence is not individual or interindividual; an accumulation not of (individual) substantial segments but of (unique) modal *potenze*. Spinozist monism is nourished by divine *potenza*. Is it not perhaps this claim – this process of making divinity *productive* [operosa], according to a strictly immanentist line of reasoning – that renders the Amsterdam Jew a 'heretic'? Consequently, positive *potenza* and negative *potenza*, the 'power to' and the 'power over', can in no sense be distinguished in Spinoza, because there is no static antinomy in his thinking... but also simply because, ontologically, *the negative does not exist*. There is only *potenza*, or freedom, that opposes itself to solitude and constructs the common. 'A man who is guided by reason is more free in a state, where he lives according to a common decision, than in solitude, where he obeys only himself' (Spinoza 1985: *Ethics* IV, Proposition 73).

The fifth point therefore concludes on the ethical centrality of the political element in Spinoza, and on the common excess that breaks with all determinism or positivism. And, to introduce what I shall be saying in the second part of this paper, let me borrow Chantal Jacquet's conclusions on the positive role of the will in Spinoza:

> Determining for the state and determined by the state, the will is thus eminently political for Spinoza. [...] Denomination of *conatus* inasmuch as it is related to spirit alone, the will designates the indefinite effort of an idea to persevere in its being. State of mind inclined to endure, it naturally finds its acme in the perennial nature of institutions. Although it is not distinguished from understanding, it possesses a specific function in the Spinozist system. It expresses the idea of right and manifests the spirit of laws. (Jacquet 2005, p. 107).

* * *

At this point I would like to make it clear that I have found my interpretation of Spinoza's *potentia* very useful in formulating concepts for the interpretation of the contemporary political world and in determining the topicality of *potenza*. So in what follows I would like to raise some questions concerning the value, utility and efficacy of this use. Such questions could be stated as follows:

A. Having examined *potentia* as being productive, collective, and common, how will it be possible to identify asymmetries and excesses? In particular, if social production is ontological constitution, how, within this radical immanence, will it be possible to express a condition of antagonism between *potenza* and *potere* (or, better from my perspective, between labour and capital, between creative activity and private appropriation of labour)? Now, in my view, this projection of a recognised *difference* within the production process (or, better, in the relationship between productive forces of labour and capitalist relations of control) is, as we have seen thus far, perfectly compatible with the strategy of the *conatus*. You cannot neutralise the latter, except by introducing 'weak' elements in the ethical context – namely elements of abstract composition or reductions of the asymmetric character of the ontological relationship, confusing modal differences with substantial individuations. But if the recognition of the relationship between *potenze* in Spinoza's thought is asymmetrical, why soften it into an ensemble of equivalences? And, consequently, why deprive it of the possibility of expressing meaning [*senso*] through conflict and an emancipatory direction?

B. Perhaps the matter is not so simple. Indeed, I have been accused of not having stated the poststructuralist premises of my interpretation of Spinoza (which, they say, now play an essential role in my political philosophy). They claim, in essence, that, together with Deleuze, I have assumed the *mos geometricus* [geometrical method] as a means of rendering Spinoza's ontology dynamic and anti-hierarchical. And then, along with Foucault, having taken on board his vocabulary, I have allegedly tried to translate the *potentia–potestas* relationship into the relation between biopolitical activity and the exercise of biopower. This would result in an absolute antinomy between an (ontologically creative) *potentia* and a (fixed or parasitic) *potestas*. It is not off the mark to assume a theoretical convergence of the thinking of Deleuze and Foucault in my work and in my use of the Spinoza corpus (although I would like to point out that, as Deleuze himself recognised, this convergence was a concomitance and not an influence). As for Foucault, it was only long after the publication of my *L'anomalia selvaggia* (Negri 1981) that I plunged into the wild universe of his thinking. But precisely for this reason – the depth of the relationship that existed between Deleuze, Foucault and my Spinozist approach – the frequent accusation raised against me is false, namely that I brought the relationship between *potentia* and *potestas* to an antinomic limit. The dichotomy of biopolitics and biopower, which nevertheless live *together* (just as labour and capital live together), is given in Deleuze in open and chaotic terms, and constructed in Foucault in genealogical terms. But then, on the other hand, how else can the interindividual construction or the 'accumulation' of *potenze* in my interlocutors be read, if not in this manner? What else can they express, if not the action of *potentia* inside or against *potestas*?

I have very much stressed this point about the interaction and dissociation of *potentia* and *potestas*, of biopolitics and biopower. Recalling the concept of habit in American pragmatists and *habitus* in the thinking of Bourdieu, I have traced the construction – *from the inside* – of the relationship, and of the difference, between *potentia* and *potestas*. The antinomy of the two effects – of the two characters – of the *potenza* that people sometimes point to as a limit in my discussions of Spinoza cannot be defined as an ontological dualism or, worse, as a kind of Manichaeism; rather it is a contrast that is continuously produced, a conflict that is continuously raised, continuously resolved, and, again, continuously repeated at other levels, an ethical tension that emerges through the difficulties and obstacles of the path that leads from *conatus*, through *cupiditas*, to the expression of *amor*. If the relationship between *potentia* and *potestas* is then recognised as 'asymmetrical', this is because *potentia*, inasmuch as it is *cupiditas*, can never be bad, and is always excedent. What is bad is that which has not been realised. *Potentia*, on the contrary, constructs the common; in other words, it directs the accumulation of passions towards the common. It conducts the struggle for the common, through a continuous production of subjectivity, towards a loving awareness of reason.

C. But, they go on to ask, what does it mean at this point to speak of the construction of a *democratia omnino absoluta* ['democracy absolute in every respect']? To assume absolute democracy at this point in the conflictual undertaking that runs through Spinoza's ethical construction – would this not constitute an undue interruption of that continuous process of conflict between singularities (understood as social forces) that, in Spinoza, characterises the ethical terrain? Is not what is being constructed in this way a kind of new political theology? An absolute democracy – on the one hand built by a multitude that, from the bottom, is drawn towards freedom and the good; and on the other hand a democracy that is no longer a form of government, but management of the freedom of all by all. Then comes the objection: outside sovereignty there is no politics. Therefore what permits one to talk about absolute democracy (and about a democratic multitude) is a theological option, while Spinoza's perspective defines an endless conflict that can have any solution, either voluntary or determined. Are we not here looking for an ontological guarantee, utopian, impossible to find, for the common emancipation of humanity? No. Here we simply state that the theory of absolute democracy in Spinoza is an attempt to invent a new form of politics, which removes itself from the theory of sovereignty and from the classic threefold division (monarchy, aristocracy, democracy) of the theories concerning the government of one. If the absolute in Spinoza is the ontological fabric of free singularities, it is logical and realistic – as he claims – to think that power-*potestas* is the result of the attempt to limit the action of singularities in their quest for freedom.

It is no coincidence that these objections come to life primarily from those interpreters who stress the legal and positivist component of the political development of *potentia* in Spinoza. In legal positivism, law is not actually qualified as *cupiditas*, as a realistic construction of 'claims' in positive law and in institutions; it is qualified rather as a second *potenza*, as a *Führung der Führungen* ['conduct of conducts']. The relation between political constitution and juridical ordering would be given here in a static relationship, in conditions of technological efficacy (so to speak). But Spinoza is not Luhmann; constitution in Spinoza is always a motor and not a result, a 'constituent power' [*'potere costituente'*] as an ongoing source of law; and therefore the legal system becomes effective through the continuous action of the constituent *potenze*.

D. It is strange to hear these objections when, in globalisation, in the relative weakening of nation-states and of European public law, juridical Spinozism, in its open version, appears more and more as a kind of anticipation of all the alternative theoretical experiments, which are now generalised in European disciplines of public law – an anticipation that has manifested constant restlessness and expression especially in Germany, from Rudolf von Jhering's 'struggle for law' to Gunther Teubner's 'constitutionalism without a state'. But here we need to add, decisively, that the political philosophy of Spinoza, albeit implanted in modernity, enacts a fundamental project against modernity: it stands radically against any modern assertion of sovereign absolutism. The atheism of Spinoza is therefore attacked with extreme violence, especially on the terrain of legal–political theory, already during the modern period, starting with Leibniz and Pufendorf. Here is a curious quotation from the latter (as reproduced in Agamben 2013, p. 108): 'Spinoza – a reckless type [*ein leichtfertiger Vogel*], *deorum hominumque irrisor* [a mocker of gods and men], who had bound in a single volume the Old and New Testament and the Koran'.

E. If we reaffirm in our own times this quality – atheism – and especially this sense of Spinoza's discourse, would that mean that we are perhaps plunging into some sort of philosophy of history? There are some who think so. The outcome, it is suggested, is that *potentia* is always more efficacious than (and historically successful over) *potestas*. Nor does it appear that the multitude – a political subjectivation of *potentia* that presents itself as a constituent historical force, as a creative power – can be or has always been extolled against the parasitic aspects of *potestas*. Once an asymmetric consistency of the conflict and an ontological meaning of antagonism are given, does one not end up guaranteeing a dubious positivity to the production of the common by the multitude? Conversely, how is one to recognise or decide whether the multitude, instead of being a producer of democracy, is a mob, or a simple occurrence of plebeian disorder?

It seems to me that the alternative proposed to the multitude, between being a mob and being a liberation movement, is an ambiguous passage – or, rather, represents a logical confusion when you take it concretely, as an ethical alternative. This statement expresses an a priori (or at least common) claim that the multitude can more easily be a mob than a liberation movement. Indeed, Spinoza refers disparagingly to the unreasoning and murderous mass as *ultimi barbarorum* [the worst barbarians]; but, on the other hand, he states explicitly that it is precisely the fear of the masses that creates barbarism. So it is not up to us, but up to the multitude to decide what it wants to be. All individuals have been too often a rabble before turning their desire towards a rational end: so, too, the multitude, which consists of a network of singularities rather than being massified from a quantitative point of view. On the other hand, if we stop laying that alternative on a practical plane and cease thinking of it as an open option but turn it into an opportunity for transcendental reflection on a theoretical plane, here, tacitly, we find reintroduced a proposal of transcendence – against and contrary to Spinozist ontology. In fact the alternative is misrepresented through a truncated version, to make the Hobbesian alienation of sovereignty appear once again as the only possibility of political construction. Within this alternative there is ample space, as we have already seen, for the movement of legal positivism; and here legal positivism is close to the philosophy of history of Hegelianism or of positivism or of both (as both are transcendental glorifications of the status quo) rather than to that ethical experimentation in immanence to which Spinoza calls us.

But there is more. Continuing in this vein, there is another possible misunderstanding that needs to be highlighted, namely that of assuming the duration of institutions as a realistic negation of resistance and of the persistence of the multitude. But, in Spinoza's ontology as in his politics, duration does not mean a blocking or withering of temporality; on the contrary. As Laurent Bove has shown, human freedom, in other words the necessity proper to self-conservation, manifests itself as constituent *potenza* in action. 'The conflicts and the balances of power which represent the anthropological condition itself, square a dynamic ontology of decision over/of problems – or rather, in the absolute actualisation of *potenza* in each singular occasion, an ontology of kairos' (Bove 1999, p. 59). Hence the possibility of considering a duration in which institutions of the multitude in the march of freedom would be manifest – without any illusion of linearity or of the destiny-oriented character of this process.

F. So we cannot talk of philosophy of history, but rather – on a terrain that is thus solidly consolidated from below, in a rigorously monistic composition – of 'production of subjectivity'. This production of subjectivity is entirely and objectively founded, materially constituted – and sometimes verifiable in the facts. The social conditions of our existence confirm this reality. The theory of the multitude (with the final 'march of freedom' that the multitude traverses) is simply the determination of a development in the material civilisation, which means throughout civilisations and cultures. The proposal here is that of an alternative: an alternative of struggle against exploitation and of pursuit of happiness. This does not alter the admission – after having stated this objective materiality of my argument – that every philosophy (assuming that it is neither philistine nor stifled by ideological baggage) must decide which side to take – with the oppressors or with the oppressed. To put it in Spinozist terms, a certain 'optimism of reason' (and ultimately a certain 'pessimism of the will') is in action here. For, even when one accepts the thesis that politics is just an attempt to control a perennial interindividual conflict, in other words when one places oneself on the terrain of an alleged 'political realism' (and thereby of a certain 'pessimism of the will'), it is not possible to look flatly at this terrain of the conflict, or to dampen its liberatory tendencies, or to remove the possibility that the struggle for freedom produces new subjectivities and anthropological metamorphoses. In his own humanistic realism, Machiavelli always pondered over the positivity of this *potenza* to act. Deleuze and Guattari in *A Thousand Plateaus* have admirably shown it to be active and multiverse. Michel Foucault, in his *Lessons*, began to construct these *dispositifs* of subjectivity from the base up. By contrast, the claim that a theory of *potentia* is only diagnostic or explanatory strips Spinozism of its essence: that of being the *praxis* of *cupiditas* and of rational *amor*, of freedom and of the common.

So I ask again: What otherness is there in Spinoza's *potentia*? If we look at it from the standpoint of politics, that otherness is, pure and simple, the point of rupture with the entire line of thought that illuminates the continuity of the transcendental concept of power, from Aristotle to Hobbes to Schmitt. But, as a friend reminded me, we have fortunately forgotten to conjugate in the aorist. From another, immanent point of view, the otherness of the concept of *potentia* lies in the fact that it constructs virtue from the ground up. Generosity and fortitude of spirit are always embodied in the city; in short, happiness is civic.

March 2012

5

Concerning the concept of multitude

The use of Spinozist concepts in politics, in political economy, in sociology, and generally in the human sciences has become noticeable today. Often this use is not subjected to evaluations that might test its historical or theoretical correctness. For Spinoza, the risk arising from this use is higher than the risk that might arise from the use of other classic writers – since the Spinozist machine is 'revolutionary' and its concepts unveil an ethical surplus, an excedence, both in ontology and in the political field, that sits badly with the methods of present-day disciplines – all social and human sciences with cold and purely analytic languages. That said, I would add that, although I am no stranger to Spinoza, my use of the concept of multitude (on which I have been invited to speak) is not neutral. When I first began to read Spinoza, it was not a reading that sought to avoid the revolutionary significance of his teaching. Rather it was precisely in that spirit that I read him – and it may well be that I took things to excess. As the scholastics might have said, perhaps I was superimposing a *distinctio rationis* [conceptual distinction] onto a *distinctio realis* [real distinction]. I had some justification, however: in the face of the tragic events in which I had been caught,* I was asking Spinoza to put me back on my feet again, to teach me how to reconstruct a terrain of political realism – while at the same time rejecting the arguments of those who were trying to persuade me that I had to bow to the harsh reality of defeat. So it was a matter of illuminating self-criticism through analysis of its causes, but

---

* Translator's note: On 7 April 1979, along with many other Italian revolutionary leftists, Negri was arrested on charges of association with the Red Brigades. A period of combined imprisonment and exile, during which he produced many of his major writings, finally ended in 2003.

also a matter of irreducible conviction (which I nurtured along with many of my comrades) about the impossibility of giving up, in the struggle for a democracy of common *potenza* [power] and of equality as a measure of freedom. This is where Spinoza's ontology helped us by giving rational clarity to the revolutionary *cupiditas* [passion, desire] that had motivated us. We were brought up on a pessimism of reason and optimism of the will – in other words, on a crude realism of political judgement and a forced voluntarism, overweening and often sectarian. By contrast, Spinoza taught us the optimism of reason, his joyous passion, and at the same time the prudence of the will, the invincible prolixity of its progress.

The fact remains that, when you study Spinoza (or any other author), there are always – I do not say two methods, but – two ways: the first is textual and historiographical; the second is critical and political. The problem is to understand what closeness and distance there is between the first and the second of these interpretative pathways; and we have to ask ourselves what is the nature of the criteria that we employ between these two choices to render topical a system of thought. I may return to this matter at the end of my presentation.

* * *

So now I turn to the concept of multitude. But it is difficult to understand it if we do not talk about democracy first. In the *Political Treatise* [*PT*], at the start of paragraph 11, democracy is defined as *omnino absolutum imperium* [a power absolute in every respect]. What does this mean? Already in his *Theological–Political Treatise* [*TPT*] Spinoza had spoken of democracy – the democracy of the Jews rather than democracy *tout court*. But there democracy was read as an ethical–political reality, all the more dense in morality as the critique – which sought to remove from the law any sign of transcendence – pointed out, at the root of the democracy of the Jews, an extraordinary humanist motif, permanently renewed. Yet in the *PT* the concept of democracy is totally secularised: secularised not only in relation to Jewish history but also in relation to that element of the transcendental that modern contractualism had introduced into the process of legitimising democracy. In *TPT* the contractualist theme is still present; in the *PT* it is no longer present. We know what the contractual theme means in the seventeenth century: at that time the theory of social contract was an explicit sociological fiction, employed to legitimise the efficiency of the transfer of power from society to the sovereign and to found the juridical concept of the state. This prepared the absolutism of the various forms of government that the modern state adopts. It follows that, in the absence of the contractual hypothesis, the *PT* shows, first, Spinoza's contribution to the tradition of republican radicalism in humanist culture and, secondly, his loyalty to the tradition of democratic radicalism in Protestantism, especially of the Calvinist and sectarian stripe. Machiavelli at one end, Althusius at the other.

In the *PT*, then, the absence of a theory of contract is matched by a radically innovative approach to imagining and building a political society. By this I mean that in the *PT* the principal claim is that law and politics participate immediately in the *potenza* of the absolute and have nothing to do with the negative, dialectical essence of the transfer of power required by contractualism. Law and politics participate directly in the truth of action.

> From this fact – that the power of natural things, by which they exist and have effects, is the very power of God – we easily understand what the right of nature is. For, since God has the right over all things, and God's right is nothing but his power itself, insofar as [his power] is considered to be absolutely free, it follows that each natural thing has as much right by nature as it has power to exist and have effects. For the power of each natural thing, by which it exists and has effects, is nothing but the very power of God, which is absolutely free. (Spinoza, 2016a: *PT* II, 3)

Let me continue with my definition of democracy. Once we exclude the possibility of the alienation of natural law, what does *omnino absolutum imperium* mean? The answer can be given at two levels. The first is directly ontological. Here the Spinozist notion of absolute can only be conceived of as a general horizon of *potenza*, as its development and actuality. Absolute refers to the democratic constitution of a social reality – political and constitutional – that is increasingly complex and increasingly open and powerful, in accordance with the magnitude of the *potentia* [power] that constitutes it. 'If two men make an agreement with one another and join forces, they can do more together, and hence, together, have more right over nature, than either does alone. The more connections they've formed in this way, the more right they'll all have together' (*PT* II, 13).

In consequence, absolute and *potenza* become, so to speak, tautological. *Potenza* as determination in motion towards that absolute that on the other hand it already constitutes is shown in *TPT* to be a progressive historical event of the Jewish people, beyond the biblical legend. In the *PT*, this human *potenza* is shown as the basis of collective existence, of its movement, in other words of sociality and civilisation. *Imperium absolutum* thus becomes a term that, in referring to the unitary nature of *potere* [power], assumes it nonetheless as the ensemble and projection of the *potentiae* of the subjects and defines their totality as life, as the always open and dynamic articulation of a combined ensemble [*un insieme*].

From this point of view a number of consequences regarding the legitimation of democratic power follow – above all, the lack of a distinction between the notions of *titulum* [title] and *exercitium* [exercise], as set forth by contractualism, in other words by the concept of sovereignty current at the time. Democracy, unlike other forms of power, is an 'absolute' form of government, since entitlement and exercise are associated from the start. Second, Spinoza breaks with the tradition that, from classical antiquity onwards, sees also the corrupt opposite to all forms of government: democracy does or will oppose itself to demagogy (or holocracy). In the *PT* this duality disappears, and the difficulty of maintaining democracy over time is considered rather as a lifegiving element, which leads to a deepening of democratic possibilities, to the continuous reinvigoration of the republic – rather than opening a state of internal war and destruction of institutions. At *PT* VIII, 5 the outcome of the various alternatives that open when contradictory options undermine sovereign unity is a confirmation of the democratic initiative.

A third point clarifies how the *absolutum imperium democraticum* removes any possibility of separating the concept of magistracy from that of magistrate. These functions have to be grasped in the unitary tendency of the system. Just as every subject can become a citizen, here every citizen can become a magistrate, and the magistracy is the revelation of a maximum potential for unity and freedom. The magistrate returns to being a *defensor pacis* [defender of the peace].

One could illustrate other points around which Spinoza tightens the concept of *potere* and that of its functions as related to absolute *potenza*: in short, democracy is the highest form in which society expresses itself, and in it natural society turns directly into political society: 'For if there's any absolute rule, it's the rule which occurs when the whole multitude rules' (*PT* VIII, 3).

Here we see the beginnings of the *multitudo* of subjects, where *potere* is set in motion from below, in the equality of all social *potenze*, according to the natural condition in which they live. From here will begin the process leading to the establishment of the constitutional figures of society. Thus, as a form of government *omnino absoluta*, 'absolute in every respect', democracy signifies that, as we have seen, there is no alienation of *potere* – be it in point of its formation and legitimation, in point of its exercise, or in point of the specificity of executive action, that is, in point of the figure of the magistracy. On the positive side, democracy is the liberation of all social energies and is a figure of a general *conatus* [striving] of the organisation – continuous and permanent – of the freedom of all.

With this, however, I have not answered a question that immediately arises here: how can there be any compatibility between absoluteness and freedom? One could in fact ask: Without further specifications and without the definition of an appropriate subject, shouldn't one think that we are in the presence of a totalitarian utopia? Or, less drastically, could not the rejection of the contract produce an absolutist projection of society, organised by the illusion of a *potenza*, such that every individual guarantee of freedom fails? To answer this question, Spinoza introduces a further step, which is foundational for democracy: he raises the problem of the subject of that collective doing that constitutes democratic absoluteness. This subject is *multitudo*.

Let it be clear from the start: *multitudo* is not something organic, not a one but a multiplicity, an ensemble of social modes of being. It appears right from the start, as a step in a dual movement. On the one hand, it moves, as we have seen, towards absoluteness, towards the oneness and indivisibility of government, towards the representation of a subject, of a single mind:

> For the first consideration is that just as [...] in the state of nature the man who is guided by reason is the most powerful and the most his own master, so a Commonwealth will also be the most powerful and the most its own master, if it is founded on and directed by reason. For the Right of a Commonwealth is determined by the power of a multitude which is led as if by one mind. But there is no way this union of minds can be conceived unless the Commonwealth aims most at what sound reason teaches to be useful to all men. (*PT* III, 7)

But on the other hand, in the concept of multitude is also expressed, in another sense, a plural *potenza* [power], matched to that continuous and unresolvable tension of democracy towards opening itself, towards constituting itself in time. From this point of view, the multitude is not so much a subject as a machine of infinite subjectivation. The life of absolute government thus knows in Spinoza a systole and diastole, a movement towards unity and a movement towards dispersion.

And in this way I have arrived at the concept of multitude.

* * *

In *TPT* the term *multitudo* appears only six times and has not yet acquired political fulness: it is, essentially, a sociological concept. As mentioned earlier, as expressed in *TPT*, the concept of democracy, whose excellence is praised, lives in a region of pure allusion to the political model – it is more of a prototype than of a regime. As for *multitudo*, already in the early parts of the *TPT* it is simply regarded as a large number of individuals, often dominated by superstition. In the *PT*, on the other hand, the perspective on the multitude is completely different: it becomes constitutive, dynamic and democratic.

It is interesting to note that *multitudo* presents itself first of all as a limit in opposition to power: the multitude as a limit vis-à-vis the solitude and action of the monarch, or as limit to aristocratic selectivity and to its justification: later on it turns into the *potenza* of democratic absoluteness. 'Absolute in every respect' [*omnino absolutum*] is therefore the *potere* [sc. *imperium*] that adapts itself to the *potenza* of *multitudo*. If it were not pleonastic, one could say, of the whole *multitude* – which thereby becomes subject: an ungraspable subject, just as any *potenza* of subjectivation, any concept of the undefined is ungraspable; it is, however, ontologically necessary.

The critics of the importance of *multitudo* as subject and as ontological attribute of Spinoza's doctrine of democracy have pointed out the elusive nature of the concept. There is no doubt that, at times, the apologists of *multitudo* (and I count myself among them) have been too zealous by treating it as an essence or as an ontological scheme of reason. But the material ungraspability of the *multitudo* subject does not prevent the effects of subjectivity from expressing themselves in Spinoza. Thus *multitudinis potentia* [the power of the multitude] is the foundation of *imperium* [power > empire] and maintains it through the direct creation of law.

> This right, which is defined by the power of a multitude, is usually called Sovereignty. Whoever, by common agreement, has responsibility for public Affairs – that is, the rights of making, interpreting, and repealing laws, fortifying cities, and making decisions about war and peace, etc. – has this right absolutely. If this responsibility is the business of a Council made up of the common multitude, then the Satate is called a Democracy. (Spinoza 2016a: *PT* II, 17)

And the whole civil law, whose expression generated the public constitution of the state, is produced and legitimated by the *multitudo*.

> Therefore, like sin and obedience, taken strictly, so also justice and injustice can be conceived only in a state. For in nature there's nothing

which can rightly be said to belong to one person and not to another. Instead, everything belongs to everyone – that is, to whoever has the power to claim it for himself. But in a state, where it's decided by a common law what belongs to one person and what to another, a person is called just if he has a constant will to give to each person his own, and unjust if he tries to make his own what belongs to someone else. (Spinoza 2016a: *PT* II, 23)

It is *multitudo* that produces a common society.

The third and final consideration is that things most people resent are less within a Commonwealth's Right. For certainly men are guided by nature to unite in one aim, either because of a common [hope or] a common fear, or because they long to avenge some common loss. Because the Commonwealth's Right is defined by the common power. (Spinoza 2016a: *PT* III, 9)

And then, finally, *multitudo* presents itself as a juridical subject, as a necessary figuration of the social, a hypothesis of oneness and political constitutivity (as we have already seen in *PT* III, Proposition 7).

Let it be clear that, in any case, this incentive towards unity in the absolute form of democracy does not take away the physical, multiple and ungraspable nature specific to the multitude: rather it reproposes it in the insoluble paradox that separates from its subjective nature and unites with it the productive *potenza* of law and of constitution. What is being built here is not a *volonté générale* [general will], because the relationship between society and *imperium* is not determined in alienation but in the direct expression of multitudinous *potenza*. The relationship between absolute and *multitudo*, between the two versions of *potenza*, is not closed: one pulls in to achieve the unity of the political, the other dissolves itself in the multiplicity of the subjects. All this is amply shown when Spinoza (in *PT* IV and V, and especially in *PT* V, Propositions 6 and 7) interprets Machiavelli's teaching as being addressed to a free multitude.

★ ★ ★

But let me now examine the nature of *multitudo* more closely. The concept of *multitudo* is first and foremost that of a physical *potenza*. In the *Ethics*, the term *multitudo* appears only once, in the Note to Proposition 20 in Part V: *in multitudine causarum* ['in the multiplicity of causes']. Here we are outside any direct reference to political thought, and yet the appearance of the term *multitudo* in this place (beyond the strict semantic reference) is not irrelevant. We are in the middle of the ascetic construction of the cognitive process in Part V. The multitude of causes, immersed in the infinite context of fluctuations and affects, sets before itself the need for the mind to regulate it, and to do so – where you would expect an extremisation of the ascetic tendency – in the perspective of a social *potenza*, of building a collective horizon. I am not intending to conflate the two passages, but all this relates to the experiment of a multiple and dynamic construction of the individual in Spinoza's physics (see *Ethics* II, Proposition 13, and in particular Corollary Lemma III, Definition). We are immersed in a fabric of interlacings and physical combinations, of associations and dissociations, of fluctuations and of concretisations, in a logic that is completely horizontal – a logic that realises the paradox of the intersection between causality and casuality, between possibility and tendency. Here is the original dimension of *multitudo*. Spinoza's political conception is consistent with his associationist and mechanist physics. The subsequent shift of this perspective from the physical to the political enriches its characteristics without obscuring the method.

Next, *multitudo* is natural power, or rather animal power. It is the dominion of fear, violence and war that is represented in it. And those passions or those affects and situations are in fact the ones that can allow us to follow the whole progression of the concept of multitude, situated as it is in a movement that is ever open and never pacified (*Ethics* IV, Proposition 45, Note; also Proposition 37, Notes 1 and 2). Here one could speak, improperly, of a 'bad multitude', when reactionary multitudes appear on the scene, laden with hate for others, and murderous... But it would be better to say *ultimi barbarorum* ['the worst barbarians']. To those who ask me about the violence that has devastated common life in recent years, I retort: Is it possible to define as 'multitudinarian' that violence, that hate of oneself and of others that the suicide bomber brings with the explosives? I do not think the answer is difficult: it is not multitude, this thing that kills others and feeds on death in order to affirm itself. Multitude is rather that mass of people who, in these days of ours, travel across Europe in search for work and happiness and in flight from that universe of grim passions, murderous superstitions, and hateful humiliations in which they were oppressed. These human swarms that traverse Europe cannot be called either 'mass' or 'crowd', but precisely 'multitude' – a non-commercial but heroic undertaking, as is said of Christopher Colombus, as is said of anyone who creates a new world. Because multitude is always the ontological *dispositif* of a multiplicity of people, and it is creative of the common. Spinoza

himself, shocked by the murderous violence perpetrated on the De
Witt brothers, wonder whether that was not a 'barbarous multitude'.
Each of us cannot help wondering about this, cannot help suffering
from it. But Spinoza's answer, and our own, consists in rejecting the
ontological consistency of this 'negative'. But it exists, they reply. No,
it does not: what we see there is fascism, sectarian violence, religious
fanaticism – it is not multitude. There is no multitude because this
concept is not descriptive but constitutive, it does not point opaquely
to a world of sad passions, but generates a world of joyous passions.
It is a politics of life against death. Here the formation of the political
subject is posited as a tendency within an indefinite interweaving of
subjectivating encounters. From this point of view, plurality prevails
over unity; and, when reason requires that *multitudo* present itself
immediately as one single mind, this request would not have a follow-
up here, because yes, reason does traverse a natural field on which
social life develops, but right now it is unable to overcome the latter's
dispersion and violence. There is no multitude in the state of nature.

This is why it is difficult to accept Balibar's reading of the multitude as an intertwining of individualities, as a transindividual subject;
for in that way what we seem to get is an identity that composes individuals, and this definition seems to introduce, albeit very cautiously,
an attempt to 'naturalise' and to pre-constitute the political process.

However, there is a third level of possible consideration: to define
the *multitudo* from the standpoint of reason. Thus far we have seen
how the requirement of reason, which moved within the project of
the absoluteness of the democratic body, did not succeed in making
itself real. There are physical and animal limits that account for
this. In Spinoza, the will of all, even were it to be given, would not
succeed in becoming general will. However, this does not mean that
the concept of *multitudo* does not have a formidable potential of
subjectivation. So how does democratic subjectivation express itself?
Multitudo, in the paradoxical nature it exhibits, is the foundation of
democracy inasmuch as it allows individuals to bring to society, each
one entirely, their own values of freedom. Each singularity is a foundation of democracy, and it is for this reason that *multitudo* will never
degrade into *vulgus* or *plebs*. François Zourabichvili rightly says that
there can be only a 'free multitude':

> Why is it that the multitude is not simply an intellectual chimera?
> Because of the natural tendency of individuals towards community
> (their common horror for solitude). We know the logic. It is that of
> common notions. So the consistency of the concept of multitude is

to be found in the tension or tendency of a common desire. And it is on this common desire that the institution is founded. (Zourabichvili 2006, p. 108)

Two or three further developments follow from here. The first is about tolerance – not as a negative force or as a residual force of morality (in *TPT*, tolerance is primarily defined within a perspective of intellectual freedom), but rather as a universal right, as a right to have rights, as a condition of democratic politics. So then: the absolute government of democracy is constructed on *multitudo*, on the foundation of the freedom of the individuals who make up *multitudo*, in mutual respect for every person's freedom. The second development that one can refer to is that related to *pietas* (see *Ethics* IV, Proposition 37, Note 1).

Pietas is the desire to do good; it is love of universality when universality is the common name of many subjects – in universality, or from universality, there is no desire to exclude any subject as would be the case if one loved the particular (*Ethics* IV, Proposition 18, Note, and Proposition 37, Note 1).

Finally, there is the concept of utility: nothing is more useful to humans than humans themselves. From this point of view, *multitudo* is an intertwining of subjects – already allowed through tolerance and rendered moral by *pietas* – that has become useful and thus makes itself into an ontological project of the collective potentiality [*potenza₂*]. It is traversed by that dynamic of imagination that is fundamental in determining the transition from passive desires to active desires, from *cupiditas* to *amor* [love]. So here we are now, at the end of the theoretical genesis of Spinozian democracy and equipped with a full definition of *multitudo*.

★ ★ ★

I said at the start that there is on the one hand a direct, textual way of approaching an author and, on the other, the possibility of bringing that reading into our present. However, the more proximate or more distant vicinity between the text and its contemporary reading can be a problem. Now, when Michael Hardt and I began to use the word 'multitude' twenty years ago, we did so, first, because the term resonated with certain specific conditions in which political subjectivation was couched in postmodernity. First we used it as a critique, undertaken in the name of multiplicity, of all identitarian notions of the political subject. In the name of a global democracy that, allegedly, had moved beyond matters of sovereignty (territorially speaking), we used the term 'multitude' against the concept of 'people' [*popolo*], against the concept of 'nation', and against the traditional concept of 'working class'. Whatever its historical importance, the concept of 'people' seemed to have been reduced to that of an unsustainable formal substrate [*ipostasi*], which functioned towards negating social and cultural differences, and in particular the class struggle. The Hobbesian origin of the concept of 'people' as a subject constructed by the ruler seemed now to qualify it as a weapon against democracy itself. As for the concept of 'nation', leaving aside the fact that it has been rendered fragile by the ongoing processes of globalisation, it seemed to us that it imposed an identitarian element, exclusivist from the point of view of migratory mobilities and of the uncontainable flows of integration given in postmodernity. Surprisingly, we rediscovered the concept of 'multitude' in Latin America, where it was used by writers who were seeking to establish democratic and multinational forms in countries where racial and colonial difference had configured the nation up to that point. As for the concept of 'working class', I shall return to it in what follows. We also used the concept of 'multitude' against any generic conception of the historical subject – generic and negative – for instance mob, common folk, mass – descriptions that stretched in ambiguous directions at the base of the political system. These descriptions offered themselves to the constantly renewed reactionary push to exclude the active movements of the population from the democratic process.

The multitude could therefore present itself and operate as a multiple subject on the global scene, but above all – and here I return to the discussion about productive classes – as a subject on the postindustrial stage. In other words the multitude appeared as a class concept in situations where the class of workers, rather than being a mass, was reconfigured in the development of production and presented itself as a set of singularities, tendentially brought together by a socialised productive activity characterised by immaterial (intellectual, cognitive, affective, linguistic, etc.) and nomadic elements. Moreover, the variety of these elements could discover a connection among them and be brought to a common measure, worked out through the growing cooperation of workers in the deterritorialised structures of the global enterprise. This social cooperation – direct and indirect, industrial and telematic – led to a change in the previous, value-creating dimensions of labour and placed itself in a precise spot, in relation to both temporal measurements of work and specific locations and spatial movements. In this perspective, production became above all cooperation, and a production surplus was created when singularities operated in association (Spinoza and Marx show this in almost the same words: see *PT* II, 13). Finally, in the biopolitical production regimes that characterise our times, cooperation proves to be a central element.

The definition of multitude was first adopted by us and, next, confirmed at first sight by the new forms of political and social struggle that became general from the end of the past century onwards. First there were movements in which thousands and thousands of people came together under peace flags, or with the aim of fighting the destructive consequences of globalisation. Then the use of the term 'multitude' spread at a later stage, with the description of the cycle of social struggles that followed in 2011: the Spanish *indignados*, Occupy Wall Street, the Arab uprisings, and so on. These struggles were characterised, apart from objectives of freedom and equality, by an agitational method that operated at the base, through social media, and with the absolute primacy of horizontal and radically democratic organisational forms. Does all this have any relation to the Spinozist definition of multitude? Not much, if we look at it from a phenomenological point of view, but a lot, if one keeps in mind the ontological figure of the concept of multitude inasmuch as it relates to that of absolute democracy. Both here and there, in the present struggles as in the Spinozian project, it is on this terrain that an open *dispositif* builds itself – a community that is coming into being, an absolute performative. All this, obviously, is problematic enough; but, as wise people say, humanity sets itself problems that it has then to solve.

6

Reflections on the immaterial

Spinoza, Marx ... and today

When Michael Hardt and I published *Empire* in 2000, we were heavily criticised for our claim that, tendentially, immaterial labour was becoming hegemonic in the postindustrial capitalist mode of production. We defended ourselves not so much at the level of economic theory – where there is evidence aplenty – as at a linguistic and philosophical level. We said that, while we were not entirely satisfied with the description 'immaterial', we felt that it could somehow capture the qualities of postindustrial labour better than terms such as 'cooperative' and 'cognitive', 'social', and 'abstract', taken separately. 'Immaterial' could embrace all of these new qualities and characteristics of labour taken together. Postindustrial labour, in fact, was located in the 'common abstraction', as Spinoza might have said; and it expressed, in Marxian language, that general intellect constituted entirely by the 'second nature' of human 'artificiality' (= production of art, work [*opera*], technology, and so on), in the 'real subsumption' of the society of capital – or, better, it appeared as immateriality = 'second matter' [*seconda materia*], as matter of matter.

As I continued to address those objections (since it is evident that the term 'immaterial' has its shortcomings), it occurred to me that, in the works of both Marx and Spinoza (these being the two philosophers whom I would like to invoke in the first instance), there is perhaps an epistemological case whose study legitimises my use of that term. And if the purpose of philosophical work is to set up a toolkit, a set of *dispositifs* for interpreting and transforming the (intellectual and material) universe, then the recovery of an immaterial function in the materialism of those authors will help us to extricate ourselves from the equivocations that the term 'immaterial' creates.

★ ★ ★

As I intend, then, to reflect on the immaterial, let me begin by comparing the thought of Spinoza with that of Marx in this respect. Let me proceed in good order. I could begin by following a philological path; in this case I would start from the Spinoza notebooks that Marx put together in 1842,* at the age of twenty-two, from 170 extracts drawn from Spinoza's *Theological–Political Treatise* (*TPT*; Spinoza 2016). The notebooks are not a commentary, but simply a set of excerpts. Examining the method of selection leads one to a number of conclusions about how the young Marx read Spinoza. Alexandre Matheron, a great specialist in Spinoza's thought, studied this notebook without drawing definitive conclusions, but noting how Marx's excerpting sought to highlight the political function of the sacral foundation of Jewish history and to establish the pre-eminence of the theological–political within it. Bruno Bongiovanni, the Italian editor of the text put together by Marx (see Marx 1987), highlights the immanentist and humanist character (as the Hegelian left understood it) of Marx's selection and reconstructs in detail the continuity between this notebook and the seven *Notebooks on Epicurean Philosophy* compiled by Marx earlier, between 1839 and 1840.

However, it is not my intention to discuss the relationship Spinoza–Marx from this archaeological point of view. I mention it rather, as I said, to clarify a central point in my discussion of our contemporary economic and political world: the hegemony of the immaterial. So let me begin with a phenomenological experience that is important for entering into Marx's system (and probably also into Spinoza's): the experience of temporality. Along with the experience and the concept of time substance, time value, and time measurement, it seems to me that we can also recognise in Marx the experience of a kind of temporal immateriality, disengaged from all measure. Grasping this will allow me to move forward in my discussion.

For my part, this is research that I began in 1982, in my book *Macchina tempo*, and then developed fifteen years later in *Kairòs, Alma Venus, Multitudo* (both of these essays were later published in an English edition entitled *Time for Revolution*: see Negri 2013). How did I proceed on that occasion? By narrating and analysing

---

* Translator's note: The notebooks of Marx's transcriptions from Spinoza were published by Dietz Verlag in Berlin in 1976, in two volumes, as 'Exzerpte aus Benedictus de Spinoza', together with excerpts from Epicurus, Aristotle, Leibniz and Hume, all under the title *Exzerpte und Notizen bis 1842*. Volume 1 contains Latin and German transcriptions, volume 2 translations from Latin into German, together with notes.

the phenomenological (and historical) experience of the different perceptions of the time that each of us can undergo. On the one hand, every temporal moment – every second, every minute of being alive – is something that is consumed in duration. For the idealist or for the 'transcendentalist', the perception of time seems to be something of this sort: a nothingness that rushes head-on towards death – especially in the Heideggerian formulation, purportedly the conclusion of modern philosophy. By contrast, for the immanentist and, a fortiori, for the materialist, the intentional *dispositif* extracted from the experience presents itself rather as an effort to stop time. Materialists undergo the indefinite movement of time but at the same time intuit it, qualify it and potentiate it, intensifying it or cooling it down with passions; when they work, they seize the second, the minute, the temporal flow from the inside, putting it in action and giving it existence. It is through *praxis* [practice], then, that time has developed (singularly or collectively) as a constructive tension. Here the moment seeks to be eternal. If you deepen this phenomenological perception still further and if, in Marxian language, you compare it with the various figures of the law of labour value, you have on the one hand, from the idealist side, a concept of value as quantitative regulation and measure of working time: it grasps the moment in the discipline of time and seeks to dominate it, establishing control over it. Such is the capitalist regime of temporality; this is how temporality is to be consumed; this is the fate of working [*operare*]! On the other hand, viewed in the light of immanence, the law of labour value presents itself as a norm of time intensified by and in work, a time valorised and valorising, a time that constitutes a form of life and a living force, productive of wealth and happiness. In *Time for Revolution* I developed these different paths, showing precisely how materialist praxis renders time creative. My reading of Marxism (in the particular tradition of *operaismo* [workerism]) can be summed up as follows: the concept of 'class struggle' is given new life when the struggle breaks the annihilating time of capitalist production and generates a time that is creative, a time that is no longer a *measure* of the labour power crushed in commodification but is, on the contrary, *living labour* and social cooperation, bodily activity (affective) and intelligent activity (cognitive) – in short, production of subjectivity, which renews life and its forms. Is this the ground on which immateriality can be concretely grasped and the work [*opera*] can be defined as 'second matter'?

★ ★ ★

Do Spinoza and Marx intersect on this ground?

To illustrate their intersecting, I would like to concentrate on the common approach that governs the way in which Spinoza and Marx open their epistemology (that is, the definition and the structuring of the instruments of a 'true knowledge') to a conception of living time [*tempo vivo*] analogous to the one presented above. By this I mean that it seems that a certain conception of the time of being could constitute the core of a comparison between Spinoza's thought and that of Marx. Not that we cannot find other common motifs – they are aplenty, and I shall point them out myself in what follows – but the suggested terrain seems to me to be central.

In their book *What Is Philosophy?* Deleuze and Guattari (1994) remind us that philosophy is neither contemplation, nor reflection, nor communication; it is an activity that creates concepts. In this light, Marx and Spinoza are philosophical brothers; in fact they create concepts in more or less the same way. Their research, first of all, reads things *realiter* [in reality] and anyway proposes to observe the constitutive tension of the concept in an ontological sense, highlighting the immanence of the relationship ('constitutive', in fact) between knowing and being. This relation is materialist, because we have (here) *cupiditas* (the desiring agent) or (there) *praxis*, both of which dominate the cognitive relation; and it is this act that determines the truth of knowledge, in other words of the construction of being.

Let me follow Spinoza, when – in *Ethics* II, Proposition 29, Note, and Proposition 27 and 40, Notes 1 and 2 – he begins to define the 'common notions'. At the beginning of the journey of knowledge, he tells us, the mind, immersed in being, will have an immediate knowledge, though confused and mutilated, of being itself [*dell'essere stesso*]: this will happen each time the mind perceives things according to the common order of nature, that is, whenever it is determined from the outside, by the chance convergence of things. By contrast, in order to know, the mind has to liberate itself of the confused, the fortuitous, and the external; and this will be possible (and true, apodeictic knowledge will be able to assert itself) only when the mind discards what is trivially common to all things, what is equally in the part and in the whole and does not constitute the essence of anything. One can say with certainty that the transcendental is the confused form of this stage of knowledge. True knowledge begins only where not the transcendental but the singular is perceived, where the particular becomes proper name. We therefore begin to step into true knowledge only through common notions that have nothing to do with ideal transcendentals. Here it is stated that what is in the part and in the whole (as pantheism would have it) is not necessarily true, because only the singularity is true. And the common notions are constructed through the activity of singularities, in other words they function to develop ontologically the desiring singularity.

Commenting on this passage in Spinoza, Deleuze (1992, ch. 17) shows very clearly that it is only within the encounters and activities of singularities that concepts can be built: the common notions (which Deleuze believes to be one of the fundamental discoveries of the *Ethics*) move from imagination and establish a curious harmony between the laws of reason and those of imagination. Reason profits here from a disposition of the imagination, which I and Spinoza can qualify with the adjective 'immaterial': that of making present to us, and disposing towards action, the things we face. Common notions, which are constructed by reason and imagination, thus become a constituent power: common notions express God, not generically, not as a deep, metaphysical source, but as the surface of the world, as the source of all the constitutive relationships of things; and therefore they affirm God's 'singularity'. God becomes the 'immaterial' means of constructing 'material' knowledge, and thus of giving us a guarantee of the being we know: common notions are the most artificial and concrete means of operating in this way. *Common does not mean more general,* in other words applicable to many modes of existence or to all the modes of a certain kind. *Common means univocal, planted in the singularity, composed of desires and form of life.* So says Deleuze. Common notions have nothing to do with signs: they simply constitute the conditions in which and the means by which we attain the third kind of knowledge – in other words true knowledge, articulated by love.

In *Ethics* IV, this same process, from its confused starting point through to the conclusions of truth, is no longer conducted with the help of imagination but on the rhythm of *cupiditas* [desire]. We know how closely imagination and desire are related in Spinoza. Since knowledge seeks the intensity of the concrete and the schematism of the imagination has transformed itself, being translated into that of constitution, we have been able to conclude that the movement of the imagination goes from the possible to the real, from the abstract to the singular. And if, in any event, this imaginative process can be dissociated from the (immaterial?) accumulation of a knowledge ruled by desire, it follows that desire is the fundamental means for orienting the path of the mind towards the concrete singular. Thus abstraction directs itself towards the concrete in order to give it, once grasped, the dignity of knowing. God has become the thing.

But now, having considered them together, let us pretend that *cupiditas* can be independent of imagination. It will not be difficult at this point to understand how, after the common notions have shown us the possibility of grasping the singularity, we can instal an analogous process, one that leads this time from *cupiditas* to the social singularities, entities and institutions that are at once collective and singular (multitudinous). The motor imagination *cupiditas*, having built the common notions, now privileges *cupiditas* and opens the common notions to the common of existence. To put it another way, the process extends and widens in the direction of the constitution of the city. So the *potenza* [power] of desire becomes a moment of political constitution. The *potenza* of *cupiditas* is absolute: in its immateriality, *cupiditas* develops a constitutive *potentia* [power] that is deployed in its entirety. *Cupiditas* neither transcends nor alters the body but completes it, develops it, expands it in the common and fills it with the common. Matter has become 'second matter', immaterial matter to be precise, passing from the body to the ensemble of bodies, to the city. And it is a process of life. So, '[a] free man thinks of nothing less than of death; and his wisdom is a meditation on life, not on death' (Spinoza 1985: *Ethics* IV, Proposition 67). *Heidegger dégage!* ['Move over, Heidegger!']

To conclude my quest for a non-trivial definition of 'immateriality' insofar as it relates to Spinoza, let us retain, then, that the common notions are on the one hand at the origin of true knowledge (they render rational knowledge capable of giving access to the singularity), making intuition the materialist function of the immaterial of reason; and on the other hand they constitute the connecting link between the theory of knowledge and the ethical–political dimension of human life, making *cupiditas* and, gradually, love the very form of politics. The common notions thus make it possible to connect desire and intuitive knowledge; they give maximum *potenza* to reason, so that it may introduce us to singularity; and at the same time they give us access to the interindividual dimension and to the immateriality of politics. (On all this, in addition to the analysis, in Deleuze 1968, of the development of the theme of common notions in the second part of Spinoza's *Ethics* II (Proposition 38, Note, Proposition 39 and Corollary, Proposition 40, Notes 1 and 2, Proposition 44 and Corollary 1 and 2 and Proposition 49, Corollary), I think one should bear in mind what I say in Negri 1981 not only about Part II, but more especially about Part IV of the *Ethics*. See also Macherey (1997, ch. 4.)

* * *

Now let me turn to Marx, starting with the 'Einleitung' ('Introduction' [*sc.* to the *Grundrisse*]) of 1857 (Marx 1975). Marx too, in constructing his epistemology, begins by considering the totality of production as a confused and mutilated totality. The dialectic of production is here immediately subordinated to a materialistic definition that sees the link between unities and differences as subjected to capitalist domination. How can one break this connection? What discontinuities and differences and crises are introduced by real processes? The answer has something of the impossible: the very category of production, Marx tells us, has to be dissolved and taken out of the harmonious capitalist figure in which it is offered to us. In this figure, it is dominated by commodity fetishism (which corrupts every category) and critique can only be constituted when that harmonious capitalist figure has been critiqued in the name of difference and singularity. So here, too, we are dealing with a materialist immersion (as was the case in Spinoza, in forms that, mutatis mutandis, were pantheistic) that looks for self-consciousness through the rupture of the abstract and apprehension of the concrete, of how singular and resistant it is, and different, when measured against any given general or generic conception of capitalist production (ibid., pp. 85–6).

The capitalist relationship that achieves the concrete in the abstract has to be traversed, then; but one must discover in it the possibility of crisis, of splitting. To tell the truth, in Marxist dialectics, there is no category that can be defined outside the *potenze* of the split. Capital is not a leviathan but a social relationship; it would not produce wealth if it could not extract it, tear it out of living labour, which it contains and commands. And this containment – which is that of exploitation – cannot be given if the components of the totality are not singularised, subjectivated. In this way their relationship becomes antagonistic, in this way the concept of capital is a concept of class struggle. But how do we arrive at this concept, when both the method of science and the method of political economy are based on the search for unity? How can critique become science, choosing singularity and antagonism against capitalist command?

This is where Marx's procedure develops – and how similar it is to that of Spinoza! It consists in the methodical affirmation of a construction of concepts that are based not on the ingenuous recovery of the 'real', of the 'concrete', but on a breakup of the 'process of synthesis' of the data of intuition and representation. A naive methodology starts from the presupposition of the concrete; Marxian methodology assumes the concrete as a result, as a 'synthesis of many determinations, unity of the multiple'. It is not the abstract that contains the singular, but the singular that contains the abstract (ibid., pp. 21–2). Such is the path that 'determined abstraction' travels – it is the capacity to relate the concept (the abstract) back to the real determination and there to establish its dynamic, the *dispositif*. The concrete thus comes about through a cognitive process of abstraction that has not only the capacity to fold back on the concrete, illuminating it, but also the capacity, implicit in abstraction, to recognise its unique and possibly antagonist *potenza*. In addition to discriminating and analysing the concrete, determined abstraction will determine the possibility and will thus place itself as a motor of transformation of the concrete into a 'tendency' of the historical process. This means that the concrete finds in abstraction not only a spatial determination and a temporal meaning, that is, a full singularisation, but also a constitutive dynamism: its own operating projection (ibid., pp. 24–8).

Let us return to ourselves. Abstraction, insofar as it is folded onto singularity, onto concrete determination, becomes force, movement of forces, subjectivation of forces; and this is how it reconquers the real: need and its force, proletarians and their labour, the social and its political determination of class. 'Practically true': this is the point of categorial development in which abstraction tightens and reaches the completeness of its relationship with historical reality. 'Practically true' is the science that becomes a concept of transformation, the possibility and actuality of a transformative force. Abstraction tightens reality, analysis becomes project, and class politics constitutes reality, a new reality. Here the constitutive principle becomes central (ibid., pp. 28–9).

⋆ ⋆ ⋆

There is thus a deep and fundamental relationship between Spinoza and Marx around the use of abstract determinations for the purpose of reaching singular (concrete) objects, and this relationship can be recognised as being implanted on the modalities of the epistemological transition: in the philosophical work of these two authors, it is around immateriality that the concept opens to the singular materiality of the thing.

Let me make a kind of summary of this procedure, which (as I see it) concludes in a kinship of method:

(a) For a start, it moves from an immersion into the natural universe or into the universe of production, to break its mute compactness.

(b) Looking for what? Looking for the practically real, in other words for the realisation of a desire or of a resistance (or both), of a *cupiditas* or of an expression of living labour (or both) – a realisation that presents itself as production of subjectivity. This subjectivation is located at the point where the real forks into experience and truth, into movement and finality, into subjection and liberation. The metaphysical block of pantheism and the political (capitalist) compact of the world of production are dissolved by the unique approach. Dialectic is recognised as antagonism and not as a synthesis, *Aufhebung*. (In order to be precise and eliminate misunderstandings, I emphasise that, a little further in the *Grundrisse*, Marx adds: 'further on, before leaving this problem, it will be necessary to correct the idealistic way of exposition, which gives the impression that it is a matter of pure conceptual determinations and the dialectic of these concepts', p. 69).

(c) 'Common concepts' or 'abstracts determinations' are names given to the cognitive means that permit us to grasp the concrete (and to construct it uniquely) as the endpoint of an unavoidable abstract passage, or as the result of a cognitive productive investment. These instruments of knowledge introduce us to a unique materiality (that is, renewed by knowledge), to the world, to the totality of singularities that constitute it, because knowledge is not discovery of an essence but opening of a common project.

(d) *Cupiditas* and *praxis* are the material *dispositifs* that construct the truth and, with it, the common.

(e) The common moves. It is constituted by a set of forces that, starting from their own construction as singularities and from their self-recognition as *potenze*, invest the world, transforming it, conquering it, and building its truth.

(f) *Cupiditas* and *praxis* operate as tendential forces; they constitute an accumulation and a motor of transformation that clashes against the abstractions of domination and condenses *potenza*. The intensity of *cupiditas* and of *praxis* is creative, it realises an ontological *potenza*. In their materiality is condensed the immateriality of the concept – and vice versa.

(g) *Cupiditas* being constructed on *conatus* [striving] and the struggle
    being produced by class consciousness, knowledge being built
    beyond the confusion of sensation and the misery of wage labour
    – this is what allows us to take practice to be the seal of truth.
    Ontology becomes practical, social ontology becomes political.
(h) And then, finally, in this development of knowledge [*conoscenza*]
    and desire, of knowledge [*sapere*] and virtue, they become princi-
    ples constitutive of reality. They become that because they invest
    the bodies, and the bodies integrate their movement.

                              ⋆ ⋆ ⋆

As always, the analysis of the thought of great philosophers (and
especially this bridging that I have created between Spinoza and
Marx) also helps to clarify important problems in the analysis of the
present. To me, for example, as I said at the start of this conversation,
the analysis of the epistemological foundation of the knowledge of
bodies in Spinoza and Marx serves to define the concept of 'immateriality' or, better, of 'immaterial labour' – in my efforts to understand
the transformations in the technical and political composition of
labour power in the postindustrial age. In the postindustrial mode
of production value-creating processes based on the autonomy of
social cooperation and on the exploitation of cognitive labour impose
themselves: in other words, what imposes itself is the thing called
'immaterial labour'. As has already been said, the use of this term
('immaterial') is somewhat ambiguous: it seems to want to describe a
raising of the quality of labour to the level of ideas, as if labour could
be imagined outside its material consistency, outside daily fatigue
and suffering, outside the wear and tear and outside its danger to
mind and body. And would this exaltation of the immaterial nature
of labour come about in the wage regime of capitalism – thus liberating us from that misery that, as the story goes, has hung over us
since divine punishment forced man and woman to leave the garden
of delights? Well, I don't think I ever fell for this mystifying illusion. Indeed, I have always used the concept of immateriality with
great caution – but also (it is true) as a result of a certain decision:
because it is the most materialist concept that has so far been created
to describe how living labour works in the postindustrial system of
production. Other terms had been proposed, but neither 'cognitive'
nor 'cooperative' (although they shed light on the concept) give a
sufficiently full picture of the relationships that are interwoven in
the new dimension of labour, nor do they adequately define the
powers installed therein. 'Immaterial' seems to work better, because

it includes 'cooperative' and 'cognitive' and places them precisely within that materialist and Spinozist definition of common notions and within that Marxian definition of abstract value ('determined abstraction') that I discussed earlier.

More than this: in those definitions we also find a kind of introduction to a concept of labour power that brings us close to the figure of biopolitical labour, where bodies are directly set to work (materially and immaterially) in the production of life, and capitalist value creation invests the whole of life, as multiplicity and as social cooperation.

★ ★ ★

Let me now allow those observations on the different phenomenological perceptions of temporality from which I began to take me to a different place. Now, a warning: both in Spinoza and in Marx, these perceptions reveal themselves to be at once an immersion of the body into temporality and a creative rupture of temporality. This is typical of revolutionary thought, when the decision of subversion and the invention of a new temporality traverse bodies in their singularity and constitute them as multitude.

By evaluating the constituent *potenza* expressed in modern revolutions, we shall be able to find that immaterial, singular and potent concept of temporality. Some have chosen to label it the 'Machiavelli moment' – a certainly correct evaluation, but one too limited to the political function. For me, against the purely political (and therefore evenemential, or isolated and unique) definition of constituent *potere* [power], the constituting [*costituenza*] seems to articulate itself materially and to determine itself through the continuous fabric of the activity of bodies. Materiality has become biopolitical. Will it not be precisely this 'modification', this passing 'from … to …', the 'discontinuity' of production that is the proper definition of the immaterial? What is certain is that it is not possible to imagine the political outside the transformations not only of the social in general, but also of bodies.

Let me briefly mention an almost archaeological moment of revolutionary political thought. A biopolitical conception of constituent power is present enough in the history of the Russian Revolution of 1917. Plekhanov, Bogdanov, Lenin, Bukharin, Trotsky himself, and above all Lunacharsky already understood constituent power biopolitically, as a transformation of the materiality of needs and desires, as the metamorphosis of bodies in the new Soviet construct. Apart from Marx, Spinoza is very present in that discussion. Then, when the revolution enters the Stalinist Thermidor, nobody speaks of

Spinoza any more and Marx is reduced to Diamat. However, as soon as dissent reawakens, lo and behold: the Spinozist joy of the revolution of bodies reappears in the Soviet philosophy of the 1950s and 1960s. Ilyenkov is the philosopher who awakens it and who opens up, through analysis, to new political passions.

In the same period, via pathways that are certainly not in common, Merleau-Ponty developed the same *dispositif* in France; it coincided with and reflected on the political action of the militants of the group Socialisme ou Barbarie. He picks up from Canguilhem intuitions and hypotheses of biological knowledge, transforms them into an epistemology of the social sciences, and assumes the epistemology of the living, of material singularity, as the basis of an epistemology of *potenza*. As Matteo Pasquinelli once observed, Deleuze's (1922) essay captures the 'pluralistic flowering' of the immaterial within materiality. I, for one, am interested in going even further, to say that in Italy too, at the base of *Quaderni Rossi*, after Hungary 1956, which marked the disintegration of Stalinism, there were philosophical reflections of a similar kind in the school of Enzo Paci and in the utopia that Husserl's unpublished papers at Louvain seemed to nurture.

★ ★ ★

As I said at the outset, I expressed similar sentiments in *Macchina tempo*; in particular, I formulated there the problem that opens when, once the whole society is absorbed by capitalist valorisation or is 'really subsumed' to capital (as is the case today), you can no longer see where and how a measure of the productivity of life, of value, can emerge. It is even harder – and one wonders whether it is still possible – to grasp, within this totalitarian tautology, its antagonistic overturning, a point of rupture, the emergence of a Machiavellian moment. One asked oneself, then: What would be a *dispositif* that could capture the innovative materiality – or rather, the immateriality – of the collective time of social cooperation, of the productive *potenza* of the working class, and could indicate its *excedence* within and against the tautological totality of real subsumption? What is the temporal *dispositif* that could constitute a revolutionary breaking point? What I was looking for – in the compact materiality of the immaterial complex that society was becoming through its global subsumption to capital – was therefore a *dispositif* that would clarify the internality of the revolutionary material within the global immaterial, and vice versa. Now, this *dispositif* on the one hand followed the figures that resulted from the extraction of surplus value and exploitation, overturning and singularising them; on the other, it posited *cupiditas* and class struggle as an ontological basis for dissecting capitalist development at this stage, for overturning its determinations and for subjectivating the antagonism. The materialism of bodies and the powerful immateriality that figured their abstraction, just as Spinoza and Marx had imagined them, became the irreducible point of contradiction of real subsumption. While the Frankfurt School and the various philosophies of alienation, with an air of resignation, decreed the tragic end of the Industrial Revolution and the beginning of the end of history in the complete capitalist subsumption of society, in the total reduction of use value to exchange value, and in the progressive immaterialisation of labour (automation in the factory, computerisation of society, hegemony of services, liquidity of production and exchanges, etc.), we were posing right there the foundations of a new revolutionary movement in a new subjectivity that was changing, 'monstrously' refounding itself in the immaterial, in desire and in imagination. Immateriality, in the two meanings it had acquired, sociological and ontological, material and excedent, proposed itself as a solution to the tautological senselessness of real subsumption – as a contradictory sign (with the aid of Spinoza and Marx) of the possibility of revolution, of the revolutionary event within and against capitalist development in the postindustrial age.

This path is completed in 'Kairos' (in Negri 2003, pp. 181–223), which shows explicitly how the immateriality of labour power, abstract in production and singularised in bodies, is now capable of building a common.

* * *

So then, have we rescued the term 'immateriality' of labour power from the dishonour heaped upon it by the 'true' materialists? I do not know. However, having shown, with Marx, how only the abstract permits us to find the singularities and, with Spinoza, how only imagination and desire are capable of expressing the material *potenza* of bodies – well, at this point I have perhaps come close, so to speak, to a materialist legitimation of the term 'immaterial'. I offer it to the revolutionary movement. It will be applied to the attempt to subvert a world in which value creation is social and productivity is cooperative, in which labour power is cognitive and wealth is becoming increasingly abstract. It is here that the analysis must begin, as always happens when the philosophical toolbox is truly materialist.

30 October 2012–4 February 2013

7

Spinoza, necessity and freedom

Some interpretational alternatives

In this chapter I shall try to demonstrate how complex Spinoza is, in the *Ethics* as a whole, especially when he addresses the theme of freedom and necessity.[1] For that reason, his so-called geometric method of proceeding has confused the minds of many – especially on this particular topic. Hegel, for example, reading in haste and perhaps limiting himself to the opening pages of the *Ethics*, could say that Spinozism was determinism (and, he would add, a determinism that was soon transfigured into acosmism). If Hegel had continued his reading (and had not been so conditioned by the preconceptions of making philosophy 'inside' Spinozism, which the previous thirty years had practised),[2] he would probably have noticed that, with regard to necessity and freedom, in the *Ethics* there coexist the same movements – sometimes contradictory, sometimes convergent – that in the tradition of materialism apply to the other ontological and ethical categories. By this I mean that at least two lines coexist in materialism: one that exalts the world in its compact effectuality, and another that makes freedom the (immanent and efficient) witness of the transformation of the real. Continuing to read the *Ethics* beyond the point at which Hegel loses patience, readers can then grasp Spinoza's discourse as it unfolds according to the second proposition of materialism – which it does eminently; and thus they can notice that freedom (which at the beginning of the *Ethics* is confused with contingency and hence forcibly resolved in necessity) conquers instead, in the 'prolix' continuation of the work, a constituent ontological *potenza* [power]. From that point on, only contingency, not freedom, is dominated by necessity; on the other hand, contingency – the real and necessary given – once invested by freedom, configures itself as the actual horizon of innovating the world. It is the real itself, the pure, absolute immanence, which presents itself untimely and forms and constitutes itself ethically (see Deleuze 1968 and 1981).

So let us move on (briefly) from the beginning of the *Ethics*, asking a very simple question. What does freedom of will mean here? This is precisely the question that Spinoza asks in Part I, Propositions 30 and following. The answer is unambiguous: '*Voluntas* ['will']* cannot be called a free cause, but only a necessary or compelled one' (Part I, Proposition 32).[3] In Corollaries I and II of this Proposition, the non-freedom of the will is ensured, both in the human being and – more importantly – in divinity, by the fact that one cannot think of will as absolute if one thinks of it as free. If it were indeed free, its efficacy would be diluted in the infinite succession of causes and would disperse itself there. On the other hand, '[t]hings could have been produced by God in no other way, and in no other order than they have been produced' (Proposition 33). The Appendix of Part I completes the argument:

> With these [demonstrations] I have explained God's nature and properties: that he exists necessarily; that he is unique; that he is and acts from the necessity alone of his nature […] and finally that all things have been predetermined by God, not from freedom of the will *or* absolute good pleasure, but from God's absolute nature, *or* infinite power.

Determinism thus presents itself here as a presupposition, and free will is restricted in the necessity of the divine substance. Wherever one looks, absolute divine nature expresses its infinite *potenza*, or cause: 'God, therefore, is the immanent, not the transitive cause of all things' (Part I, Proposition 18)[4] – and all the more so of every act of will. At the end of this reflection, freedom appears as an illusion of being free, because people, while aware of their actions, are 'ignorant of the causes by which they are determined. This, then, is their idea of freedom – that they do not know any cause of their actions' (Part II, Proposition 35, Note).

At the end of this first section of the *Ethics*, Hegel would therefore be right. It is precisely here, however, that the picture of determinism begins to shake; and from this point on Hegel is no longer right. If freedom is an illusion, one has to understand whether there is a way that allows us to overcome the illusion and to arrive at the heart of truth – here, to give a new meaning to freedom. It is not uncommon

---

* Translator's note: Giancotti (quoted in the Italian original) translates *voluntas* here with 'freedom' (*la libertà*).

to find the pantheist philosopher asking himself this question. Here
it happens with great force: pantheism brushes aside any catatonic
aspect and Spinoza's materialism, 'cautiously' but no less overwhelmingly, comes to light. A first act of breathing? Maybe. Let us see
how it works. The first transition takes place between Propositions
41 and 49 of Part II of the *Ethics*. The argument is simple: when
we gather appropriate ideas, or ideas that express the truth, at that
moment reason perceives being 'under some kind of eternity' [*sub
quadam æternitatis specie*]. Here 'the will and the intellect are one
and the same' (Part II, Proposition 49, Corollary). This means that
will establishes itself again, on that ontological fabric from which the
illusion of free will had expelled it.[5] What is actually happening? It is
this: recognising itself in the eternal, will takes away from the intellect
(at the very moment of confirming that it is ontologically intrinsic to
it) the privileged position of being the destroyer of illusion. Now, it
is will itself that overturns the illusion of freedom; it is will itself that
feeds on the eternal. But if God is the production of being and truth
consists in the recognition of this production, will (and true freedom)
will now be placed on that terrain of production of being that divinity had shown us. Under 'some kind of eternity', will reveals itself
as a machine of truth, albeit within the absolute determinism of the
sequences of being.[6]

As we progress in our reading of the *Ethics*, we shall find other, ever
wider breathing moments for freedom. We have already seen what the
central displacement is: it consists of the fact that will, after having
been subordinated to intellect, is now placed at its base. In Part III of
the *Ethics* this displacement is further specified, or rather shown to be
a constitutive *dispositif*. In fact will and freedom are transformed into
each other, to the extent that *cupiditas* [passion, desire], moving from
appetitus [longing], grows (increases, strengthens) into *amor* [love].
The Note to Part III, Proposition 47 – but in general this whole articulation of Part III – introduces the transition, showing how will
and freedom condition each other in the process of liberation – or
rather of ontological constitution in the joy of freedom. From here
on there will be a continuous deepening of this process throughout
the entire development of the *Ethics*. Here are three passages, by way
of illustration: Proposition 49 in Part III; Proposition 11 in Part IV;
and Proposition 5 in Part V. The first passage indicates that, in the
human being, the passion for freedom is more powerful than awareness of necessity. But the second passage corrects and completes this
indication, showing how the free passion for something that is necessary may be more intense than that which leads to the contingent

or the possible. This amounts to saying: the passion for freedom has nothing to do with the contingent and the possible but rather has to do, immediately, with adherence to the absolute. However, if one wanted to preserve some contradictoriness in the first two steps, the third would reveal the full and complete appearance of that contradictoriness. In fact '[a]n affect towards a thing we imagine to be free is greater than that towards a thing we imagine to be necessary, and consequently is still greater than that towards a thing we imagine as possible or contingent' (*Ethics*, Part V, Proposition 5). So – and this happens at the very heart of Parts IV and V – we have the definition of the free person as the one whose *cupiditas*, born as it is of reason, will never have excess, since it is given [unqualifiedly].[7]

What is there to say, except that here the determinist picture is strongly shaken? And what is there to add, except that there is no trace of 'acosmism' and that, in this sort of metaphysical determination, ontological constitution is paradoxically arranged by reason and love, which is almost to say by freedom? And therefore that Spinozist pantheism is a true machine of freedom?[8]

Part V of the *Ethics* will give further confirmation of the reversal of perspective that has taken place between the beginning and the end of the process, where the emancipation lived by human freedom is affirmed – until human freedom comes to be installed in divinity, as happens precisely in Part V.[9]

The theme of ontological innovation is central and unresolved in classical materialism. Between Democritus and Epicurus, the atomistic construction of the world is immersed in eternity. As for freedom, that is the ethical conduct of life, played in terms of a metaphor of the cosmos. In this flattening, freedom is extinguished and innovation is incomprehensible. Only in Lucretius does liberty strive to break the trivial [*insignificante*] metaphor and to act autonomously in the physical totality of atomism, to impose a tear on eternity. And yet Lucretius posits his *clinamen* [swerve] on tiptoes, in a whisper, almost as if he wanted to cancel the violence of the tear through the imperceptibility of the deviation that makes it possible to innovate the world – to grasp the singular, and thereby the sense of freedom. The rain of atoms opens to a very small, but at the same time huge glow: poetry is exalted by it, philosophy humbled, the problem raised. Modernity will inherit that problem, unsolved.

It is only in Spinoza that the problem is transformed. Here in fact the ontology of materialism is not interrupted by the *clinamen* but is invested and refounded by desire. The rhythm of the constitution of the world is supported – in a confusion of forms – by a living force that develops in the world to constitute itself as divine. Freedom is built in this ontological development, whose continuity it interprets in an absolute immanence, productive of a *vis viva* that develops from physical *conatus* [striving] to human *cupiditas*, and then to divine *amor*. Ethics constitutes the physical world, before interpreting (acting) the human world and reaching (revealing itself in) the divine world. Eternity is lived as a presence, and here – in this presence – freedom and innovation, ethics and ontology build the world together. Or, better, they strive in this direction (as Spinoza would say).

The shift of the problem between classical and Spinozian materialism is powerful. The problem of innovation is not in fact formulated as that of a deviation of the course of life within the horizon of eternity. Absolute immanence is the dynamism of life and gives life its *potenza*. The singularity begins to stand out in the sea of being – or, if you prefer, it begins to reveal itself in the overall dynamics of materialist teleology. But is this radical shift enough to solve the problem? Is a physics of desire sufficient to give eternity the figure of freedom? Is it enough to imprint on the world the discontinuity of innovation, and thus to go beyond those heavy and repeated aporias of materialism? Spinozist ascetics has something of a *coup de force*. In fact it imposes immanence as the only horizon (singular and concrete) of materialist discourse; and it instils the force of life there. Freedom is affirmed therein as liberation. And yet, having said this, it must be added that Spinozist asceticism is incapable of giving full meaning to its own progression. As already happened in Lucretius, in Spinoza, too, in order to proceed, one relies on a series of imperceptible leaps of quality that seek to break every blockage, every limit that stands against freedom. Thus in Spinoza we move between physics, ethics and theology with the same uncertainty with which being (and the *clinamen*) moved in the atomic turbulence of Lucretius.

In the grip of the cold necessity of the given, of a materialism that is almost transcendental, the modification introduced by Spinozism is therefore still too cautious, indeed rather insignificant. In fact, here again, no creative meaning is given to the progression of the real, to the unity of innovation and eternity. For this is the problem: to produce freedom on the same lines as eternity, and to make it not a flat result but the active key to the construction or reconstruction of the world. On the contrary, a necessity that aspired to be axiological and an assumed image of the world represented themselves surreptitiously even in these philosophies of absolute immanence. Classical and Christian teleology, the idea of infinity, sprayed their transcendental (or rather transcendent) poison onto the radicality of materialist procedure. Freedom, when it approaches the eternal, is still broken by an external determination of value, by an order, by a measure, by an identity that come from somewhere else (and we do not know wherefrom). In the modern period, in the age of humanist ascesis, some kind of axiological transcendence (and a phantom of ontological transcendentalism) percolates in even through the most powerful materialist teleologies.

Spinoza's *Ethics* is tightly limited by these conditions of development. And if, as we have seen elsewhere, it is true that Spinozist causality is subordinated to the random nature of the surface (and every element of internal necessity is removed, and all finality is ignored) for the simple reason that only the effect qualifies the cause – still, having said this, we should also admit that the formidable leap forward that Spinoza forces modern philosophy as a whole to make[10] comes to a halt before the necessity of a pre-established order and measure. And if, as we have seen, it is true that in Spinoza freedom is built through desire (in the various natural and intellectual figures that represent it) and that consequently nothing affects it if not the naked givenness of passion – that said, the fact still remains that freedom ends in an idea of mystical, abstract beatitude. In short, if the determinism that the materialism of antiquity had produced is here, in Spinoza, decisively overcome (as we saw in the first paragraph of this chapter), there still remains in the *Ethics* the shadow, the pledge (evanescent and yet real) of an order and of a measure that are transcendental.

So is the problem of freedom not really resolvable from the point of view of a materialist approach to the themes of ethics and ontology?

★ ★ ★

Having tested the intrinsic limit of the Spinozist conception of freedom in the context of the difficulties that the materialist tradition presents to the solution of those problems, it is nevertheless possible to define another point of view or, better, to effect a different entry into the problematic (materialist) field of Spinozist freedom. In fact, for some time now, Spinozist philology has revealed the many curvatures of the 'experience' of Spinoza, which make it possible not only to follow the deductive and geometric path of his work, but also to unravel its complexity, indeed its prolixity.[11] It is from this perspective that it will probably be possible in what follows – proceeding from below, precisely from the context of the 'Spinozist' experience – to avoid the transcendental limit to the Spinozist conception of freedom that I just recognised: it will be possible to follow the path of freedom and of ontological innovation in its immediacy. The question, then, is no longer 'What is freedom?', but 'Who is free?'. That is, how, in the experience of singularity, do necessity and freedom interrelate? How does this interrelation come about, a singular relationship between mind and nature? Anyone with a sudden desire to object to this possibility could of course appeal to the tribunal of metaphysical 'parallelism' and could accuse me of forgetting the logical preconstitution of singularity and its ontological prefiguration (parallelism precisely when you consider it to be the keystone of Spinoza's theoretical edifice). Without forgetting them, there is still the possibility of grasping these interrelations in the dynamics of singularity and life, in the genealogy of freedom – rather than in their violent, transcendental conjunction.[12]

There is an episode, in some sense paradoxical, that can allow me to proceed in the direction of singularisation within the *Ethics*. This is where Spinoza speaks of 'laughter' [*ridere*]. (Before going into this argument in detail, I might note that laughter – the same that Spinoza assumes as a pivotal point in the phenomenology of passions – is today increasingly seen as a place of ontological revelation or of confrontation – or both – in the definition of singularity).[13]

Let me turn directly to Spinoza. In Spinoza, and in particular in the *Ethics*, laughter has various functions. The first is the rhetorical one that shows it to be a fundamental weapon of freedom. Laughter allows us to oppose superstition by mocking it and to free ourselves of the fear that is the source, the nutriment and the scheme of superstition. In the Note to Proposition 45 in Part IV one comes across a beautiful exercise of this demystifying laughter. 'For laughter and joking are pure Joy'; and

> Nothing forbids our pleasure except a savage and sad superstition. [...] No deity, nor anyone else, unless he is envious, takes pleasure in my lack of power and my misfortune; nor does he ascribe to virtue our tears, sighs, fear, and other things of that kind, which are signs of a weak mind. On the contrary, the greater the Joy with which we are affected, the greater the perfection to which we pass, i.e., the more we must participate in the divine nature. To use things, therefore, and take pleasure in them as far as possible [...] this is the part of a wise man. (*Ethics*, Part IV, Proposition 45)

But this is not enough. Beyond the polemical function, or perhaps because of the force that it expresses, we can grasp the true ontological function of laughter, since it disposes both the body and the mind and urges them radically towards that very high state of virtue that is *laetitia* (or joy). Therefore laughter has a central function in Spinoza's phenomenology of passions, as a constituent of the dynamic forces that bind together mind and nature – which is another way of saying freedom and necessity.[14]

But let us see, succinctly, exactly how Spinoza's discourse on laughter is articulated. We are in Part IV of the *Ethics*, at the centre of that strange phenomenology of the passions that describes a super-abundant development of being. At one point Spinoza asks how freedom disposes itself on that appetite that leads the human to the highest good. The first qualification of this disposition is joyfulness. 'Joy is an affect by which the body's power of acting is increased or aided. Sadness, on the other hand, is an affect by which the body's power of acting is diminished or restrained. And so joy is directly good' (Proposition 41). But this is not enough. Where joy relates to the body, we call it 'hilarity'. Spinoza had already defined hilarity as a 'pleasure' [*titillatio*] in Part III – 'the affect of Joy which is related to the Mind and Body at once I call Pleasure [*titillatio*] or cheerfulness [*hilaritas*]' (Proposition 11, Note)[15] – but now, retaining that involvement, he distinguishes and raises laughter above *titillatio*, because the former (unlike the latter, which is partial) involves *all* parts of the body homogeneously... So, laughter appears to us – or, better, it *is* – a passion constitutive of being and that places itself at the intersection of the parallel lines that run through the substance, and it determines a powerful equilibrium of substance. While therefore *titillatio* (or 'pleasure') 'can be excessive and evil' (Part IV, Proposition 43) 'cheerfulness [*hilaritas*] cannot be excessive but is always good' (Part IV, Proposition 42). Whatever the limits, the cautions, the reservations that Spinoza applies in the discussion,[16] we have an awareness (and we appreciate it with the mind as much as we construct it with the body) of being inside the production of singularity, that is, in a place where the material process constitutive of being emerges from a thousand points: when we laugh, we inhabit that point from which reality is produced. Laughter is here, then, perfection in body and soul – and consequently we understand why its capacity for demystifying superstition (as we already saw in the Note to Proposition 45 in Part IV) lies here; and also its capacity to develop freedom:

He who rightly knows that all things follow from the necessity of the divine nature and happen according to the eternal laws and rules of nature will surely find nothing worthy of Hate, Mockery or Disdain, nor anyone whom he will pity. Instead he will strive, as far as human virtue allows, to act well, as they say, and rejoice. (Part IV, Proposition 50, Note)

Freedom is in fact liberation from all the baleful passions that block the creativity of being – from hatred, mockery, contempt, as we have seen; but also from fear and hope (Proposition 47), from indignation (Proposition 51), from humility (Proposition 53), from repentance (Proposition 54)... And one could continue, as indeed I shall, in part, in the next paragraph.

So who is free? A point of definition is given here, which is not a break with the general Spinozist system but is certainly different from the traditional parameters of constructing a materialist system of nature: it is almost the anticipation of a Faustian topos, of that materialism of the Enlightenment that was to be in Diderot was to dream.[17] I set out to find a place from which there would emanate – from below – the innovative immanence of mind and of body, the invention of life, the event in its singularity. The theme of laughter seems to fit the bill... to attack the problem. Blessed Spinoza!* He has this capacity to overturn every preconceived reading of his thought... And now, in this case, he is able to offer us an ethical and ontological point of view that allows materialist thought to slip out of the furrows within which freedom had been traced in modernity.

* * *

Is it not going too far (since it is acceptable only relatively, from a correct philological perspective) to rely like this on laughter for grasping a path of subjectivation within Spinoza's *Ethics*? One would have to admit that there is something paradoxical about this line of argumentation. And yet...

... And yet in the whole *Ethics* (and particularly in Part IV) there is a constant pressure to find ways of subjectivation – which means to reconstruct the order of the world starting from the bottom of the *potenza* of ethical action (singular, individual or collective). Spinozist pantheism has become the destiny of philosophical materialism precisely because Spinoza was the only one during the modern period, at its highest moment between the crisis of the Renaissance and the Enlightenment, to take the task of putting philosophy back on its

---

* Translator's note: Benedictus, the Latin form of Spinoza's first name Benedetto (Baruch in Hebrew), is a nominalisation of the adjective *benedictus*, which meant 'well spoken of' (in classical Latin) and 'blessed' (in medieval and scholastic Latin).

feet. It is in fact no coincidence that in Part IV of the *Ethics*, before the discussion arrives at laughter, we can observe the founding of the democratic concept of state, and hence the collective subjectivation of the political, in the series of Propositions 37–40, which broadly address the question of the constitution of a body and a mind in which everything is of everyone. Now, we think (and Spinoza thought so too) that the definition of the concept of democracy and, in general, progress in the area of an 'absolutely' democratic politics constitute the highest distiction of metaphysics (when to talk about politics is to talk about freedom); but in doing so we underestimate the problem of subjectivation in Spinoza. With him, the theme of politics and democracy is certainly fundamental, but more fundamental is the solution of the problem that materialism raises – the problem of subjectivation as innovation of being; and we have seen how central that problem is to the *Ethics*. The solution that goes through the political seems to Spinoza to be the simplest (and he traverses it entirely).[18] But it is not enough. Freedom must be discovered as a constituent force; liberation must be built as *potenza*$_2$ [potentiality]; the production of subjectivity must be recognised as an ontological machine. So, *after* having built the political, Spinoza starts to work around the subject of subjectivation and advances, as we have seen, in that phenomenology of the passions that has one of its productive nodes in the discovery of *hilaritas*. He therefore recognises the process of subjectivation (or the identification, around the subject, of the matrix of the innovation of being) as having a fundamental ontological intensity for the process (or in the 'experience') that leads the human being to liberation.

We have, in a recent work by Laurent Bove, one of the most effective efforts to show how Spinoza's *Ethics* is actually organised through a series of strategic decisions of *conatus* that construct a dynamic ontology or dispose ontologically a series of affirmative acts (Bove 1996). The meaning of this movement is the realisation of that to which everyone (every singularity, individual or collective) is held by his nature – so that a paradoxical teleology comes about: one defined by *acquiescentia in se ipso* [self-satisfaction/esteem], or one built by the resistance (insistence) of subjectivity (individual or collective). Now, within the framework of this strategy, the Spinozist theory of emotions is revisited by Laurent Bove around two apexes: *habitudo* in the *Theological–Political Treatise* and *hilaritas* in the *Ethics*. What the two categories have in common is that they put together mind and nature, freedom and necessity, at the moment when subjective being (collective or individual) is being produced. These categories therefore open

(or close) the metaphysical parallelism from the bottom of the constitutive process and capture within the subjective decision (individual
or collective) the powerful key to the innovation of being.

This demonstration seems to me to correspond entirely to what I
have been expressing up until now. But I would suggest a small step
forward (whether it really is that will be up to us all to assess later).
This step consists in replacing 'affirmative' potentiality with 'constitutive' potentiality. Let me explain. If we return to Proposition 44 in
Part IV – the Proposition at the end of the development of the analysis that, through *hilaritas*, had constituted the new regime (or the new
strategy) of the emotions – we read: 'Love and desire can be excessive.'
The demonstration rests on the fact that love and desire can have an
external cause, and therefore can be taken off their own measure by
it. And yet, once the development of the argument on joy comes to
its conclusion, we are presented with a new definition: 'a desire that
arises from reason [...] cannot be excessive' (Part IV, Proposition
61). That this proposition does not contradict the preceding one is
made clear by the proof, where precisely 'this' desire is shown to be,
unlike the 'other', a direct expression of human essence – that is, of
human nature. It therefore has no excess because it has no 'external'
(in other words no external cause that might take away its power of
expression). So here we arrive at the problem: What does it mean to
have no 'external'? What does it mean to be 'autonomous'? Is this a
purely 'affirmative' experience (in other words a self-declaration of
essence) or a 'constitutive' experience (that is, expressive, innovative)? In short, does 'not having excess' mean that *cupiditas* and desire
are related to a natural, static and essential dimension? Or does this
'not having excess' mean, on the contrary, an 'excedence', autonomous and constitutive, of *cupiditas* – a '*potenza* of desire'?

Perhaps at this point I don't need to add my own answer[19] – but
it is, I think, the same as that of Spinoza. Just read the titles of the
Propositions that come next in Part IV. Proposition 63: 'He who
is guided by fear, and does good to avoid evil, is not guided by
reason'; Proposition 64: 'Knowledge of evil is an inadequate knowledge'; Proposition 67: 'A free person thinks of nothing less than
death, and such a person's wisdom is a meditation on life, not on
death'; Proposition 68: ' If people were born free, they would form no
concept of good and evil so long as they remained free'.

Putting materialist philosophy back on its feet means therefore
examining very closely the experience of classical materialism, in its
cold affirmation of necessity; it means grasping, in Proposition 61 of
Part IV ('a Desire that arises from reason [...] cannot be excessive'),

the meaning of that 'arises from' [*ex ... oritur*]. It transforms freedom into *potenza₂* or, better, it absolutely exalts *cupiditas*, desire, in the face of any possible negation, that is, of the negation of its power to act, which is then a 'lack of power' (which is the name of evil). Here, then, what is affirmative is only and unqualifiedly [*simpliciter*] constitutive. Nature, to which the will of reason relates, has been completely constituted. Nature, far from being a model, is a product of freedom. The eternity of nature is a consequence of the productivity of singularities, of the freedom of the minds that produce and constitute being. This (among other things) is Spinoza's conclusion. In fact, 'he who has a body capable of a great many things has a mind whose greatest part is eternal' (Part V, Proposition 39).[20]

And now, to conclude, something of a digression.

> In the sense in which I can ever bring anything about (such as stomach-ache through over-eating), I can also bring about an act of willing. In this sense I bring about the act of willing to swim by jumping into the water. Doubtless I was trying to say: I can't will willing; that is, it makes no sense to speak of willing willing. 'Willing' is not the name of an action; and so not the name of any voluntary action either. And my use of a wrong expression came from our wanting to think of willing as an immediate non-causal bringing about. (Wittgenstein 1958, §613)

These are the terms in which Wittgenstein, stimulated by profound philosophical recollections (the indiscernibility of the cause with regard to the effect), opens his research on free will, denying consistency to the problem. Here I am not able to pursue the argument as a whole; suffice it to point to its conclusion. 'Our mistake is to look for an explanation where we ought to look at what happens as a "proto-phenomenon". That is, where we ought to have said: this language-game is played' (ibid., p. 654).

In Wittgenstein, the impossibility of distinguishing cause from effect in the mechanism of the passions is therefore entirely Spinozist, so to speak. But immediately a big difference emerges: here the originary phenomenon, and the game, are not joyous (nor are they productive), whereas they are for Spinoza. In Spinoza, joy fuses with origin – and what an origin! Liberation is a game, says Spinoza, in which the fact of wishing 'acutely' implants itself whole on our intellect, and sustains it in its openness to the absolute. Indeed, it simply leads it there, with joy. In Wittgenstein, however, too often the game is sad: a sad passion. Perhaps, in demystifying free will with a Spinozist line of argument, Wittgenstein does not understand what is fundamental in Spinoza: the excedence of being that is connected to the expression of freedom, the joy that crowns the expression of freedom. So, 'if that famous humourist lived today, he would certainly die laughing' (Spinoza 1951, p. 163) when he heard that will is originary, but without joy.

There is, however, a humourist, an ironic hero who transforms Wittgenstein's analytic hieroglyphs into biopolitical prose; and we know him. Here he is, albeit incidentally, proposing his point of view on the whole question.

> A point, live dog, grew into sight running across the sweep of sand. Lord, is he going to attack me? Respect his liberty. You will not be master of others or their slave. I have my stick. Sit tight. [...] From farther away, walking shoreward across from the crested tide, figures, two. The two maries. They have tucked it safe among the bulrushes. Peekaboo. I see you. No, the dog. He is running back to them. Who? [...] The dog's bark ran towards him, stopped, ran back. Dog of my enemy. I just simply stood pale, silent, bayed about. *Terribilia meditans*. (Joyce 1993, p. 45)

I can perhaps close these very limited reflections on the interpretative alternatives for the pair freedom–necessity in Spinoza by commenting on this well-known passage from Chapter 3 of *Ulysses*. So pay attention to the literary game. Between the distant sighting of the snarling dog and the configuration of a proximate danger, there are in fact other fantastic images (which I cannot reproduce here): the landing of the terrible Danes (the Vikings) on this selfsame Dublin beach, the massacres and horrors that follow... Then, after that, lightning flashes, warning of present danger, and the tormenting memory, the nightmare of the death of Joyce's mother – a great trauma of imagination (and freedom). Well, that brings us right back to Spinoza – where, within a necessity that comes from afar and envelops everything, in the face of danger, the choice of freedom arises as an untimely [*intempestivo*] act. Effect and cause are twisted together. *Terribilia meditans*. I arm myself with sticks, to defend myself from the bad dog that is approaching – I respect your freedom but I defend my own. So says Joycean irony. So is freedom a stick? Continue ... In Spinoza's political philosophy it was. Here, in the place of *hilaritas*, around the effort of the coupling of mind and body – a coupling that is productive of being – it is still, as resistance, as the capacity to respond to danger; but it is not any longer so (on the other hand, this transformation takes place even in political philosophy, in different times and forms) because *this* resistance, untimely, is now excedence over causality, the effect that triumphs over the cause, innovating the necessary rhythm of production of the world. Give me a lever and I will move the world; give me a stick and I shall reshape Hobbesian fear; give me a game and I shall destroy every fiction; give me a tool and I shall reinvent being. It is difficult to express materialism in a more effective way – and I mean the freedom of or in materialism. Give me the tool. In other words, let us build a prosthesis of the body and of the mind that forces the world, from lack of being to excedence of being. Or let us build freedom as ontological excess. Spinoza defined freedom as innovation, innovation as freedom, and freedom and innovation as an excedent ontological constitution. He translated, that is, the materialist *clinamen* of classical antiquity into the modern language of production.

Perhaps, like Wittgenstein and Joyce, Spinoza too offers some arguments for going beyond the modern.

Notes

1 I will do so without adding much to what I have already written in my essays on Spinoza from 1981 to 1998, now collected in Negri 1998. In the 1995 essay 'Democrazia ed eternità in Spinoza', included in that collection, I delivered a deep self-criticism of the too rigid periodisation of Spinoza's thinking and of its internal contradictions, two features present in *L'Anomalia selvaggia* (Negri 1981).

2 What Hegel had read of Spinoza (and in what cultural milieu) is well covered in Chiereghin 1961. What Hegel had *not* read of Spinoza is systematically noted in Martial Gueroult's commentary to his two-volume *Spinoza* (Gueroult 1968, 1974).

3 The original quotations from Spinoza's *Ethics* were taken from the Italian translation prepared by Emilia Giancotti (Spinoza 1988); the English passages are quoted from Spinoza 1985 (with slight modifications).

4 But see Spinoza, *Ethics*, Part I, 17, Corollary ii and Note; and, previously, Proposition 7; Proposition 8, Note ii; and then Part I, 35.

5 On this passage, see Macherey 1997a, pp. 367–407.

6 I permit myself another reference to my article 'Democrazia ed eternità in Spinoza', in Negri 1998, for a list of places in Spinoza where this problematic is raised and discussed.

7 Spinoza, *Ethics*, Part IV, Propositions 61–2. On this passage, see Macherey 1997a, pp. 321–431.

8 For a defence of the free human being, see Spinoza, *Ethics*, Part IV, Propositions 68, 69, 70, 71, 72, 73, where the basis of the full realisation of political freedom is also discussed. On these propositions, see Macherey 1997b.

9 In addition to Spinoza, *Ethics*, Part V, Proposition 10 and Note,

Proposition 22, and Proposition 29 and Note 42, see the commentaries
by G. Deleuze cited here in n. 3, as well as Matheron 1969 and Chaui
1999.

10 Nietzsche is perhaps the person who understood this best. For the
Spinozist breakpoint in modern philosophy, see my essay 'Spinoza e i
postmoderni', now in Negri 1998.

11 See Moreau 1994: this book is certainly the most important one in the
new generation of studies on Spinoza that developed after the work of
refounding Spinozist critique between 1960 and 1980.

12 Deleuze indicates several times the possibility of following Spinoza's
argument along two lines: one that starts with the formalisation of the
Ethics' Propositions, another that develops in the informal discussion in
the the *Ethics*' Notes. In my view, Deleuze's point (often confirmed by
the critical tradition) can be interpreted more broadly than the simple
philosophical reference to the difference between the Propositions and
the Notes permits.

13 See, for example, Deleuze 1967. For an opposite position, see G. Bataille,
as correctly expounded in Perniola 1998, esp. pp. 132–3. On the historical background to the negative view of laughter in the medieval tradition
of the church, see Le Goff 1999, and in particular the sections 'Le Rire
au Moyen Age' (pp. 1343ff.) and 'Le Rire dans le règles monastiques du
haut Moyen Age' (pp. 1357ff.).

14 On laughter or laughing as a constitutive potentiality, and thus against
Bergson's (1924) theorisation of laughter, see Certeau 1986.

15 For the much contested translation of *titillatio*, see Emila Giancotti's
note in her translation of the *Ethics* (Spinoza 1988, pp. 400–1). Pierre
Macherey (who upholds the French tradition of translating it as *chatouil-
lement*, which is entirely inappropriate) offers an intelligent discussion of
the concept in Macherey 1995, pp. 120ff.

16 See in particular Part III, Proposition 59, Note; and Explicatio, Definition
III in Appendix, Part III.

17 See Diderot 1961 and Vernière 1954.

18 Spinoza, *Ethics*, Part IV, Propositions 37–40 and passim. But on this
development of Spinoza's thinking, see Negri 1981 (now also in Negri
1998).

19 In the various successive interpretations at the end of the 1960s, the
experience of Spinoza's *potentia* has generally been read, by Deleuze and
also by Matheron, as one of an ontological excedence. In particular, this
does not mean that a certain naturalism (and thus a transcendental idea
of measure and of order) does not remain in Spinoza's thinking, as I have
strongly argued in the present section of this chapter.

20 And again: 'In this life, then, we strive especially that the infant's body
may change (as much as its nature allows and assists) into another,
capable of a great many things and related to a mind very much con-
scious of itself, of God, and of things. We strive, that is, that whatever is

related to its memory or imagination is of hardly any moment in relation to its intellect' (Spinoza 1985: *Ethics*, Part V, Proposition 39, Note). But '[d]eath is less harmful to us, the greater the mind's clear and distinct knowledge, and hence the more the mind loves God. [...] Next, because the highest satisfaction there can be arises from the third kind of knowledge, it follows from this that the human mind can be of such a nature that the part of the mind which we have shown perishes with the body is of no moment in relation to what remains' (Proposition 38, Note).

8

Justice

Spinoza and others

1

In November 1971 Michel Foucault and Noam Chomsky met in Eindhoven. The [televised] debate between them was labelled at the time 'Human nature: justice against power' (Foucault 2001; Chomsky and Foucault 2011). Chomsky, taking his theory of language as a starting point, proposed that linguistic structures have a natural foundation and considered this naturalness to be enacted (and traversed) by human creativity. Human beings, endowed as they are with a given biological organisation, have in their heads a set of intellectual structures, open to possibility, free for invention. Foucault objected to this naturalistic concept of language and, in particular, expressed his difficulty with the view that, in the human spirit or – to put it in Chomsky's way – in human nature, those innate conditions of existence and expression of language are a given. He suggested that the systems of rules that make science possible (together with the language on which science is based) consist rather in social forms, in relations of production, in class struggles: these would constitute *grids* within which historical determinations find their consistency. When the discussion moves from analysis of language and the origin of science into political analysis and the definition of justice, the differences between Foucault and Chomsky became more marked. Chomsky argued that the creative drive inherent in human nature can realise itself fully outside any constraint from the social organisation and that struggle consists in setting this possibility free; Foucault, on the other hand, maintained that social institutions are only apparently neutral and independent; in fact they are shot through with political violence, which masks their oppressive function and allows them to operate obscurely and omnilaterally. Foucault attacked Chomsky (Chomsky and Foucault, 2011):

FOUCAULT So it is in the name of a purer justice that you criticise the functioning of justice [...] It is true that in all social struggles, there is a question of 'justice'. [...] Rather than thinking of the social struggle in terms of 'justice', one has to emphasise justice in terms of the social struggle.

CHOMSKY It seems to me that the difference isn't between legality and ideal justice; it's rather between legality and better justice. (2011, pp. 60–1)

FOUCAULT If you like, I will be a little bit Nietzschean about this; in other words, it seems to me that the idea of justice in itself is an idea which in effect has been invented and put to work in different types of societies as an instrument of a certain political and economic power or as a weapon against that power. But it seems to me that, in any case, the notion of justice itself functions within a society of classes as a claim made by the oppressed class and as a justification for it. [...] [T]hese notions of human nature, of justice, of the realisation of the essence of human beings, are all notions and concepts which have been formed within our civilisation, within our type of knowledge and our form of philosophy, and that as a result form part of our class system; and one can't [...] put forward these notions to describe or justify a fight which should – and shall in principle – overthrow the very fundaments of our society. This is an extrapolation for which I can't find the historical justification. (2011, pp. 66–70)

Here Chomsky's utopia collides with Foucault's Marxism and Nietzscheanism.

2

It is curious how the theories of natural law disengage justice from law. Chomsky operates this separation in optimistic terms – I mean that his conception of natural law, albeit individualist, voluntarist and democratic (and also rather anarchist) is fundamentally open and is oriented towards eudaemonism. However, any theory of natural law can only admit and justify law as 'political justice'. The validity and the truth of law are therefore always 'relative' (if compared to the ontological absoluteness of truth), but they constitute a 'necessary' figure of justice (when confronted with the urgencies and the contingency of history). But, while so far we have seen in Chomsky the positive, decisively utopian version of justice, there is also there especially a negative version of natural justice, when the latter is realistically compared with positive law – a version that cannot be called pessimistic because it is basically 'mystical' (and hence religious, whether theistic or not).

> *Justice, might.* It is right that what is just should be obeyed; it is neces-
> sary that what is strongest should be obeyed. Justice without might is
> helpless; might without justice is tyrannical. Justice without might is
> gainsaid, because there are always offenders; might without justice
> is condemned. We must then combine justice and might, and to this
> end make what is just strong, or what is strong just. (Pascal 1958:
> *Pensées*, para 298; translation slightly modified)

But in fact Pascal's reasoning goes beyond this, seeking the cause of this reduction:

> one affirms the essence of justice to be the authority of the legislator;
> another, the interest of the sovereign; another, present custom, and this
> is the most sure. Nothing, according to reason alone, is just in itself; all
> changes with time. Custom creates the whole of equity, for the simple
> reason that it is accepted. It is the *mystical foundation* of its *authority*;
> whoever carries it back to first principles destroys it. (*Pensées*, para 294)

Here Pascal takes up a notion contained in Montaigne: 'And so laws keep up their good standing not because they are just, but because they are laws: that is the mystical foundation of their authority, they have no other… Anyone who obeys them because they are just is not obeying them the way they should be obeyed' (Montaigne, *Essais* 3, ch. 13; cf. also the quotation of this passage in Derrida 1992, p. 12).

Jacques Derrida offered a powerful commentary on the structure of Pascal's pessimism. Justice would not be put simply at the service of a force or social power but, at its deepest structural level, would consist of a *coup de force* [act of force], a performative violence without any pre-existing foundation: 'No justification may or may not take on the role of meta-language in relation to the performativity of the institution's language or its dominant interpretation' (Derrida 1994, p. 13). In taking up Pascal's critique, Derrida thus puts together a *dispositif* generally critical of legal ideology:

> it turns out to be a nonviolent violence. This does not mean that the
> laws are unjust in their own, in the sense of illegal or illegitimate. They
> are neither legal nor illegal in their founding moment. They go beyond
> the opposition of the well-founded and unfounded … even if the
> success of performative founders of a law presupposes pre-established
> conditions or conventions, the same 'mystic' limit will be the source of
> those conditions, rules or conventions. (Ibid., p. 34)

Inasmuch as the law is an element of calculation and, hence, cannot be justice, the hiatus is insuperable. Inasmuch as the law is an element of calculation, justice is incalculable.

The only terrain on which we can advance in analysing justice is thus that of deconstruction. 'Justice is deconstruction' – it is, in other words, critique of the concept and location of a possible *excedence*. A possible reconstruction? We shall see. Moving forward, Derrida relies on the theorists of the critical legal studies school and, with them, digs into the difference between justice and law and signals the aporias that show up there. The first aporia – the *epochē* [suspension] of the rule – consists in the fact that the foundation on which a law is established will never be reached: the determination of justice, which should have been the foundation of law, cannot, in reality, be traced back – and that foundation will therefore be buried, dissimulated, deferred, and at the same time violently proposed, as if it were a real foundation. 'Here the best paradigm is the founding of the nation-states or the institutive act of a constitution that establishes what one calls in French *l'état de droit*' (ibid., pp. 23–4). The second aporia – the ghost of the undecidable – consists in deciding to calculate what is not calculable. 'The undecidable is [...] the experience of that which, though heterogeneous, foreign to the order of the calculable and the rule, is still obliged [...] to give itself up to the impossible decision, while taking account of law and rules' (ibid., p. 24). A third aporia – the urgency that obstructs the horizon of knowledge – is that every decision in law is always required immediately, as soon as possible. But a performative can be just, especially in the case of justice, only if it is based on other performatives. If justice commands to calculate, it forgets that it is uncalculable; if justice demands to calculate immediately, within a defined time, it forgets that its decision is based on the undefined.

There emerges here a grand idea, of an infinite horizon with which the practice of justice confronts itself: the Pascalian mystical is overturned into the infinity that has to be traversed. But in Derrida this overturning is posited in ontologically inconsistent terms: the infinite appears here not as a perspective but as an inaccessible horizon; it is not a terrain for operating on, it is not the edge of a determinate being that has to be left behind, but a void into which one falls; and it is interpretable as a *myth* rather than as a *dispositif*. Derrida's version – that separation between law and justice that relies on deconstruction – represents an element of modernity: individualism, naturalism and universality (based on nature) constitute the base of that contradiction between justice and law, which remains as it is – fixed in the pessimistic logic of the mystical, of the inexpressible. Sign of a 'libertine' condition? Sceptical expression of an absolute rejection of ontology? No, because, whatever the limits of the reasoning, what is marked here is a detachment: justice exceeds law, and this excedence has to be grasped and followed through. Along this transition, deconstruction has the possibility of becoming an opening to the production of subjectivity, in other words to a mode of operating in and beyond the limit marked by the aporias of law in the face of justice. Let me recall Foucault again, in the debate with Chomsky, when he responds definitively to the latter's naturalist framing:

> I would like to answer you in terms of Spinoza and say that the proletariat doesn't wage war against the ruling class because it considers such a war to be just. The proletariat makes war with the ruling class because, for the first time in history, it wants to take power. And because it will overthrow the power of the ruling class it considers such a war to be just. (Chomsky and Foucault 2011, p. 62)

3

'The exploration of logic means the exploration of *everything that is subject to law*. And outside logic everything is accidental' (Wittgenstein 2001: *Tractatus*, 6.3). But this applies only to the logic of libertinistic individualism that leads, pessimistically and sceptically, to the mystical. It is dominant in the *modern age*, where individualism triumphs – but it is valid only for that logic. Not only deconstruction – the philosophical critique of *postmodernity* – discovers it; this problematic places itself in a generalised way at the head of the aporias of law and justice, in an era – postmodernism – when those aporias are no longer permitted and when the composition of law and justice is made necessary by the compacting of production and forms of living – in short, when normativity is attracted unreservedly to immanence. *There is no longer an outside*. Here opens, therefore, a new field of research. Calculable–non-calculable: what the relation between justice and law (and therefore traditional aporetics) proposes to us is not a problem of measurement, but rather a situation of exception, an indeterminacy, something in consequence not measurable. And this does not happen simply because it is not currently possible to provide a measure but because, on the horizon of that totalisation, there is no measure. In today's social reality, a realistic semantics will recognise that contradictory (naturalist and individualist) function of law and justice, reduced to zero through immersion in the immanence of any normative determination.

But this same semantics restores the relation between justice and law as effectiveness. In what form? Outside any possibility of transcendence, of any tendency to the transcendent. Justice as an ideal is annulled in the tautology of present being; but its annulment is redeemed [*riscattata*] by the presence of the tension between justice and law as an immanent and compact relationship.

It is the economists who have grasped this condition with the greatest clarity. The horizon of social conflictuality (in which the justice relationship lives) cannot be resolved except through acts of authority. Pascalian mysticism is reintroduced into the figure of the state, which is not content with declaring itself to be an authority but claims to be a function (technical and immanent) of reality. In this way, because it is *within*, it is a function that has the power to resolve the problem. Keynes says that money is what the state declares periodically, to make an honest, legal settling of monetary contracts; yet at some point (and in the present) the state demanded not only the right to enforce compliance with the dictionary, but also the right to write it. As the state does this, as it eliminates every outside, the monetary function becomes a balance – fragile and always prey to manipulation – between supply and demand, between production and ways of living. Polanyi, too, repeats the same notion, insisting that the antinomic elements that live in the social can at most be balanced through state regulation (it is only in this balancing that the state defines, through law, a certain justice).

A series of problems arises here. They constitute aporias that are no longer radical but mobile, fragmented, and yet historically effective and recorded by experience. For example, how can law be subjected to deconstruction (to justice), when society has become increasingly massified and justice seems to be nothing but a contingent rule of balance and distribution? Or, better, how can an excedence of justice emerge in such a society any more? Here law and justice can at best be made to coincide in the form of administration.

And yet people still suffer injustice and die from justice, with increasing frequency. This leads to further thoughts. On the one hand, the postmodern society of mature (financial) capitalism presents itself as a compacted, institutionally balanced structure, and claims to be a fabric, a product of self-regulation. This self-regulation is a tautology that has eliminated all measure, all possibility of measurement. In this tautology everything is in fact transferable to everything and interchangeable: there is no difference, only repetition. And yet – and this is a second fundamental aspect – something has happened, namely the change of form that the problem of justice takes. The demand for justice arises here in the 'common' – no longer on parts that are making themselves a whole, no longer on the ambiguous dialectics between justice and law, but on the articulations of a 'common' that pulls law and justice into one reality. This means that here, at the centre of the definition of justice, there is now the theme of social order, of the distribution of wealth, of the measure of work and non-work, of happiness. The mystical is overturned at the impossibility of disolving the compactedness of these objects. Measure no longer exists, but there is a 'common', a common that is corrupt, for sure, yet effective, implanted in the present of the life of all humanity.

4

So I have referred to a repositioning of the question of justice in postmodernity. This repositioning in the *immanence* of the relation between justice and law was expressed (and was crucial) in the doctrines that had the lead in the Anglo-Saxon world in the 1960s, when a revolutionary élan was passing through society. The revolutionary aspect of that theoretical expression can be said to have been shown by the extent to which the theory has addressed these themes and has placed them, in immanent fashion, on an institutional terrain.

The work of John Rawls (1999) is central in this respect. He regards the relationship between justice and law as a systemic movement that, within a process of reflection and equilibrium – the genius of the system – compacts individuals and the social into an 'original position', productive of justice. The original position is covered by a 'veil of ignorance' that needs, however, to be torn away, so that the procedure can be put into motion. *A Theory of Justice*, the title of Rawls's foundational work of critique, does not mention any transcendental source of production of norms; nor does it assume any unconditional and categorical imperative – or any *Grundnorm* – as foundation of the system. The juridical system is rather based on an original position that corresponds to the construction of identity and principles expressed in the Declaration of Independence and in the Bill of Rights of the United States. It is by entering into this mechanism and by following through the genetic process of social institutions that the veil of ignorance is partially but progressively raised – until one arrives at the direct application of laws to particular cases by judges and administrators: here the veil is definitively removed, since the decision of justice takes place by completing the process of applying the law. We encounter here a dynamic formalism, or rather a historicised transcendentalism that allows us to grasp the process of justice in concrete ways, through institutions, within the common.

This model has been widely criticised as being grounded in idealistic or universalist positions and sustained by a quasi-metaphysical moral theory (Walzer 1981, p. 393). Also, especially in the 'communitarian' schools (Sandel 1982; Taylor 1989), it has been attacked for its inability to develop an ontology of the social. Further, in a sometimes suggestive critique, Rawls's positions have been disparaged, for example by Robert P. Wolff, for putting in place a distributive rather than productive system. Each of these assessments may in some way be substantiated and justified, but this is not my problem here. My problem is to grasp in this theory (and, in general, in the development of Anglo-Saxon thought during that phase of renewal that the 1960s represented) the introduction to a new way of putting the matter of justice and of its relationship with law.

Paul Ricoeur vigorously emphasises this when, in answer to those who attacked Rawls on the grounds that his theory of justice constitutes a *circle*, he replies that this circle is a circle of institutions.

> The theory assigns the virtue of justice to *institutions* and not, in the first place, to intersubjective relationships; and this is said in the first lines of the book: that the object of justice is the basic structure of society, its pattern of cooperation; this requires that, in the order of the reasons, one should proceed from institutions to individuals. (Ricoeur 1988, pp. 79–80)

Close to this circle there are other circles: the one from which the social bond of the contract arises, or the one that guarantees a process of distribution of rights and goods, or, finally, the one that strengthens the freedoms of citizenship through terms of equality. But that, Paul Ricoeur continues, is not important; it even risks confusing things. The fundamental result of Rawls's work is, on the contrary, essentially to place the institution *before* justice. Hence, from this perspective, we must move against the 'centrifugal forces' that tend to ruin the search for a reflective balance, that attack the synthesis of descriptive and normative elements, and that seek to deconstruct the composition of the economic and political–juridical sphere.

5

We know that Rawles's juridical theory is 'weak', that its ontological reference is fragile, that its moral theory is ambiguously positioned between liberal attitudes and tendencies to conservatism, and so on. We consider it to be a purely introductory work. Its importance

comes more from the 1960s that it interprets than from its theoretical thickness. And yet we agree with Ricoeur. The establishment of
an institutional level as an ontological premise for the development
of the debate on justice became, with Rawls's theory, a point of no
return. This (if I may put it this way) happened in the perspective of a
historical and specific redefinition of the problem of 'justice'. Today
we cannot discuss law unless we take as our starting point an institutional ontology in which justice and law are coupled. Can the same
be said about the definition of law – that law can now be defined only
as the form and language of justice? That the problem of defining the
law separately from justice (legitimacy, not simple legality) does not
exist?

Another current of juridical thought, heavily influenced by the
upheavals of the 1960s and subsequent years, should be noted
around the same theoretical convention. Luhmann and his disci-
ples, Teubner in particular, have given an answer to that question:
'just' is only that which is produced *qua* just by agents of the law.
Here, then, immanence becomes the space – empty but always filled
anew with juridical actions – on which justice is defined. As we
know, the system, according to Luhmann, reacts to the *Umwelt* and
is self-productive, capable of self-organisation only in relation to
the environment. According to Luhmann, a right becomes binding
if the horizontal effect of fundamental rights is transferred from
interpersonal conflicts to conflicts between the social system and
its environment. It appears that in this way the tendency to abstraction of legal formalism is exacerbated; but this is not so. By resisting
the environment, justice stands as a self-referential and autopoietic
product. It constitutes, in its closure to the *Umwelt*, an 'internal
totality', capable of resistance, of course, but also of productivity. In
a world created by the operations of this system, each item looks as
if it were contingent and could be different; but in reality it is not,
because the law reconstructs itself precisely on this separating edge.

In Teubner, Luhmann's approach is experienced in the globalised
dimension. Global society is a chaotic society with a thousand forms
of law and a thousand autopoieses of justice. According to Teubner,
the state is not to be confused with the constitution. Constitutions
are plural and the state stands to them as a real 'epistemological
obstacle'. Here Derrida's aporias, which I have acknowledged above,
are grasped and redefined, namely as a 'knot' that must be cut if it
can't be untied; but only the effectiveness of the institution has that
power of decision. Will it be possible to develop a form of constitutionalism without a state? For Teubner, it is impossible to make

the constitution (of a world society) coincide with only one people, with only one structure of representative institutions, with only one schema of interests: the law cannot be defined as justice in this way. Justice appears rather as completely disengaged from law when it is postulated as a system endowed with force, as a good that is 'enforced', 'empowered'.

And here is the most interesting aspect of Teubner's discourse: the sense of justice is postulated not merely as a *dispositif* and a constituent part of the law but especially as an institutional materiality, which the law discovers and develops: the law becomes *object* of a *subject* called *justice*. It is here that a theory of the common begins to form; it is here that the common begins to be recognised and conceptually developed. The common appears as the ensemble of the efforts of justice that a multitude of subjects produces. This is one side of the story. On the other side, the common opens itself to the institution as a subjective modality of justice. There seems to be here a reprise of Spinoza's *tantum iuris quantum potentiae* ['there is law inasmuch as there is power'].

6

People have talked about retributive justice and commutative justice for centuries; but the real problem has never been the distinction between these two figures of justice and their different functions; it has been the *measure* of justice – and this measure is called law. How is this measure today?

Now, as we saw at the beginning, following the debate between Chomsky and Foucault and the critical integration that Derrida makes of it, it is clear that, in the absence of measure, the only solution to the problem of justice is to do it, to assume the 'deconstruction' of law as the product of a just subjectivity. But, if this is where the path of modernity stops, with this insistence on an individual pragmatics of the just, postmodernity reveals a new trajectory for the definition of justice: to consider it as not having a possible 'outside', and hence to take it always and only as an institution (in its historical materiality), and thereby as law. What drives the fulfilment of this action is not a positivist residue but, on the contrary, an assumption that shows any definition of justice outside the collective and institutional *dispositifs* of the production of subjectivity to be unacceptable. The contemporary postmodern world (which is postindustrial, postnational, post-state, as Teubner says) offers a new ontological basis for the relationship between justice and right and for the solution to the problem of measure – and this is what it owes to Rawls's thought: the 'reflective equilibrium' that Rawls claims to build moves from an original position (situation), which composes ontologically what the struggles for freedom and equality have built over the centuries. Thus the 'reflective equilibrium' sought for combines with the production of subjectivity, and deconstruction is valid when it allows the law to *make itself* just, in that figure imposed by the struggles for equality and freedom. The originary position is (ontologically) collective, multitudinous. The production of subjectivity and the collective foundation *make* the law. What takes place here is a synthesis, not dialectical but constructive – hence the difficulties and the uncertainties that accumulate around the transition from modernity to postmodernity, from the increasingly operational emergence of subjective rights to their multitudinous consolidation around the contradictions that traverse the transformation of human rights into 'institutions of the common'.

To put it another way, we are facing the demystification of the transcendental illusion of a sovereign measure. What does 'common measure' mean, and how can it be constituted, on the measureless terrain in which we move? The imperative 'do justice' inherited from Derrida urges us here to build links and *dispositifs* that build a new 'original position' by creating networks, by appearing as constellations. Rawls's formalism is perhaps less transcendental than it has appeared to be on other occasions. In any case, whatever the nature of Rawlsian reasoning (which is probably more ambiguous than in our interpretation of it), it seems to me useful to refer to his theory, because it posits the necessity for this game of foundation and of production. I say nothing here about its intensity – I'm using only the critical opening that his thought offers. It is therefore on the materiality of that position that the cooperation of singularities can express and integrate a new ensemble of measures. Common? The point is to move in this direction. Perhaps it is the desire of the many that affirms in its development a measure of the common – having traversed an ontologically common basis of social activity and a productive composition of labour that becomes part and parcel with the form of life. What is essential, however, is that it will not be possible to derive the conquest of a common measure and the construction of institutions of the common from the development of public law, from the will of the state; rather they have to be the result of the expression and expansion, of the cooperation and coordination of subjective rights. It is in a Spinozist perspective – and I shall return on this point later – that the concept of justice can be developed and transformed into the practice of a just law.

In the North American debate, this field had been established not so much by Sandel's and Taylor's communitarianism, which too often falls back on Hegelian positions, but – albeit with great uncertainty – by the jurists of the 'critical legal studies' movement (Unger 1983 and Fish 1999 are the works that Derrida debated), through the progressive use they make of deconstructionism. This school is, at the institutional level, the most important product of the revolts on US campuses during the 1960s and 1970s. Defending deconstruction against the charge of cynicism and showing that it has, on the contrary, something positive to say about justice and social transformation – this was the goal of the students of the critical school when, at the Cardozo School of Law, they set themselves the task of defining 'justice' (Cornell et al. 1992). They sought to pursue a programme of substantial (material) justice and, as someone once observed, a deconstructionist criticism of the law carries an inbuilt alternative legal system that can't limit itself to ideal reference points – it must offer an alternative to the social and economic system as well. And, while it is nonetheless true that, when you look for a foundation of justice in excedence, as highlighted by deconstruction-ism, there sometimes appears a theological overtone that threatens to annul the power of the completed discourse (an accusation that many of these authors level at one another), the fact remains that the constitutional immanence – anthropologically meaningful – of the multitude as an open structure designed to transform justice into law [*fare della giustizia diritto*] is here finally determined.

7

The modern anomaly, the subversive 'second modernity', the one that leads from Machiavelli to Spinoza and from Marx to Foucault, had already moved on this terrain. Just one example – and I return to it here after many quotations: What is justice in Spinoza? It is, in this case too, the institutional intersection of the quest for the useful, of one's own utility, and of interindividual consensus between singular-ity and multitude, or rather between nature and reason, between a common nature and a rational and productive singularity – and this is what determines justice. I permit myself this reference to classical thought of the modern period not because I think that my research needs to receive theoretical or historical pregnancy from it but simply because in this way I can illustrate not only my own theoretical expressions but also those of our contemporaries, and give them greater consistency: 'we are dwarfs, but on the shoulders of giants' (Derrida 1994, p. 33).

Let me comment on this passage in Spinoza: 'Only insofar as men live according to the guidance of reason, must they always agree in nature' (Spinoza 1985: *Ethics* IV, Proposition 35). Spinoza says that people's will to preserve themselves – their search for utility for themselves – becomes increasingly powerful as people, reasonably, reach agreement about that end. In other words, if people, by their nature, pursue utility as their purpose, as their own good, they live according to reason and build a common society. In the Note to the same Proposition, Spinoza adds that, in this light, 'man is a God to man'. However, a human is not a solitary God – only with difficulty do humans succeed in living alone: the human being is also 'a social animal' – in fact, things are such that from the common society of people 'are born many more benefits than harms'. Nature and reason work together, then, in the construction of society. And, since nature here designates an 'original position' in which we locate ourselves, reason, inasmuch as it embraces that original position, develops an understanding of 'that good', rendering it 'common to all'. We are in *Ethics* IV, Proposition 37 (Spinoza 1985): 'The good that all those who seek virtue want for themselves, they also desire for others; and this desire is greater as their knowledge of God is greater.' Proof:

> The good that people want for themselves and love, they will love more constantly if they see that others love it. So they will strive to have the others love the same thing. And, because this good is common to all and all can enjoy it, they will therefore (by the same reason) strive that all may enjoy it. And this striving will be the greater, the more they enjoy this good.

So then: when this good, having been built by the individual, begins to be built by many, it becomes 'common good'. But, you can object to Spinoza, this does not happen often; and he admits it without difficulty (*Ethics* IV, Proposition 37, Note 1): There are many individuals around who 'are not balanced in their minds', people who are selfish and impetuous rather than reasonable – but there are also persons who act 'not by impulse, but kindly, generously, and with the greatest steadfastness of mind'. Well, these turn their existential *conatus* [striving] into an ethical *cupiditas* [desire] for the common. For this is how virtue is defined: as *cupiditas* for the common; since virtue is the power to live according to the guidance of reason alone. This is the reasoning that leads us to discover the genesis of the state as desire for the just that makes itself society, as desire of the common that makes itself institution; and in the subsequent Note 2 Spinoza stresses the point that, if people 'lived according to the guidance of reason, everyone would possess this right ... without any injury to anyone else'; but, since they are subject to conflicting effects that veil their fundamental capacity for 'true virtue', in other words for the common which is their nature, in order that they 'may be able to live harmoniously and be of assistance to one another, it is necessary for them to give up their natural right and to make one another confident that they will do nothing which could harm others'.

So is this a typical natural law solution, a rabbit pulled from the hat of a magician? Has Spinoza, too, fallen for the ideology of an 'alienation' of the natural law, which puts every law and the entire power of justice in the hands of the alienating power? This cannot be, because in Spinoza that desire that reason expresses as a virtue, that common good that reason excavates in nature in order to inaugurate it as an institution, is not given but is built. The good, both the concept of it and the right to it, is not drawn as such from nature but constructed – it exists only 'in the civil state ... where it is decided by common consent what belongs to this person and what to that'. But, far more importantly, '[f]rom this it is clear that just and unjust, sin and merit, are extrinsic notions, not attributes that explain the nature of the mind'.

The good and the just are thus at our backs, in the sense that they are the ontological fabric of which we are made; and they become law only when our acting makes them actual. This is like saying that they become 'common' – not only because they are good but because they are common expressions – and this becoming common is a kind of justice making. Justice is thus a common making – 'Things that are of assistance to the common society of people, or that bring it about that people live harmoniously, are useful; those, on the other hand, are evil that bring discord to the state' (Spinoza 1985: *Ethics* IV, Proposition 40) – and 'concord' and 'discord' should be interpreted as a 'constructing' or a 'pulling down' of the multitudinous process that produces justice.

To put it another way: this passage from the expression of subjective rights, which are often collective (e.g. these calls for justice), to the formation of law also needs to be analysed in historical and material terms. When, for example, the 'right of Mother Earth' – *pachamama* – is proposed as the basis of human rights, this means that the common is treated as the silent base that 'human rights' can and should make to speak – not in order to deny the rights of singularities, but in order to make them live productively in the common. All this means not isolating human rights as unnegotiable 'individual' realities (and this is especially true of what is called 'property rights')

but regarding them as reasonable functions in an ensemble of consensus and juridical norms.

Finally, human beings are not born free. At birth they have no
concept, either of evil or of good. 'If humans were born free, they
would form no concept of good and evil so long as they remained
free' (Spinoza 1985: *Ethics* IV, Proposition 68). But they will build
these ideas, and society and justice are born in this process. Law is
what is true [*il vero*], and it is always in tension with justice. Humans
become free by living in accordance with the dictates of reason – by
bringing to light and by expressing as a necessity what they, *qua*
humans in search of freedom, seek to bring about.

9

A small note on fear in Spinoza

1

Let me start from Spinoza's definition of fear: 'Fear is an inconstant sadness born of the idea of a future or past thing concerning which the cause of doubting has been removed' (Spinoza 1985: *Ethics* III, Definition 13). But note immediately that the definition of fear goes hand in hand with that of hope: 'Hope is nothing but an inconstant joy which has arisen from the image of a future or past thing whose outcome we doubt' (Spinoza 1985: *Ethics* III, Proposition 18, Note 2). Fear and hope are therefore related in the same way as sadness and joy. Both fear and hope, being thus connected, are affects that live in a state of uncertainty, doubt, and chiaroscuro. If doubt is not there, hope becomes certainty and fear becomes desperation. If you take away doubt, hope and fear consolidate into a state that annuls their original inconsistency. In short, it is always doubt that puts into play these two affects or passions, projecting and stretching them beyond any possible direct construction of happiness. Consequently, the affects 'of Fear [...] and Hope [...] cannot be good of themselves' (Spinoza 1985: *Ethics* IV, Proposition 47). But, if this is how things are, fear and hope have to be done away with. They are uncertain phantasms of reason; they are signs of an impotent soul. To achieve certainty and joy, we need to have overcome this situation of uncertainty: to live under the guidance of reason, we need to have been placed beyond hope and fear. We have to depend less and less on hope and free ourselves from fear; we have to impose ourselves over and against fortune and direct our actions only according to the certain counsel of reason. Will this ever be possible?

Here is another classic definition of fear. We are in Goethe's *Faust* (Part II, Act I, lines 5,394ff.). It is carnival time, and in the vast hall of the imperial palace great mythological figures arrive, allegorical characters. First comes wisdom, represented as a huge elephant (you can think of it as the large creature that dominates *The Triumph of Julius Caesar* by Andrea Mantegna). Here fear and hope are tied to the elephant, two noble ladies in chains, one sad, the other joyous ... This is what fear tells us:

> FEAR: Smoking torches, flares and lights,
> Are burning at the troubled feast:
> Among all these deceptive sights,
> Ah, I'm held fast by the feet.
> Away, you ridiculous smilers!
> I suspect those grins so bright:
> All my enemies, beguilers,
> Press towards me through the night.
> Here! A friend becomes a foe,
> Yet I know that mask, I'd say:
> One that wants to kill me, though,
> Now unmasked he creeps away.
> Gladly, heedless of direction
> I'd escape from out this world:
> But, beyond, there roars destruction:
> In mists of terror I am furled. (5,407–22)

And this is what we hear from hope, who, as in Spinoza, is tied to fear:

> HOPE: I greet you, sisters! Though today,
> And the whole of yesterday,
> You enjoyed the masquerade,
> I know all will be displayed:
> In the morning you'll unveil.
> And if, in the torchlight, we
> Don't feel particular delight,
> Yet the days to come, so bright,
> More wholly suited, we shall hail,
> Now as one, now solitary,
> Through fair fields, we'll roam loose,
> To act, or rest, as we choose,
> And in that carefree way of living,
> Dispense with nothing, go on striving:
> Guests are welcome everywhere,
> Confidently, let's appear:
> Surely, the best anywhere,
> Must be somewhere, here. (5,423–40)

Finally, wisdom, with its *Überwindung* [overcoming] of doubt and of doubt-ridden affects, could not have been left out:

INTELLIGENCE: Two of Man's worst enemies,
Fear and Hope, I bind for you,
Now this country worries me.
Make room! I'll rescue you.
I lead the living Colossus,
Turret-crowned, as you see,
Step by step, he crosses,
The highest passes, tirelessly.
But above me, on the summit,
Is a goddess, there, who's bearing
Outspread wings, and turns about,
Everywhere, to see who's winning.
Ringed by splendour, and by glory,
Shining far, on every side:
She calls herself – Victory,
Goddess of the active life. (5,441–56)

Be reassured against fear and hope, then! In Goethe too, as in Spinoza, the fear–hope coupling is defined and fixed within a mutual relationship. And, again as in Spinoza, it is only wisdom that enables us to emerge, in both cases, from the uncertainty of an affective imagination (of fear or hope). It is incredible, this similarity between Spinoza and Goethe in the phenomenology of fear, even though we know how intensely Goethe thought of himself as a Spinozist. Sadness, but above all uncertainty and doubt, colour, define and fix fear just as much as joy, and mostly uncertainty and doubt, give form to hope. Childhood and youth live in doubt and in the uncertainty of fear and hope; will maturity represent their overcoming? Being wise is to be in a mature state of certainty.

2

In some ways fear is banal. Each one of us knows what fear is; each one of us has experienced moments of fear. Not always, however – indeed rarely – can one accept the definition given thus far by following in the footsteps of the authors of modernity. As far as I am concerned, after having reread these two great authors, Spinoza and Goethe, companions to my life and thought, I find it difficult to adjust to their definition of fear. For example, at a particular moment in my life I was assailed by accusations that had no truth in them but that promised horizons of suffering and punishment. I was afraid,

and it was a fear separated from hope. There certainly were elements
of uncertainty and doubt in my fear; but there were more than frag-
ments [*morceaux*] of hope, and clear statements of truth that I was
opposing to the falsehoods, and claims to justice that sustained me
and pushed me to resist and to survive. And then fear was completely
cut off from hope; the wisdom and power of living were not balancing
between fear and hope but, as they sank into whirlpools of injustice,
they were projected forward, in the strong tension of a desire for
justice. No, there was no despair, no sense of despair at all: there
was struggle. Is it necessary that there be no fear, or is it necessary
that there be hope, for there to be struggle? Or, on the contrary, is it
sufficient to have a desire not to succumb to untruth? Is it enough to
have a passion for truth and a will not to surrender to the imposition
of falsehood, not to give in to the provocations of authority and to
terrorist intimidation?

To overcome fear, both Spinoza and Goethe put their trust not
so much in struggle as in wisdom. They see wisdom as the triumph
of reason, as serenity, as a lucid awareness of natural events and of
the mechanics of emotions. But this does not correspond to my own
experience. On the contrary, fear can spin on itself, and wisdom
can miss every single appointment. Fear can have a pressing and
unsurmountable logic. When I am in uncertainty, I can find myself
wandering endlessly. Huge instruments of power and monstrous
figures of repression can whirl up in my path and remove all possibility of my being wise. There is a prejudice in the conceptions of
Spinoza and Goethe: that there is a balance of passions! In reality,
wisdom is far removed from any ideal balance and can present itself
as balance only when it already contains force, realistically. This call
to reality is a call to the social, to its determinations, and to the passions that emerge in and from the social. On this terrain we can begin
to question ourselves once again. If you are poor, if you are unarmed,
how can you ever be wise? How will you ever be able to appeal to the
sweetness of reason when you are subjected to the violence of power?
The classic element that dominates the modern image of wisdom – as
between Spinoza and Goethe – is (and this needs to be recognised)
disembodied; and, if it were not disembodied, it would anyway be
dehistoricised; and, when it is not dehistoricised, it is hypocritical.
Here we need to change register in our attempt to define the fear
we experience in the social, in the belief that it is only in the social,
in politics, that we shall be able to solve the problem. And so let us
say, on the one hand, that the relationships that life knots up in the
social don't necessarily have wisdom. Indeed, if fear is separated from

uncertainty, it does not mean that it will resurface as wisdom; it can still remain permanently sunk in a terror without reason and without outlet. On the other hand, we can say: only struggle, only the recognition of violence of and in life (and of our being active in it) will give us a way out of fear.

If we come back now to consider Spinoza, how static his conception of wisdom seems to be, in the bracketing that holds together both hope and fear! (The tearing of the continuity of the process from *cupiditas* [desire] to *amor* [love] in Part V of *Ethics* will change the definition of wisdom.) And again, if we go back to Goethe, how empty that exaltation is that elephant wisdom makes of itself ... If a mouse came up, what would happen? We know the elephant's allergy to mice. If, then, a rat were to appear, dirty and horrible (of the kind many of us meet in life), what would happen? The neoclassical discourse, where wisdom is neatly presented as victory over fear and hope, does not go much beyond the exhibition of an empty and ideal equilibrium, in reality a 'bourgeois' hope for a peaceful solution to any drama. This victory really does not know how to fly. On the pivotal point of equivocal passions, the great wings of bourgeois equilibrium are weighed down by unforeseeable chance events and Goethe's dialectical solution comes nowhere near acting out the tragic story of Hegel's dialectical solution.

3

However, in the thought of the bourgeoisie (that is, in the dominant ideology of modernity) fear (thus unresolved) fulfils an essential political function. Hobbes reminds us of this, in a grand and highly impressive scenario: the human is a wolf to the human, and it is in order to overcome fear that humans, wishing to enter into association but unable to do so spontaneously, transfer their natural right to a sovereign, to whom they offer an indiscriminate obligation to defend life. Overcoming fear is here not entrusted to wisdom but to the state. The dialectic of fear has shifted entirely onto the political terrain; it has become a genealogy of power, and it indicates a path that leads exclusively from the bottom up, from the impotences of life to the transcendent power of the state. This function of fear as a creator of order has now become so commonplace and is repeated so often that it is almost trivial to mention it. Today the political insistence on security, the threat of permanent insecurity, the need for the state of emergency, and the urgency of exceptional circumstances renew with great effectiveness that genealogical insight of the modern conceptions of the state.

Here again, however, we have a chance of reviewing the alternatives to the model.

When the repetition of the word 'fear' and the heightened sense
of its fragility lead to a transcendent transfer, is this not a fearful
and humiliated reaction of self-defence, of a desperate trust willing
to countenance the expropriation of the creative *potenza* [power] of
the singularities? In short, is it not what others have called superstition? Here we return again to Spinoza. In the *Theological–Political
Treatise* [*TPT*] he launches his ironic and anti-authoritarian wisdom
against fear, when the later becomes the foundation of the state.
'Superstition, then, is engendered, preserved, and fostered by fear
... only while under the governance of fear do humans fall a prey to
superstition ... There is nothing more effective than superstition to
hold the multitude' (*TPT*, Preface, 11). On the other hand,

> From the foundations of the Republic explained above it follows most
> clearly that its ultimate end is not to dominate, restraining men by fear,
> and making them subject to another's control, but on the contrary to
> free each person from fear so that he can live securely, as far as pos-
> sible, i.e., so that he retains to the utmost his natural right to exist and
> operate without harm to himself or anyone else. [...] The end of the
> Republic, I say, is not to change men from rational beings into beasts
> or automata [...] So the end of the Republic is really freedom. (Spinoza
> 2016b: *TPT*, ch. 20: 11–12)

And, again, peace is not what remains when fear is removed, but
is the force that overcomes fear: peace is virtue. There is only one
dimension of fear, one aspect of fearful dependence, that remains
and is developed in Spinoza's discussion of building a social life of
peace and happiness – the fear of solitude: 'all men fear being alone,
because no one alone has the strength to defend himself, and no one
alone can provide the things necessary for life. So by nature men
desire a civil order. It can't happen by nature that they'll ever completely dissolve it' (Spinoza 2016a: *Political Treatise* [*PT*], ch. 6: 1).

This Spinozist line of thought, so intensely anti-Hobbesian, has
its origins in Machiavelli: in reconstructing the history of republican
democracy, Machiavelli recognises the art of despotic government in
the use of techniques of fear and identifies the basis of all resistance,
struggle, and hence democratic institution in the rejection of a peace
imposed through fear and in the indignation against those who use
such means. In the play of democratic political action, fear does not
represent, then, a pole that can be mediated, that can be summed up
within a higher wisdom; it is not something that can be dialectically

subsumed – fear is rather an emotion that politics and a full life in the *polis* should remove.

This is all the more so as, in postmodern terms, we stopped addressing the relationship between fear and hope simply as a tension between poverty and wealth (expressed in the economic horizon of class struggle); we address it as a confrontation between poverty and activity, between desire and *potenza* of creative expression – terms that now characterise the language of biopolitics. In this case a positive, creative tension arises against fear. It is not only the tension that accompanies us in an alternative between conditions of social being (poverty *versus* wealth), but the tension that is embodied in activity: work as a potentiality for producing increasingly free and happy forms of life. *Vita activa*.

4

Yet, contrary to what appears (namely that work and knowledge can allow for happiness today), social life is now broached almost exclusively in terms of security. The daily bread of a humankind that has reached well-being seems to be fear. We are haunted by an obsessive repetitiveness of journalism and by endless news reports about the pitfalls of daily life. If we are good workers, we are threatened by clandestine migrants; if we are good citizens, our tranquility is endangered by all kinds of delinquents who infiltrate the metropolis; in short, there are others of every colour and race who threaten the moral certainties of our existence, the religious roots of our culture, and the very foundations of our own relative privileges, the self-referentiality, unaccompanied by states of mind, of our knowledge, and the routine of our practices of life. Fear reinvents society and once again imposes the need to trust authority. Postmodernism goes back to its roots, but rather underhandedly: the idea that each person is the enemy of the other (which, paradoxically, is supposed to have made possible the birth of society) is now accompanied by the idea that our society is threatened by the other and that the future viability of our social life depends on dealing with this threat. Here fear becomes part of the biopolitical order of society. Foucault imagined a type of society (a system of biopowers) in which the passions of the population are ordered and made functional for the economic and moral reproduction of existence. If this hypothesis is correct, then fear extends as both effect and cause of the proposed order, of the required normativity, of the penality imposed on the collective totality of the passions of the citizenry.

Fear thus becomes something very different from what Spinoza and Goethe describe. Modernity is left behind. In the liquid order of postmodernity, fear is liquid too: it does not connect to hope (ambiguously, in an uncertain but real manner), but sinks us into the all-embracing generality of fear of the other, into the liquid abyss of an alterity that creates fear. There is no balance anymore; we are all at risk. Spinoza tells us that 'there is neither Hope without Fear, nor Fear without Hope' (Spinoza 1985: *Ethics* III, Proposition 50, and Note and Definition XIII). But, contradicting what he suggests here, fear no longer has fluctuations of mood. Danger, the state of being afraid, is present at every moment. Phantasms, nightmares? Maybe. However, the time and the space of metropolitan life and citizen existence are now defined by insecurity. Past and future are linked by an agonising anxiety to live. It is interesting to note how reactionary philosophies (à la Heidegger) had anticipated this metaphysical sense; but we were still in the era of the state, and in its territory. Today, under global deterritorialisation, that terror and trembling are becoming universal. The pathologisation in society opens spaces for threats that present themselves on a global scale. Economic and financial risks, ecological risks and risks of pandemics, and the risk of terrorism and war take turns in reminding us how much fragility our lives have to reckon with. Terrorism and famines, contagious diseases and tsunamis... You have to be scared. The good globalised citizen is afraid.

There arises a certain nostalgia for that impossible balance of wisdom of which the classics gave us a glimpse, alongside fear and hope, doubt and uncertainty. Human beings pursued that dream with a pure mind, and it is of little concern that it was bourgeois. The present condition, on the other hand, leaves us only one alternative: to live in a state of fear or to fight against fear. But fear is a biopolitical product, a structural condition of present-day being; it traverses ways of life and is made up of them. So what is to be done, then? Struggle? Of course, struggle against fear. But if fear is so intimately tied to social being, what probability of success can our struggle ever have? Maybe, if we wish to liberate ourselves from fear, we shall have to liberate ourselves from biopower as a whole. As a whole – easier said than done... As a whole? If fear is everywhere, then it has to be pursued and destroyed everywhere. If it has become one with power, then life has to be hurled against it. Thus the only possibility left to us is to break the opaque mirror of that securitarian paradigm, of that phantasm of fear, and to make our existences and their excedences – alternative, and full of passion – the terrain of our refusal... Are these extreme and delusional proposals? Perhaps. It is true that, if fear is now the queen of all passions, then the struggle for liberation may itself have become an illusion.

Naturally, what I have written here is only the record of what is often said of fear by educated and intelligent people who, having known fear in all the forms in which it is expressed and can express itself, feel its effects with suffering and register with indignation its impact on their own conscience. And then these same people, understanding the effectiveness of fear, confess to be prey to it themselves – in short, they adjust to it. In today's conformism, we experience again that fear has become an independent force and that it is no longer linked to hope. However, the discussion cannot end here.

5

Johann Wolfgang von Goethe reminds us that strange and very deep things can happen in life. On 20 September 1792, accompanying the duke of Weimar in the military expedition against Paris and the French revolutionaries, Goethe personally witnessed how the largest and strongest European armies were inexplicably thrown back at Valmy by bands of unlikely *sansculottes*, French armed popular forces: 'In that place and on that day, a new era began in the history of the world, and we will be proud to say that we witnessed it at its start' (*Von hier und heute geht eine neue Epoche der Weltgeschichte aus, und ihr könnt sagen, ihr seid dabei gewesen*, Goethe 1822). Borges notes that often our eyes see only what they are accustomed to seeing. Tacitus had not perceived the devastating power of the crucifixion of Jesus, even though he mentions it in his *Histories*. And Goethe is here overwhelmed by an amazement that leaves him passive, astonished. Perhaps fear needs other eyes to look at it. Perhaps fear needs new Dionysian *sansculottes* to push it beyond the frontiers of our limited imagination.

According to this limited imagination, it is realistic, for example, to agree with Spinoza when he states: 'The mob is terrifying, if unafraid' (Spinoza 1985: *Ethics* IV, Proposition 54, Note). 'If weak-minded men were all equally proud, ashamed of nothing, and afraid of nothing, how could they be united or restrained by any bonds?' (ibid.). A strict affirmation of *raison d'état*, this! It is an indication of government to the powerful; a reading – as Spinoza himself emphasises – of the directive 'to do politics' that the prophets aimed at the Jewish people; a typical expression of thinking from above, proper to princes – as Machiavelli says in the 'dedication' of *The Prince* – as against the thinking from below that is proper to democratic knowledge. How will this imperative, 'impose fear if you do not wish to

experience terror', ever be preached to the rebels of Valmy? They
freed themselves from fear by imposing terror on those who were the
enemies of their freedom: *libera seditio vel libera multitudo* [free sedition or free multitude].

6

So let us try to understand better that excessive attention that Spinoza
pays to Tacitus' statement *nihil in vulgo modicum: terrere, ni paveant*
– 'nothing is moderate in a crowd; it terrorises unless it is in fear'
(*Annals* 1.29; but see also Spinoza, *PT*, ch. 7, Proposition 27). We
could show its incidental, superfluous character in the prolixity of the
Spinozist method. That statement is obviously built through a series
of annotations that precede it, follow it, and come together around
the degradation of *cupiditas* into 'fear', into 'inconstant sadness'
(*Ethics* III, Proposition 18, Note 2), its being prey to presages and
superstitions (III, Proposition 50, Note), to terroristic imaginaries
considered possible and close (IV, Proposition 2), and so on. But
'the affects of Hope or Fear [...] cannot be good of themselves' (IV,
Proposition 47), because what dominates us when we are affected
by them is impotence. 'He who is guided by Fear, and does good
to avoid evil, is not guided by reason' (IV, Proposition 63; quoted
from Spinoza 1985). Here, then, the axis of the Spinozist discourse
reverses: the discussion of reason sets aside fear and any unsteady or
oscillating option of passion in order to find again its constructive
matrix:

> A free man, i.e., one who lives according to the dictates of reason alone,
> is not led by Fear, but desires the good directly, i.e., acts, lives, and
> preserves his being from the function of seeking his own advantage.
> And so he thinks of nothing less than of death. Instead his wisdom is a
> meditation on life. (Spinoza 1985: *Ethics* IV, Proposition 67)

And from here on Spinoza will talk about how virtue can be won
by eliminating fear (*Ethics* IV, Proposition 73 and Demonstration;
Appendix: chs 16 and 25; *Ethics* V, Proposition 10, Note; Proposition
41, Note).

The individualist and liberal interpreters of Spinozist immanentism have always maintained that the political in Spinoza is a
polyvalent mediator of the social; hence it cannot be defined either
as an element of action or as a structural property. It seems to me,
however, that in Spinoza the political is not a medium of the social
but is its permanent source and its continuous constitutive rupture,
an excedent *potenza* in relation to any measure, and this excedence

is an ontological asymmetry. If this were not so, we would be really condemned to acosmism – not just an acosmism of the pantheistic conception of being, as Hegel wanted, but also an acosmism of the conception of the political or, more respectably, one restricted to the Goetheian elephant.

The commentators who insist on the fact that the political in Spinoza cannot be substantial but is built on the dialectic between individuals and groups are right. But this is not enough to define the 'event' of Spinozist politics. In this dialectic (which is not a dialectic), there is always a surplus of the constitutive process, an institutive and communicating surplus (and therefore one that is neither individual nor interindividual), an accumulation not of substantial (individual) segments but of (singular) modal *potenze*. Spinozist monism is nourished by divine *potenza*. Is it not perhaps this claim, this way of making the divinity active [*operosa*] – according to a strictly immanentist line – that renders the Amsterdam Jew a 'heretic'? It is no coincidence that positive potentiality [*potenza$_2$*] and negative potentiality, the 'power over' and the 'power to', are in no way distinguished in Spinoza, because there is no static antinomy in his thinking... and, again, simply because, ontologically, *the negative does not exist*. There is only potentiality, in other words freedom, which opposes the nothing and constructs – outside solitude – the ever new measure of the common. 'A man who is guided by reason is more free in a state, where he lives according to a common decision, than in solitude, where he obeys only himself' (Spinoza 1985: *Ethics*, IV, Proposition 73). This is how fear is expelled from the language of the passions and, with even greater purpose, from the language of politics.

10
Hatred as a passion

Definition of hatred

Let me start from the definition of hatred in Spinoza:

> When the Mind imagines those things that diminish or restrain the Body's power of acting, it strives, as far as it can, to recollect things that exclude their existence. (*Ethics*, III, Proposition 13)*

and the annotation to it:

> From this we understand clearly what Love and Hate are. Love is nothing but Joy with the accompanying idea of an external cause, and Hate is nothing but Sadness with the accompanying idea of an external cause. We see, then, that one who loves necessarily strives to have present and preserve the things he loves; and on the other hand, one who hates strives to remove and destroy the thing he hates.

As always in the *Ethics*, the systematic definition is then discussed in experimental and phenomenological terms and at the same time in ontological terms.

In phenomenological and descriptive terms: from Proposition 20 to Proposition 49 in the third part of *Ethics*, Spinoza analyses hatred in the variations of its intensity and in the extent of its fluctuations, be they towards the other or towards the social other. What is central in

---

* Translator's note: All translations from the *Ethics* given in this chapter are taken from Spinoza 1985.

this approach is the relationship between love and hate: intensity and fluctuations are fixed in the relationship that ties the 'variable' – the external cause – to the 'invariable' of holding closely or distancing, of absorbing or destroying the external effect. Loving and hating are two poles of a continuous wave-like movement of mind and body that reject or accept the effect–affect of an external cause, of an other outside us. I shall return in the next section to these oscillations and give a name to each variation of the affect.

For the moment let me pause on the ontological definition of hatred. Let me start by taking up Definition III at the opening of *Ethics* III. It is a definition of affect or emotion in general, but love and hate are the matrix: 'By affect I understand affections of the Body by which the Body's power of acting is increased or diminished, aided or restrained, and at the same time, the ideas of these affections.' And in the Note to Proposition 11 we read:

We see, then, that the Mind can undergo great changes, and pass now to a greater, now to a lesser perfection. These passions, indeed, explain to us the affects of Joy and Sadness. By Joy, therefore, I shall understand in what follows that passion by which the Mind passes to a greater perfection. And by Sadness, that passion by which it passes to a lesser perfection.

We immediately ask what it means to say that sadness constitutes a person's transition from a greater to a lesser perfection, and we also have to ask what is meant by the transition to greater perfection implicit in joy. Are we faced with a radical asymmetry between joy and sadness, between love and hate, such that joy-love leads to the positivity of being, while sadness-hate is attracted to the negativity of being? Proposition III, 11 answers this question in the affirmative: 'The idea of any thing that increases or diminishes, aids or retrains, our Body's power of acting, increases or diminishes, aids or restrains, our Mind's power of thinking.' And Proposition 12 gives a further confirmation: 'When the Mind imagines those things that diminish or restrain the Body's power of acting, it strives, as far as it can, to recollect things that exclude their existence'; and, to conclude, '[h]ate can never be good' (*Ethics* IV, Proposition 45).

With this definition we are in ethics in the proper sense, where action is always qualified and fluctuation can always be determinate. While hatred can never be good, we have the possibility of lessening it; or, better, we can strive to transform hatred through love. The note accompanying Proposition 46 in *Ethics* III gives a clear sign of this project:

He who wishes to avenge wrongs by hating in return surely lives miserably. On the other hand, one who is eager to overcome Hate by Love, strives joyously and confidently, resists many men as easily as one, and requires the least help from fortune. Those whom he conquers yield joyously, not from a lack of strength, but from an increase in their powers.

But Spinoza goes further in his reasoning: 'If we separate emotions, or affects, from the thought of an external cause, and join them to other thoughts, then the Love, or Hate, toward the external cause is destroyed, as are the vacillations of mind arising from these affects' (*Ethics* V, Proposition 2). And immediately he shows how desires, whether born from adequate or from inadequate ideas, can always be traced back to the *potenza* [power] of the mind and thus oriented towards building a state of happiness (*Ethics* V, Proposition 4, Note): happiness in freedom, in solidarity, in love. The political dimension (for the political is the apex of the ethical) underlying the whole discussion of love and hate reappears here after having made the transition from the last Propositions of *Ethics* IV to the Preface of *Ethics* V, 'which concerns the means, or way, leading to Freedom'.

Articulations of hatred: indignation

Let me take one step back from the Spinozist proposition about proceeding to overcome hatred through the good use of love. Because we know that, in Spinozist ontology, the path that leads to perfection – and in consequence places love in a privileged position in relation to hatred ('No one can hate God': *Ethics* V, Proposition 18) – is mixed with and indistinguishable from the urgencies of passion, let us try to understand how, in the emotions that follow on hatred – in other words, in the genealogy of the passions headed by hate – there is an interplay of heteronomy and confused determinations; but also how the passions that diminish the body's *potenza* of acting can and must function in the construction of the ethical and political order.

The specificity of Spinoza's ontology is not solely that it makes love triumph over the passions that do not increase the *potenza* of the body and of the mind, but also (and mainly, one may add) that it uses the entire system of the passions to build the conduct of a good life – and its institutional projection. This is how some of the subordinates of hatred come to function towards building a path that leads to a good life. Fear and hope – and, as Chantal Jacquet has recently shown, even the passion of revenge, albeit in subordinate fashion

(Jacquet 2017, ch. 6) – are at the forefront of this transition. A good example here is that provided by indignation, as highlighted by important interpreters of Spinoza's thought (particularly Matheron 2011, pp. 219ff. and Bove 1996). So let me, in my turn, try to see what happens with indignation. First, it appears as a 'reactive passion': it is 'a Hate toward someone who has done evil to another' (*Ethics* III, Definition of the Affects, 20) – especially if we love this other (*Ethics* III, Proposition 22, Note). Indignation appears therefore as rage, anger, hatred towards those who operate in shameful ways, yet – and here is a first reversal, or an important 'fluctuation of passion' – it may not be repugnant to reason if it wishes to re-educate or reintroduce into the social order those who have been expelled (*Ethics* IV, Proposition 51, Note). Secondly, indignation may appear as an 'overbearing hate' – overbearing because the passion for the other, with the other (whether positive or negative), is born out of a desire for participation and communion (*Ethics* III, Proposition 31, Corollary) that is itself the effect of love. So when someone, becoming indignant, builds community, that person follows the dictates of reason in this community building (*Ethics* IV, Proposition 37, Note I). In fact, this 'overbearing hatred' can be converted into 'overpowering love' if we hold to the definition of good and evil that (although these are 'extrinsic notions' and not 'attributes' of the mind) bases the good on 'concord and in mutual help' and defines it through 'common consent' (*Ethics* IV, Proposition 37, Note II).

Thirdly, indignation – as Spinoza continually reminds us – is a fluctuation of passion. Is it predominantly positive or is it not? After having seen previously, in two examples, how in some respects indignation may be positive, in the end we shall have to make the decision. After Proposition 45 of *Ethics* IV – after having stated (as we have seen) that 'hatred can never be good' and after having renewed, in Corollary I, the condemnation of 'Envy, Mockery, Disdain, Anger, Vengeance, and the rest of the affects which are related to Hate or arise from it, are evil' – the Note offers a quite different opening. It is here that Spinoza develops his famous discussion of laughter, *hilaritas* – which comes so close to the highest humanist definition of 'happy living'. It is in the critical function of *hilaritas*, when it turns against 'a savage and sad superstition', against '[ascribing] to virtue our tears, sighs, fear, and other things of that kind, which are signs of a weak mind' – it is precisely there that *hilaritas* meets with indignation. *Hilaritas* liberates indignation from the parent hatred, or – better – it holds hatred within the ambit of the critique of reason. So here we really do have a maximal fluctuation imposed on the story of love and hate, almost a jump from the one to the other that the 'common praxis' oriented by reason provokes. On this basis, and in this place, we shall be able to see hatred acquiring a positivity when ethical–political analysis orients the reading of the concept of 'sedition against the tyrant'. Implicit in *TPT*, chapter 20 (6 and 11), the revolt in the name of freedom that arises from contempt for unjust laws and from a refusal of the command of the magistrate is legitimised entirely by the combined effect of what is expressed in *TP*, chapter 5 (2, 4 and 6) and in the splendid page of realistic indignation about the operations of power in *TP*, chapter 7 (27).

But in other passages indignation is a passion that develops in political action against tyranny (*TP*, ch. 3: 9, 4 and 6; ch. 6: 1 and 2). I do not need to examine all those passages here. It's enough to recall the section in *TP*, chapter 8 (4) where, in explaining why the aristocratically governed state can never attain the absolutism of democracy, Spinoza writes: 'The only reason [aristocracy's] rule is not absolute is that the multitude is terrifying to its rulers. So it maintains some freedom for itself. If it doesn't claim that freedom for itself by an explicit law, it still claims it tacitly and maintains it.'

The hatred of solitude

> What we have just shown is confirmed by daily experience, which provides so much and such clear evidence that this saying is in almost everyone's mouth: man is a God to man. Still, it rarely happens that men live according to the guidance of reason. Instead, their lives are so constituted that they are usually envious and burdensome to one another. They can hardly, however, live a solitary live; hence, that definition which makes man a social animal has been quite pleasing to most. And surely we do derive from the society of our fellow men many more advantages than disadvantages. So let the Satirists laugh as much as they like at human affairs, let the Theologians curse them, let Melancholics praise as much as they can a life that is uncultivated and wild, let them disdain men and admire the lower animals. Men still find from experience that by helping one another they can provide themselves much more easily with the things they require, and that only by joining forces can they avoid the dangers that threaten on all sides – not to mention that it is much preferable and more worthy of our knowledge to consider the deeds of men, rather than those of the lower animals. (*Ethics* IV, Proposition 35, Note)

The thing most useful to the human – the thing that agrees best with human nature – is humans themselves: the fact of coming to agree with the nature of the other human; in consequence, 'among singular things there is nothing more useful to a human than a human'. In short, the most useful thing is living in society.

In view of this, can we talk about a 'hatred' of solitude? Certainly we can, if we go along with the definition of hate as a '[s]adness with the accompanying idea of an external cause'; and 'one who hates strives to remove and destroy the thing he hates' (*Ethics* III, Proposition 13, Note), to distance and destroy solitude – which means building society. In the *TPT* (ch. 5: 7, 8, 9) and in the *PT* (ch. 2: 15 and ch. 6: 4) this dynamic is strongly underlined. Suffice to quote this passage:

> A social order is very useful, and even most necessary, not only for living securely from enemies, but also for doing many things more easily. For if men were not willing to give mutual assistance to one another, they would lack both skill and time to sustain and preserve themselves as far as possible. Not all men are capable of all things, and no one would be able to provide the things which a man alone needs most. Everyone, I say, would lack both the strength and the time, if he had alone to plow, to sow, to reap, to grind, to cook, to weave, to sew, and to do the many things necessary to support life – not to mention now the arts and sciences which are also supremely necessary for the perfection of human nature and for its blessedness. For we see that those who live barbarously, without an organised community, lead a wretched and almost brutal life, and that still it is not without mutual assistance, such as it is, that they are able to provide themselves with the few wretched and crude things they have. (Spinoza 2016b: *TPT*, ch. 5: 18–20)

And he continues in this spirit: when we, humans, social by nature, have laws imposed upon us that go against nature, they have the name of slavery, barbarism, and in fact loneliness: one should rebel against this; and the power that is in the hands of 'one alone' is equivalent to slavery, which cannot be imposed either in the name of peace or if that 'one' is called 'the people'.

If we were looking for effects of love that, in confused or contradictory fashion, traverse hatred in a state of fluctuation, here they are presented in extreme forms. It is through hatred that human community is built.

It is is obvious that Hobbes became Spinoza's adversary in this area:

> With regard to political theory, the difference between Hobbes and myself, which is the subject of your inquiry, consists in this, that I always preserve the natural right in its entirety, and I hold that the

sovereign power in a State has right over a subject only in proportion to the excess of its power over that of a subject. This is always the case in a state of nature. (Spinoza 2002)

In reality, behind the hatred of solitude there lies in Spinoza a historical drama that humanity was experiencing: that of being reduced again to solitude, as in the paradigmatic times proposed by the theory of social contract – reduced, that is, through capitalist appropriation or, rather, through the primitive accumulation of capital, which in Spinoza's century was investing the whole of society. In Spinoza's rejection of solitude there is a rejection of the new capitalist accumulation, of the misery it imposes on humans. And there is also the affirmation that the world must be appropriated by humans as a human collective, as an institution of love that is an absolute alternative to hatred – and in this case its singular complement. To exit from solitude is to qualify *conatus* [the striving], to develop *appetitus* [desire] in terms of *cupiditas* [passion] – and '*cupiditas* is man's very essence, insofar as it is conceived to be determined, from any given affection of it, to do something' (*Ethics* III, Definition of Affects, 1). So here *cupiditas* stands for passion, but also for appropriation: 'Appetite is the very essence of man, insofar as it is determined to do what promotes his preservation' (ibid., Explicatio), in other words, *cupiditas* explains the essence of the human being in the dynamic order of reproduction and constitution. This 'doing', this 'acting' of *cupiditas* is not in any sense solitary: in this movement, individual action constitutes itself into a collective entity: 'By singular things I understand things that are finite and have a determinate existence. And if a number of individuals so concur in one action that together they are all the cause of one effect, I consider them all, to that extent, as one singular thing' (*Ethics* II, Definition VII). And it is in this process that hatred turns completely into love, on the path from the hatred of solitude to the collective constitution of society.

But with what articulations, in what unique ways can the hatred of solitude transform itself into love, when by love we understand an appropriation of the world collectively performed?

Love and class hatred

In the history of the class struggle, hatred has a fundamental role. The hatred of the bourgeois against the workers in revolt, from 1848 onwards (that June that was 'damned' by the bosses, as Marx says), exercised itself in orgies of blood. In 1871, the repression of the Paris Commune developed perverse passions of the bourgeois against the proletariat. Passions of hatred, which the 'short' twentieth century – on the bourgeois side – took to extremes through the creation of fascist regimes that turned the hatred of the proletariat into a hatred of humanity. But what else could be expected of those who, since the period of the primary accumulation of capital, had developed a blind and boundless passion for surplus value and an indescribable violence in sucking the blood of living labour, in both the central and the subaltern countries? What could be expected, except a destructive hatred towards any desire for happiness? This hatred cannot be recuperated by love.

On the other hand, there is a class hatred, that of the proletariat against exploiters, against colonial masters, and against finance capitalists, which enacts to a maximum extent the possible conversion of hatred into love. The hatred of the proletariat against the exploitative tyrant is in fact the engine of the emancipation of labour, as Marx describes it – or of the liberation of labour and of its transformation into free activity.

Why is it that proletarian class hatred has the capacity to produce love? Here I offer a commentary on the Proof of Proposition 46 in *Ethics* IV:

> All affects of Hate are evil. So he who lives according to the guidance of reason will strive, as far as he can, to bring it about that he is not troubled with affects of Hate, and consequently will strive that the other also should not undergo those affects. Now Hate is increased by being returned, and on the other hand, can be destroyed by Love, so that the Hate passes into Love. Therefore, one who lives according to the guidance of reason will strive to repay the other's Hate, etc., with love, i.e., with Nobility.

Who, then, can replace hatred with love, through generosity? Certainly not the capitalist, whose existence is tied to the exploitation of the other. And equally certainly the proletarian, who, albeit subjected to bourgeois hatred, builds community and organisation through a practice of cooperation in labour and of solidarity among workers. For generosity is a passion defined by love for the other, that is, by the capacity to be 'active together'. And then 'those actions, therefore, which aim only at the agent's advantage, I relate to Tenacity, and those which aim at another's advantage, I relate to Nobility. So, Moderation, Sobriety, presence of mind in danger, etc., are species of Tenacity whereas Courtesy, Mercy, etc., are species of Nobility'

(*Ethics* III, 59, Note). So hate, anger, fear (and courage), which are the basis of the struggles against capitalist exploitation, are – in the machine of generosity – brought to be effective moments of concatenation and organisation; and in this way they become 'rules of life', 'the command of reason' in the generous construction of a common (*Ethics* V, Proposition 10, and Note). Getting together, emerging from solitude by generously generating a community recycles bad passions and predisposes them to struggle. 'A man who is guided by reason is more free in a state, where he lives according to a common decision, than in solitude, where he obeys only himself' (*Ethics* IV, Proposition 73). All forces must be employed to build, in the struggle for the common, our association that frees us from exploitation.

A new difficulty:

> But to achieve these things the powers of each man would hardly be sufficient if men did not help one another. And indeed, money has provided a convenient instrument for acquiring all these aids. That is why its image usually occupies the Mind of the multitude more than anything else. For they can imagine hardly any species of Joy without the accompanying idea of money as its cause. (*Ethics* IV, Appendix, Chapter 28)

But this difficulty, too, will be overcome if generosity becomes the fundamental virtue – more than piety and religion (*Ethics* V, Proposition 41). It is generosity that turns hate into love, destroys solitude, and unites human beings in a free commune, in constituent activity. Victorious class struggle on the part of the proletariat? Certainly, because it unites us and, against the hateful other who is exploiting us, makes it possible for us to construct a 'we' that cooperates and loves.

All the big social movements of today arise from an emotion of indignation: a dominant emotion, an articulation of hatred that brings many individuals into a powerful civic passion. The Spanish 15M movement is a characteristic example of this emergence. It can be characterised, from its aspects of protest and indignation, as a process of massive politicisation, of a reappropriation of politics by the multitude. Within it, one finds the solution to many problems that generally arise in the relationship between unity and political differences, to many difficulties that stand against the building of consensus within any given multiplicity, to the solution of that dilemma that lies between force and legality. To follow the process of constitution of a movement that becomes dominant in the public sphere and to observe how assemblies are created from the *acampadas* [pitch camps] and, from there, to follow the possibility of a political system that is autopoietic and open is to give form to Spinoza's dictate about the construction of the political. One avoids the risk of spontaneity, which has no place in Spinoza; one realises the *potenza* of a democratic regeneration that is aware (if only intermittently) of the non-representability of the multitude. Thus these processes show an extraordinary convergence with Spinoza's writings. When the movement sets itself in motion, the hatred for *potere* [power] that drives it and the anti-capitalist urgency that organises it make a 'leap': hatred is overwhelmed by love, by the joy of uprising, by the joy of being together. We find in the movements generated since 2011 an unexpected but fundamental discovery – that hatred can turn into love through the construction of the common by the multitude.

Part III

Spinoza in the Seventeenth Century

11

Politics of immanence, politics of transcendence

A people's essay

Many years ago, working on the political resonances of the philosophy of Descartes, I began to describe what I defined as the 'rational politics' of the ideology of the modern (Negri 1970, in English as Negri 2006b). On that occasion I also described the various different lines of development, the various alternative options. Looking again at what I wrote thirty years ago and taking into account new historiographic readings that have developed in the meantime, I have recently been able to confirm those positions. They addressed both the genesis and early development of capitalism, and the options of bourgeois ideology in constructing political forms that were appropriate, on the one hand, to the primary accumulation of capital (the absolutist state), and, on the other, to the formation and consolidation, through time, of the third estate within that development (see the afterword to Negri 2006b, pp. 317–38).

It is clear that, within the 'rational ideology' of the third estate, there was a privileged place for the instruments of repression of the peasant and urban revolts (of the artisans, or simply of proletarians) that threatened capitalist development. Wherever you look in that period, you find that, in order to guarantee absolute sovereignty and the efficacy of its action, there was a necessary recourse to transcendence. The power that sustained the development of capital required an ideology that would cause divinity to be present in history. The power that organised itself into capital and made possible and encouraged its development needed to be (in fact unavoidably had to be, given the intensity of the resistance) implanted in the absolute of transcendence.

Theological necessity, then, invested completely the development of capital and the philosophies of the present: this is where the onto-theological metaphysics of modernity was instituted.

By this I mean that, when modernity opened up to capitalist development, *the new forces of production* (and in the first place living labour) had to be subjected to an ancient and perennial stamp of power, to the absolute character of a command that legitimated *the new relations of production*. And then any attempt to break this framework was viewed as reprehensible and heretical, and aspirations aimed at modifying it were admitted only through a theoretical initiative that intervened in the relations of production with moderation and with prudent foresight: thus Descartes. With this it was stated that modern metaphysics (and when one says metaphysics one always says theology in some sense) sharpened its political claim. *Since that time metaphysics has always been in effect political.*

It is in the climate produced by positions similar to those of Descartes that the theory of domination develops in the modern period. As a consequence, the politics of transcendence become hegemonic. With Hobbes we have the birth of the modern theory of sovereignty. Bodin had already attempted it (and with what intelligence!). Logically, any form of government – he claimed – is monarchic. Both aristocratic and democratic forms of government are monarchic because they are governments of the one: thus they are monarchic regardless of the hypocritical form in which the exercise of power legitimates itself. But it is only Hobbes who considers citizens themselves as fundamental to the construction of the absolute of dominion. What Hobbes narrates is the transfer of *potenza* [power] from civil subjects to the sovereign.

It is a strange transfer, this, of the power of citizens to the sovereign. Who knows why...? Perhaps because of the civil war? But is it not the case that only the existence of Leviathan allows the very existence of civil society, through the birth of sovereign power? How, then, can there be civil war without civil society...? If this story were not enough, then there is always in Hobbes the divine *potenza* that dominates and legitimises the power of Leviathan. The civil war, the real war that primary accumulation had produced, and the surplus of violence that the expropriation of the commons had created – is all this shown here critically? No. Far from being critiqued, it was immediately justified, assumed as necessary, and finally legitimised by the theological power of the sovereign.

But the process doesn't end there. In order to develop the rising power of capital, in addition to imposing a sovereign rule, it was also necessary to remove from the subjects any recognition of their unique *potenza* and to lock its expropriation and the consciousness of alienation within a state of necessity, thus removing all possible justification from eventual rebellions and possible forms of resistance. Alienation becomes inevitable and, paradoxically, useful. Constructing this condition comes to be the essential transition in the political theories that develop around the transcendence of sovereignty. This transition is *the invention of the public*. The expropriation of the commons, as developed during the process of primary accumulation, is transfigured, and therefore mystified, into the invention of public utility. The theory of 'general will' in Rousseau is in some ways related to this operation.

Finally, it is on this basis that Hegel will effect the synthesis of the public and the sovereign, of command and progress, through the dialectical *Aufhebung* of civil society into the state, thus completing, in the metaphysical image, the necessary subjection of living labour to the command of the sovereign.

* * *

But in the modern period another philosophy arises and affirms itself. This is a mode of thought coterminous with the struggles, the revolts and revolutions that run through the modern period. It invokes the rule of immanence and embodies a politics of immanence.

But what does immanence mean? It means that there is no *outside* to this world; that in this world it is possible to live (and move and create) only *right here*. And it means that the being in which we are, and from which we cannot free ourselves (because we are made of this being and everything we do is nothing but an acting on, or of, this being of ours), is a becoming – and is not closed, not prefigured or preformed, but produced. Putting ourselves in the situation, can we therefore conclude, from this point of view, that production relations do not dominate but are dominated by the forces of production? Yes, of course. It is precisely the opposite, then, of what the politics of transcendence prescribed, namely that relations of production – the fact that, if you are born a slave, then you will die a slave – constitute a necessity guaranteed by the good God. If – so say the theologians and the politicians of absolutism – the power of humans over humans is the DNA of creation, then we reply that immanence is the *being against* [l'essere contro].

And so, within the theoretical episode of modernity, what the authors of immanence offer, with respect to absolute sovereignty, is great anomalies, exceptions and ruptures. Machiavelli is an early example of a conflictual theory of power, reversing – precisely through an anticipation – the theory of civil war that Hobbes had used, in a naturalistic and contractual manner, to construct his absolute theory of power, inventing a history of individualistic and proprietary relations.

No, says Machiavelli, conflict is always open, power is always a relationship, there are winners and losers, but let's not tell fairy stories: those who hold the power are only those who have greater force. But if this is our experience, it follows that power cannot exist without a subject, and command must always be exercised over and against a resistance. But then, theoretically, this resistance can always overthrow command. But if this is the case, does it not open the door to a *democratic theory* of power?

And this is where Spinoza comes into this short history of mine (Negri 2006a). In order to constitute itself, he says, society does not need power. Only subjects can build society, or, better, can produce every form of the state, insisting on the *potenza* of singularities, through the passions that pass through the multitudes. And any form of state, therefore, can only be legitimated by the relationship that is established between the subjects and the sovereign or vice versa, between the sovereign and the subjects; this is always the way things go. There is no 'sacred history' unless as a narration of this human event and, if there is a God, it is that being that the desire for happiness invents through the movements and transformations of the multitude. In Spinoza, the forces of production produce the relations of production. But, since the forces of production are in effect *cupiditates*, passional forces, multitudes open to the constitution of the political, what Machiavellian theory anticipated comes about: the forms of command are subject to the activity of the multitude.

With Marx, conflict–becoming and production–*potenza* are recomposed through the critique of political economy. Marx gives *direction* to this 'exceptional' process that the anomalies of modernity had produced: *this direction is communism*. However, it would be a serious mistake to confuse this political *direction* with a *telos* [end] of history. In Marx, it is the struggles that shape institutions, and it is the forces of production that produce, and eventually overturn, the social relations within which they are confined and contained.

★ ★ ★

After Marx, the alternatives to communism, too, will often try to set themselves on the terrain of immanence. Thus transcendence seems to be definitively disqualified. The great Hegelian synthesis (transcendental in origin, then, soon, within the logic of absolute spirit, entirely transcendent) is swept up by the materiality of historical processes (of resistance, of struggle, of revolution) in which the politics of immanence are expressed, at an alarming rate for the sovereign. Opportuneness and prudence thus require that alternatives be given in immanence as well, on that terrain that has definitively imposed itself. But take care! That terrain has been falsified. We are presented, in the new fetish of immanence, with theoretical experiences that, against communism, surreptitiously reintroduce into political discourse those facts about *necessity* that negate and block the processes of *liberation*.

Kant, a philosopher too often associated with idealism who is instead very much a figure (and an essential author) of the Enlightenment, had foreseen, in his 'Conflicts of the Faculties', that, through and beyond the affirmation of freedom, there would be new outbursts of repression of the forces of production – in the definition of the historical process and in the organisation of its aims and of the consequent structures of power. They are reactionary experiences, he adds. Let us classify some of them, following Kant's suggestion. First of all, there are the experiences of Abderism. These are experiences of an *opaque materialism* that reduces the world to a set of irrational contingencies, of conjunctures – in the context of a metaphysical necessity that dominates the existent – and thus subordinates historical development to a determinist finality (in which one assumes the equivalence between chance and necessity, as for example Louis Althusser has sometimes done). Well before Althusser, and certainly with less elegance and conceptual subtlety, so-called scientific socialism and so-called dialectical materialism were formidable examples of this way of using immanence to eliminate the ontological creativity that constituted its salient character in the 'anomalous' philosophies of modernity – the sign of freedom. It is evident that, when we say freedom, we are not talking about spiritual essences but about resistance and rebellion, or imagination and invention... not so much of the soul as of bodies and of cooperation, of labour and of revolution. Enormous tragedies of knowledge and of politics will be inscribed in this horizon in the course of the twenty-first century.

On the other side, Kant tells us, there is *terrorism*. What is terrorism for Kant? It is any theory that considers revolution to be impossible and that therefore terrorises human beings by subjecting them to the presence of death as their inevitable destiny and to the flattening of their every desire onto death. Far away from Kant, these positions and these authors constitute a second group of mystifying experiences of immanence in twentieth-century thought. The passivity that arises from necessity, and the inoperativity that arises from the disconcerting awareness of the inevitable defeat of desire, or from compliance with this condition, are the sign of a new ethic of transcendence on this philosophical stage. From Heidegger to the

weak and marginal variants of postmodernity, it is in these forms that
reactionary ideology now expresses itself. We are at the antipode of
the thinking of immanence, as it had appeared – anomaly, exception,
rupture – in the theoretical clash that had characterised modernity
(see Negri 2006c and 2007).

* * *

How many other events, small and large, could – and not marginally
– be laid at the door of this great reactionary line! They are not stories
or philosophies, practices or ideologies that end up in the most terrible and black points of fascist or Stalinist terror. However, they are
tendencies (often rhetorically or politically hegemonic) whose central
meaning translates into impotence, or even into an incapacity (which
sees itself as critical) to express force. Some of these positions (I
mean for example those of Derrida or Agamben in the contemporary
world) seek sometimes to present themselves as *heretical* positions,
as adversaries of the dominant ideology. But they are far from being
that. For heresy is always a rupture of the order of knowledge, and
indeed a positive excedence, the product of a theoretical invention
that expresses itself creatively and thus enhances the ontological
uniqueness of the existing, whereas in the positions I have just mentioned, on the contrary, the sad passions that triumph are weak,
marginal variations, ethically inoperative, or bewilderment in the face
of the sublime, more or less aesthetic, the beautiful life and flight
from struggle, contempt for historical determination, or destructive–
libertine scepticism opposed to excedence and resistance.

Secondly, heresy is a rejection of transcendence in all its forms
– a dissidence in relation to the very nature of the concept, which
seeks to be not universal but common and does not want to accept
the customary nature of command and knowledge, having verified
and resisted critically, point by point, to the very end. Therefore
the heretic is an intellectual who moves from a specific, particular
point of view, which is not that of the totality but that of rupture,
which therefore assumes knowledge as *situated knowledge* and acting
as being conditioned by a common project of resistance and struggle. Here the excedence of heresy begins to open... to what? To the
generous construction of the *common*.

Thus I arrive at a crucial point, where today it is perhaps possible
to separate, with great clarity, the politics of transcendence from the
politics of immanence.

But before delving into what the *common* is, I would like to focus
on one group (among many) of arch-heretics who have, so to speak,

built the bridge between the critique of modernity and our current philosophical–political condition. Here I want to highlight the subversive thought that, in France, through a thousand rivulets (from Socialisme ou Barbarie through to situationism), leads to the joyful creations of Deleuze and Guattari and, in more difficult and politically central ways, to Michel Foucault. I leave aside those other blocs of subversive thought that were collaborating in different places during that period, in the construction of that heresy that allows us to live at the same time the communist struggle and the exercise of libertarian passion: for example, Soviet critical thought between the rejection of dialectical materialism and the alternative management of socialist planning; Italian workerism [*operaismo*]; the various currents of colonial and postcolonial critical thought, and so on. We should pay more attention to all these authors, not only on the terrain of political debate (obviously), but also on that of the construction of a new philosophical horizon.

★ ★ ★

So then: here are a few aspects of French subversive thought of the postwar period. There are, for example, pages written by Maurice Merleau-Ponty in 1960 that seem to clarify what might be, from within the class struggle, the redefinition of a critical and creative horizon. I refer to them in order to show the place of critique or, better, of a 'point of view' in wielding the philosophical weapon of immanence. When we rebel, says Merleau-Ponty (1960), referring to the insurrection of the workers of Budapest, we do not do it in the name of freedom of conscience or philosophical idealism, but *qua* Marxists, and hence inasmuch as we are inserted into a conjuncture, into a specific situation: we break with a universe to which we want to oppose a new direction. Those Hungarian workers who interest us here, Merleau-Ponty continues, have rejected a certain idea of the being-object – and thus have introduced a critique of socialist identity and a practice of difference for free human beings, for singularities in struggle, a practice of constituent rebellion. They have adopted the conception and the practice of a being endowed with many dimensions, of a multiverse, of a being that is produced, built collectively... The problem of being inside or outside the party, or rather of placing oneself inside or outside outside of concrete history, is something wholly subordinated to a common action that transgresses the rules and reinvents history. Being-object, being-subject: these are philosophical barbarisms from which we hope to free ourselves soon... probably by inventing others... But our task is to reveal their *potenza*

– if there is any. And here we can do it, because other writers and militants have walked this road, giving to this elementary but strong expression of resistance the materiality of a *production of subjectivity*. *Dispositifs* of organisation, tendencies that relate the future to be built to the moving realities of the present struggle, plans for a joyful future that deconstruct the violence of the present suffering: we are not people of dialectics and not of impotence either; our every behaviour is disutopic, affirmative and constituent.

It's no coincidence – adds Merleau-Ponty, citing Paul Nizan's 'Aden Arabie' – 'that is why many Marxists have been tempted by Spinozism' (Toadvine and Lawlor 2007, p. 343): because the thought of the infinite here makes it possible to dissolve necessity and reinvent the world. A surprising conclusion? Not particularly. Here, actually, there is *a method that allows one to move between historical determinism and the ontology of creative* potenza. To be 'in the situation', but to be there on condition of being able to break, critically to invest the real, and to determine an action that traverses the real in critical terms.

Here one might add, taking a small leap forward and moving on through the story that we are living: who would ever have thought that a proletarian movement could realistically be defined in terms of *bios*, a political activity of liberation in terms that concretely invest life – what later came to be called the *biopolitical* context, an interweaving of bodies and of the institution of common life... who would have thought that this perspective could arise from the strong affirmation of a particular and irreducible *point of view*? From a specific act of imagination, located 'inside' a vital process of struggle? Irreducible, not only because it is matched – this point of view – to a causality that is specific and determinate, and therefore true, but because it is practical, produced by *dispositifs* of a creative *potenza*. It happens here as it happened for Moses – when, as Spinoza shows (in the *Theological–Political Treatise*), his making of a constitution for the rebellious Jewish people in flight from Egypt could not be founded on fear but had to be founded on hope, on a strong act of imagination...

So we no longer find ourselves in an abstract condition, in the metaphysical alternative (for example) between necessity and freedom, but in a historical condition of life, in which resistance and the constitution of the common are proposed as a tension to be resolved.

Let us place ourselves in this condition, and also consider the various directions and deviations from this path. Deleuze, for example, immerses himself in this same story; and, like him, Debord, in parallel. How different, however, their answers are to the same question! Deleuze wonders: To what extent is resistance something 'outside' history? And he replies that the minority is *never* out of history, because minority and concrete resistance are one and the same. For Debord, on the other hand, resistance is an 'outside', an extraordinary event. To him resistance is joyous, history sad. Of course, we cannot deny that there is also in Deleuze an 'outside' that appears somewhere, irreducible... schizophrenia, the emergence or the overcoming of a limit... a horizon that sometimes is almost naturalist... Deleuze and Guattari in search of the utopia of 'use value'...? Sometimes it seems that we must think this, in other words that even in great philosophy there persists the illusion of reaching a fixed point, a *measure*, or anyway something that might save us... in short, the reasoning sometimes seems to hinge on waiting for an epiphany... The event devalues history. But all this is episodic. In the course of their *récit* [narrative], Deleuze and Guattari reinvent the concreteness of *disutopia* and bend the passions of the creative subjects to the actuality of the struggle, of the clash. Immanence: but what will immanence ever be when the theory of transcendence, the practice of obedience, the recognition of identity have been subverted?

By asking the question, I am not returning to the analysis of the metaphysical relationship between freedom and necessity. On the contrary, here we are already entirely within that perspective that makes the *ontology of actuality* the basis of the *production of subjectivity*. There is no nostalgia here for an 'outside', we are now totally in the 'inside'; there is no memory of use value here, we are completely immersed in 'exchange value'. Is it ugly, all this? No. It is our reality. it is our life... It is in this 'inside', within these historical relationships, that the *reappropriation* of exchange value presents itself as a central objective, because only here does the relation of *potenza* express itself in a topical fashion.

Mind you: 'exchange value' is a very dignified thing. It is a common reality; it is built and consolidated in such a way that it can no longer be related back to the world of pure exchange; it is given in common form. This is because the product of labour has become consolidated. *It is here*. There's nothing else, *there is no outside*. Consider for example the world of finance: who can think of doing without it? But it is now earth [*terra*] – just as it was in the commons expropriated at the start of the modern era – a common reality in which we live, but that has been taken from us. So we want to take it back, this land. Spinoza explains to us the importance of the Jubilee in Jewish history, when all debts are lifted and the material equality of citizens is restored. Or again, there is Machiavelli insisting on the centrality of agrarian laws in the history of the Roman republic – it is there, in the plebeian reappropriation of the earth, that sovereignty bends to the democracy of the producers! There should therefore be no nostalgia for 'use value'; on the contrary, it is essential to recognise that we live in the world of exchange, and goods, and their circulation and that we do not need to reach – or, better, we do not need to return to – something pure and primal but only to continue to rebel, here and now, within and against this reality. To free oneself from exchange value will mean, then, to reappropriate to ourselves the common reality (the reality that, at one time, was created by labour and exploitation, by cooperation and by profit and sale, by the one against the other, the one inside and in place of the other), to reappropriate that common reality that we produce and that stands against us as power; to reverse that reality that sees us living as exploited poor, subjects in the common of valorisation, in the communism of capital – a reality that we ourselves can reappropriate as the common of living labour.

I have looked at things from various angles here. However, it should not be considered strange that I am here for the first time in a position to reconnect the common: not the common that, in its genesis, had been torn from us in primitive accumulation – and with how much pain! – and not simply the use value of labour power, but the new consistency of the value of labour, multiplied by the experience of struggles and by the common reappropriation of knowledge.

It is a common that goes beyond both private and public appropriation and that proposes itself today rather as a subject of struggle against public authorities, since these are nothing but an instrument of the private sector, as they have always been. The *common against the public*. The common is therefore that excedence, that *potenza* that people have built, that they can continue to build in the activity of liberation from command and from exploitation. The common is both the ambit and the result of the break that we operate vis-à-vis the power that dominates us. An ontology of actuality is thus asserted at the moment in which subjectivities produce and build themselves in the common – or, better, at the moment in which the multitude of singularities finds in the common the sign of the constructive efficacy of being. Only through the deconstruction of sovereignty, of that subject or figure of transcendence, does the multitude succeed in the construction of the common. *Democratic construction?* Yes, if we consider that the multitude is not a 'conjuncture' but a *cupiditas* – the tension of many singularities in a process of constitution that is always open, in an effort, never interrupted, to constitute the common. The multitude is an *ensemble of institutions*, always alive. Leaving aside the Spinozist analysis of the history of the Jews, this is also shown by the philosophical anthropology that stresses the processes of transformation that exist between the ontology of actuality and the production of subjectivity. *Potentia multitudinis* [the potentiality/power of the multitude]!

And so we reach the conclusion of that reasoning that had begun, in modernity, with Machiavelli and Spinoza, together with and beyond other thinkers, prophets and combatants, in resistance and rebellion, when critique attempted for the first time to put *the hegemony of the forces of production* above and against the relations of production. Today, finally, the forces of production are given in the powerful virtuality of their liberation from the domination of the relations of production. This is the immanence of which Deleuze spoke: not a thought system about an eternity that disperses itself into the infinite, but a powerful action, realised in the here and now. Absolutely. This is the soul of the politics of immanence, where making politics acquires meaning in the recognition of the common, or rather in the explicit construction or production of the common.

12

Rereading Hegel, the philosopher of right*

Foreword

This text, first published in 1970, was written in 1967; which makes it fifty years old. Rereading it with a view to republication, I feel a certain pride, as a militant philosopher, about having maintained coherence in defining the critical object of my analyses. My thinking has since progressed in many respects – I focused on different contexts and authors and I extended the times and horizons of my research – but on Hegel, right from those years, my critique has remained firm, irreducibly hostile, unrepentant in its opposition to bourgeois dialectics. As befits a philosophical militancy built in the fabulous 1960s.

1

1.1

It seems that nowadays the theoretical problem, and also the political problem, of both state and right tend to focus on the issue of social control over living labour – or rather on the question of legal control over social labour. In other words, if it is the case that the contemporary state has become increasingly socialised, if its action is increasingly diffuse, and if this is due to the extreme importance

* SOURCE: Antonio Negri, 1970. 'Rileggendo Hegel, filosofo di diritto', in Fulvio Tessitore, ed., *Incidenza di Hegel: studi raccolti nel secondo centenario della nascita del filosofo*. Naples: Morano Edizioni, pp. 251–70.

that the movements in the world of labour have gradually assumed, then it follows that the juridical essence of the contemporary state tends liminally to merge with the form of the social organisation of labour. Thus the planned state, both in the case where the fiction of the private property relationship is maintained and in the case where it is denied (e.g. the social state, the socialist state), really grounds its legitimacy in the overall framework of the nexuses of coercion and consensus it extends and through which it informs the mode of social production. Insofar as it has become the exclusive foundation of social wealth, organised labour has also become the foundation of constitutions, the material condition of legality. The contemporary state is above all control over social labour and organisation of living labour.

To reread today a philosopher of right whose contemporary relevance is claimed – in the sense that the problems he addresses can objectively be translated for the contemporary reader – means asking him how he deals with the problems mentioned above. We need to ask how he conceives of control over social labour and to what extent these kinds of problems are present in his thinking. The history of the philosophy of right begins to be interesting only at the point where it begins to express itself as a philosophy of the organisation of social labour.

1.2

Hegel's *Philosophy of Right* is perhaps the first philosophical text of modernity for which such an approach can be valid – and valid in an exclusive way. Hegel as philosopher of right is, from this point of view, very much a contemporary author.

Right is the organisation of and control over social labour, the form in which *civiltà* [civilisation] is constituted through labour: this is a recurring and fundamental concept in Hegel:

> *Education* [Bildung],* in its absolute determination, is therefore *libera-tion* and *work* towards a higher liberation; it is the absolute transition to the infinitely subjective substantiality of ethical life, which is no longer immediate and natural, but spiritual and at the same time raised to the form of universality. Within the subject, this liberation is *hard work*

---

* Translator's note: The Italian translation used by the author in this article (Hegel 1965, p. 171) renders Hegel's original *Bildung* (education, learn-ing, culture, formation) with the Italian *civiltà* (civilisation, civility, culture, education).

against the simple subjectivity of conduct, against the immediacy of
desire as well as the subjective vanity of feeling and the arbitrariness
of caprice. The fact that it is such hard work accounts for some of the
disfavour that it incurs. But it is through this work of education that
the subjective will attains objectivity within itself, the objectivity in
which it alone is for its part worthy, and capable, of being the actuality
of the Idea. (Hegel 1967a: §187)

Thus global labour is the substance of education [*civiltà*], of civilisation as rational organisation of the idea, as objectivity of the idea
and of its new need for an ethical universe. And right is entirely
framed within this objectivation – through labour – of the idea: 'the
system of right is the realm of freedom made actual, the world of
mind brought forth out of itself like a second nature' (Hegel 1967a:
§4): a nature not found but radically constructed, by the social activity of human beings, all jointly engaged in the profound necessity of
the labour of the idea. The hard work of single individuals is included
and contained in the design of the absolute labour of the spirit.
Labour is the substance of the spiritual world.

1.3
Now, this substantiality of labour as a foundation of the civil world,
as Hegel puts it in *Philosophy of Right*, is even more explicitly stated
in the writings of the formative period of his thought – particularly in
the writings that shaped his legal philosophical thought.

Between Frankfurt and Jena, through economic analysis and
through an explicit reference to the classics of English economics,
labour (as the source of value) and wealth (as an outcome of labour)
are integrated into the story of the spirit and are considered terms of a
positive qualification of objectivity. Society is constituted as a totality
through the laborious synthesis of material motivations, through the
valorisation of the precise determinations [*determinatezze*] of overall
human labour. The previous, youthful image of an ethical community
in which individuality and rationality flowed together harmoniously,
in classic form, an image on which Hegel's early research had focused,
was dissolved by the Jena Hegel into a process that figured stages of
human industriousness – from need to interdependence from needs,
from labour to the social collectivities that manage global labour. A
rationale of the overall picture:

Physical needs and pleasures ... asserted by themselves in the totality,
in their infinite interweavings obey a necessity, and build that system of

general interdependence that considers the physical needs, and labour, and accumulation for the same, as a science; the system of so-called political economy. (Hegel 1975: 94; translation slightly modified)

But here the picture is excavated further, and the excavation is perfected to the point of finding in individual labour the substantial source of ethical value, in its universality. A few years later, in the *Phenomenology of Spirit*, Hegel was to say:

> The labour of the individual for his needs is a satisfaction of his own needs, no less than that of others; and the individual only achieves the satisfaction of his needs through the labour of others. As the single man in his individual labour already accomplishes unconsciously a universal labour, so, conversely, he accomplishes universal labour as his object of which he is aware; the entity becomes his labour as entire; and precisely thus, in labour, he re-establishes himself. (Hegel 1967b, p. 213)

1.4

Thus we have the substantiality of labour as foundation of human civilisation. However,

> Need and labor, elevated into this universality, then form on their own account a monstrous system of community and mutual interdependence in a great people; life of the dead body, that moves itself within itself, one which ebbs and flows in its motion blindly, like the elements, and which requires continual strict dominance and taming like a wild beast. (Hegel 1979a, p. 249)

This is the point where Hegel's thought takes on even more expressly a contemporary figure. The recovery of the positivity of labour for the life of the spirit, its deep inherence therein, its very fundamentality, cannot be given as such. Civilisation is not simply labour, but labour that is regulated, organised and controlled. Without right, without a state, labour becomes chaos, the life of a dead body, a particularity that arrogates universality to itself – whereas on the other hand labour can and must be universal, but only through the mediation of the state. The fundamentality of labour is dialecticised, subsumed and sublimated. Already during Hegel's Jena period, the inherence of the economic in the entire development of ethical life is subordinated to the necessity of its regulation. Indeed, the regulation is gradually abstracted from the content to which it applies; the economic and the juridical are born together, from within the elementary processes of the socialisation of need and enjoyment, through the system of needs.

However, this proceeding together goes only as far as the 'second state', the acquisitive class; then the right emancipates itself. Only through denying its commonality with the process of socialisation of labour can it regulate this process and hence declare, definitively, the substantiality of labour to the human world. Right is contract, punitive justice, institution; in this it is still mixed with the direct necessity of the economic; but then it becomes constitution, state, government, in other words a regulative and simultaneously exalting reality of that regulated world. From now on labour will present itself in the command of the state.

1.5

The framework that *Philosophy of Right* presents is that of the complete hegemony of right over labour – which is nevertheless the substance of the ethical world. Command over social labour ends up constituting here the schema of the state itself; the assumption of labour into the absolute takes place in the form of command, in the form of the state's articulation of social labour – as an articulation by means of social classes. Here the division of labour has a figure that is immediately functional for command over labour. The capitalist mode of production in the phase of primitive accumulation is sanctified and assumed as the substance of the general social relation; and in control within it are the political forces that are the guarantors of this phase of development. Idealism triumphs over economic analysis, exalting into spirituality the forces that exercise command in the reality of economics.

So here in *Philosophy of Right* the system of needs – albeit conceived of in the richness of its internal dialectic:

> In this dependence and reciprocity of labour and the fulfillment of needs, subjective egoism turns into the contribution of the satisfaction of the needs of all others – in the mediation of the individual, through the universal, as a dialectical movement, so that, since everyone acquires, produces and enjoys for himself, and precisely thus he produces and buys for the enjoyment of others. (Hegel 1967a: §200)

– is immediately bent to the dialectic of capitalist 'participation' in wealth:

> The possibility of sharing in general wealth, particular wealth, is however conditioned, in part by a particular immediate base (capital), and in part by the attitude that, for its part, is itself once again conditioned by that, but then by contingent circumstances, whose multiplicity pro-

duces diversity in the development of the natural bodily and spiritual dispositions that are already in themselves unequal – a diversity that, in this sphere of particularity, comes out in all the tendencies and in all the grades and, with the other contingencies and arbitrarinesses, has, as a necessary consequence, inequalities in the heritage and the aptitude of individuals. (Ibid.)

Nor is differentiated participation in wealth an individual fact, an exception of singularity: the universality of the process must equally express diversity in 'universal masses' [*masse generali*], in diverse collectivities of participation and of command over social living labour (ibid., §21). Thus right is superimposed on the living community of social cooperation in the organisation of wealth.

1.6

The nexus of unity and division, of cooperation and subordination that the capitalist organisation of social living labour offers thus ends up constituting also the inner nexus of the Hegelian conception of right.

In fact, right presents itself in *Philosophy of Right* under three aspects: it is an abstract right, a norm and a prohibition, a moment of negative protection of the personality, an element that conditions the constitution of society as such; but, secondly, it is also, immediately, subjective right – a claim: the person becomes a subject and will conforms itself positively, as action. The auroral life of right constitutes itself through this intertwining, in a form completely analogous to that of the constitution of social cooperation in the world of production. Right confers here, to the particularity, capacity – the possibility – 'of developing and of launching forth on all sides' (ibid., §184). It is a freedom of action that the particularity develops in the world as collective intention of a given sociality – the particular reflected in itself is in general well-being (according to a note to §113 in the German edition) – in other words, the collective growth of labour from the system of needs to the production of wealth. Labour, as a constructed world and as a forming force, as a second nature, as produced objectivity, thus constitutes the fabric on which society and right are simultaneously developed.

But in *Philosophy of Right* right is also presented in a third, definitive figure: as an organic nexus of the ethical world, as an ethical institution, as a given articulation of the overall social world. Now, the rising of what, for Hegel, is 'the real spirit', the transition from particularity to universality, from the finite to the infinite, means that the entire process of defining right is modified and that the nexus that united right and social cooperation is completed and sublimated in the nexus that sees cooperation in subordination. Freedom, in making itself 'substantial freedom', completely subordinates – almost driving it into the background of an unreachable negativity – the world already seen as a human construction, as a collective enterprise of freedom. Cooperation and its dialectic of positive production of the collective come to be dissolved within a framework that sees them totally locked in the subordination of their process to the absolute – to an absolute that is prior to any process: 'this idea is the being, eternal in itself and for itself, and necessary, of the spirit' (ibid., §258).

Of course,

> in relation to the spheres of private right and private welfare, of the family and civil society, the state is, on the one hand, an external neces- sity, and their higher authority, to whose nature their laws, and also their interests, are subordinated and depend on them; on the other hand, however, it is the objective immanent within them and has its own force in the unity of its ultimate universal goal and of the particular interests of individuals, in the fact that they have duties in relation to it, at the same time as they have rights. (Ibid., §261)

But this duality of the relationship between civil society and state, whereby the state would be both the negation and the fulfilment of civil society, is a duality only in appearance – because the fulfilment is in subordination, and the process is real only in negation. Thus the system of social labour, which is assumed, within the system of right, to constitute its reality, can definitively exercise its substantial function, can continue to be its condition, only by subordinating itself completely to the state. In the final instance the state is the true ethical reality; society and the world of cooperation acquire reality only by subordinating themselves to it. Subordination penetrates the very process of cooperation, giving it its own sign. Subordination, the reality of the state, is ontologically immanent to the dialectical process that constitutes it; it is present in the moment of social coop- eration and gives it its determinate being. Labour is the foundation of the state; it is the foundation of overall legality inasmuch as it is the material of state control. The work of the state is control over social living labour.

2

2.1

The conception of right and of the state as a conception of labour and of its organisation is thus entirely explicit in *Philosophy of Right*: it is a conception of labour and of its given organisation – bourgeois and capitalist.

This is immediately evident in the assumptions present in Hegel's analysis, excessively conditioned as they are by Smith and Ricardo's conception of the foundations of political economy. Thus value is certainly addressed in its labourist origins (ibid., §189), but it is also translated, on this basis, into universality of exchange value:

> The thing, in use, is a single thing, determined qualitatively and quantitatively and in relation to a specific need. But its specific utility, like those that are quantitatively determined, is, at the same time, comparable with other things of the same utility, just as the specific need, which it serves, is, at the same time, a need in general... This universality, whose simple determinacy derives from the particularity of the thing, so that it abstracts itself, at the same time, from this specific quality, is the value of the thing, in which its true substantiality is determined and is an object of consciousness. (Ibid., §63)

Secondly, the bourgeois and capitalist specificity of Hegel's discourse on labour and its organisation spring from the assumption of inequality as a fundamental condition of the subjects of the labouring process. And this is not a simple, naturalistic inequality (ibid., §§57–8), but an exaltation (in terms of having to be) of the various functions of the production process. Association demands subordination; cooperation in labour requires differentiation in the process of value creation; labour necessitates command and capital (ibid., §§196–7).

Thirdly and consequently, Hegel's very conception of the civilian sees the rule of exchange as being predominant. The citizen, as a 'bourgeois' (ibid., §190, note), is the meeting point between the necessity of having value [*valere*] as an abstract interchangeable need (all people in society are, first of all, commodities) and the possibility of playing a given role – and a collective role as a class – in the mechanism of overall social subordination.

So we have Hegel, the philosopher of right, as a philosopher of the bourgeois and capitalist organisation of labour.

2.2

But in Hegel there is not only the theorisation – and the justification – of the given situation of the capitalist process. There is not
only the recovery of the theoretical intuition of classical economics,
as between Smith and Ricardo. There is, in addition, the utopia of
capital, the perfect definition of the transcendental and driving relationship of the two propositions: the reality of the rational and the
rationality of the real. If the reality of the rational is the apotheosis of
the de facto state, the absolute immanentism of the pacification of the
idea with the real and the determinateness conquered as pacification,
and thus capital as an absolute ordering in the bourgeois categories
that Hegel was given to grasp – well, alongside all this there is the
affirmation, entirely dialectical, of the rationality of the real. In this
the revolutionary passion of the Enlightenment is consciously bent to
the necessities of capital.

The state is the reality of ethical life; it is the reality of labour. And
it is, above all, the driving rationality of this absolute identity, the
world in which that which is rational, and given, and justified comes
to be shaken by the tension that emanates from the inner essence
of rationality. A kind of unfulfilled will to understand, to dominate through doing [il fare] and through the intelligence of doing,
is thus a constant presence in the overall picture. Where it seems
that everything is completed, everything is uncompleted. Where it
seems that precision triumphs, the margins of possibility of the real
turn out to be unlimited. But all this occurs within the measure of
a control and management of development that have to find their
own definitive condition in the realised ethical idea, in the state. It
is the essence of the state; it is the essence of capital as completeness of the subordination of the world of labour: it is all this – the
absolute, the autonomous, the moving self. The non-movingness of
the abstract ethical idea has refound itself as engine of the real. And
if the real is labour, if the rational order is 'capital', if the relationship between cooperation and subordination, between the particular
and the universal, is a given, then here we have the state as development, as capital in a condition of necessary development. The state
as capital is the state as development. Il potere [power] is exercised in
development and through development. The state is a dynamic institution that sees how right develops as determinate action, within the
framework of society, in order to relate every social action back to the
overall determinations of the given rational order.

At this point, the rediscovery of universality in the discontinuous
seriality of events, the connection of actions into a coherent universe

of inner experience, the fixation of a necessary nexus between individual meanings and overall meaning – all this becomes a task that will find an answer. Science fills itself to satisfaction with this process, which feels within itself the absolute: even as it works, it justifies itself, offering itself again and again as an objective, although each time it is a result. The balance of the whole triumphs over the tension of the parts and vice versa, the precision of the parts finds its location and composition in the movement of the whole. The capitalist urgency to exalt the world, taking it to pieces, rebuilding it, dominating it completely – never a moment of peace, but always solid command – in Hegelianism, this urgency comes to be translated into science. From Giovanni Gentile to Carl Schmitt, interwar European intellectuals learned this to be their apologetic mission.

2.3

This image of a rationality that is simultaneously given and continuously transcendent – unfinished *qua* development but also complete *qua* state – this also embodies the centuries-old bourgeois and capitalist fortune of Hegelianism. This image corresponds precisely to the image that capital produces of itself, in the perpetual alternation of development and crisis, of reformism and repression that its existence determines. And nowhere is this overall and dynamic projection of the state of capital offered better than it is in *Philosophy of Right*. Neither Hegel's aesthetics nor his logic, let alone his philosophy of religion or of history, succeed in producing this completeness of the image. In *Philosophy of Right*, in fact, the conciliation of positivity with the idea is given without incoherences: the indeterminateness of religious intuition, the coarseness of historical typology, the instability of the aesthetic vision, and the formalism of the logical process – all fail to upset the picture. In fact in *Philosophy of Right* neither the mere positivity of right nor the mere normativity of the state are able to prevail in the face of the idea; in play here is rather the complete positivity of social production through labour. This compact social reality, unitarily assumed and resolved in the process of the idea, is the measure of the dynamic positivity that the universal configuration of *Philosophy of Right* manages to achieve. It is an image that interprets as positive the rigidity of the social structures it reads and that interprets as dynamic the necessity that emanates from those same social structures, in order to understand ever more deeply and rationally this given world of capital within which the contemporary individual is entirely contained.

2.4

This inner completeness of *Philosophy of Right* has simultaneously nourished and imprisoned the philosophical and political thought of the nineteenth and twentieth centuries: a largely positive imprisonment, when one considers the continuous self-critical initiative that the living nexus of rationality and positivity imposed on bourgeois thought. The nineteenth-century conception of progress, which was closely linked to it, in its positive aspects (and eighteenth-century rationalism was overcome in the process); historicist optimism; and also the great wave of scientific thought – all this is perhaps not understandable if not linked to the intuition that the real can be moved from within, without thereby losing its positive composure. For the first time in the history of humankind, order has become progressive, power has become reformist – in Hegel's sense. In the name of Hegelianism the bourgeoisie has found the possibility of renewing an old, Renaissance revolutionary case – for which perhaps it had never lost its nostalgia until then.

But a prison is still a prison, even when it is gilded – particularly if it contains bourgeois thought only insofar as it subordinates and crushes the society of labour, only to the extent that the bourgeois discourse of development within order rests on the exploitation of overall social living labour. Development, domination, wealth: but it 'has to deal with a material which presents infinite resistance, in other words with external means, having that particular character, which is the property of free will, and therefore absolutely unyielding' (Hegel 1967a, §195). Here the cage of the absolute wavers and really finds its antithesis. The 'absolutely unyielding' does not accept the orderliness of reason's plan, the state's plan.

2.5

Bourgeois thought feels all this like a crisis in the bowels of the absolute in which it reposes but is not able to free itself. The imprisonment that Hegelian thought imposes here is no longer gilded but dramatic – an unresolved and absolutely unyielding determination, which is experienced, received and endured. Yet the cage of the absolute does not want to be, cannot be, and must not be broken. After the nineteenth-century apotheosis of Hegelianism, here is the twentieth-century nemesis of the frame of reference, of the absolute as a project of reason that the most lucid bourgeois theory has inherited from Hegel. This new hard-won determinacy is not such as to accept subordination. A new dialectic opens up, within and against the Hegelian absolute; this one is no longer triumphal but, depending on circumstances, mystic or ascetic and always tragic and increasingly negative.

Here the totality of the Hegelian process of reason can no longer constitute itself; the process is given as interrupted. And yet it wants to be given. Philosophical science moves from the determinate and wants to reconstitute it in the perspective of the absolute. But now the 'absolutely unyielding', the reality of an irreducible conflictuality, becomes apparent. The need for totality cuts loose and detaches itself from the recompositional mechanism; and process and result are unable to reach identity. So here the totality is pursued along the lines of an unresolved dualism: it will be the ascesis of a functioning intentionality that repeats the models of transcendental schematism, but with a charge of phenomenological weight that does not permit the apprehension of the absolute. It will be, on the contrary, the acceptance of a world of meanings, historically given, that one holds onto in the absence of an overall and ontologically probative meaning. Here the absolute becomes convention, the given is mystically validated, in amazement and submission to its *potenza* [power], which cannot be broken. Finally, it will be the awareness that the nexus between meanings and sense of the ontological situation cannot be resolved, that the relationship between determinacy and totality does not come to conclusion: the whole is the untruth. What a terrible destiny lies behind this discovery! Negation is qualified painfully by nostalgia for the absolute content on which it is exercised. Hegelian phenomenology is relived entirely in reverse: not in the process that brings it to the height of the capitalistic composition of *Philosophy of Right* but the other way round, starting from a critique of the latter, within the series of contradictions that constitute the process – contradictions that today are irresolvable and have indeed become even deeper. The Hegelian totality is dissolved in the contradictions that constituted it; it has no possibility of overcoming them. The tragedy in the ethical is no longer the condition of the totality but the result of the process.

3

3.1

The trajectory of Hegel's thought on the state and on right is not only bourgeois and capitalist; his impact is so complex that it also reverberates and applies in areas that are far more contradictory – at least potentially more contradictory.

If it is true that the insubordinate determinacy of labour left its mark on the development of bourgeois philosophy to the point of imposing desperate outcomes there, even more so does this particularity erect itself historically, in the real world, against the general capitalist interest that seeks to be represented in the figure of the Hegelian state. When – from 1848 on, and then in the great revolutionary undertakings of the working class in 1870 and 1917 – particular workers qualified themselves as subjects, proposing or implementing the destruction of the machine of statal domination over subordinated labour, it appears that the Hegelian ideology of the state has closed its account with history.

> Capital stands on one side and labour on the other, both as independent forms relative to each other; both hence also alien to one another. The labour which stands opposite capital is *alien* labour, and the capital which stands opposite labour is *alien* capital. The extremes which stand opposite one another are *specifically* different. (Marx 1973, p. 266)

And yet this did not happen, or happened only in the utopian form of revolutionary hope. In effect, the real experience of realised socialism comes across as a continuity – a paradoxical continuity, as we shall see – of a Hegelianising practice of the state. The revolution reorganises itself as a capitalist institution and socialism takes the figure of the state. The militant cooperation of revolutionary workers identifies and foregrounds the mismatch between egalitarian participation in the structure of the state and a subordinate participation to the structure of the economic process, in conformity with the requirements and positivity of productive functions. Gradually – within this historical framework – free participation in the formation and management of political will is destroyed and subordinates itself to the needs of the economic mechanism. Socialism is given in the form of the Hegelian state; the interest of individual workers and its unyieldingness do not succeed in liberating themselves from the general interest, from the plane of general subordination. And yet Marx had already noted this in the *Grundrisse*: 'The demand that wage labour be continued but capital suspended is self-contradictory, self-dissolving' (ibid.).

3.2
Certainly something has changed. Right and the state do not have here – as they did in the development of Hegel's thought and in that crucial phase of the construction of the contemporary capitalist state – the need to transcend the world of labour, if only at the end of the dialectical process, in those pages of *Philosophy of Right* that see the transition from civil society to the state, or the transition from

the second acquisitive class to the general class (Hegel 1967a, §§202–4). Here labour is extended through to the sphere of the general class, but only to discover within itself that dialectic of cooperation and subordination of which Hegel at this point interrupted the continuity by arguing, outside the labour process, for its political autonomy and sublimation. Paradoxically, in this new experience, which wanted to be one of negation, Hegelianism stands up and finds a more intimate coherence. The absolute does not need to cut its roots with labour; order does not need to break away from the dialectic that proposes it and constitutes it. Realised socialism gives us the continuity of the formative schema of the state entirely within labour. Labour and right, cooperation and subordination, society and state develop together, in a tight and integrated commonality, at all the levels of dialectical development.

In this way the prison of *Philosophy of Right* extends to one of its potential negation here as well – and triumphs over it. It triumphs over it at the point where negation, rather than proposing doubt, deepens the coherence of the picture. What seems to be an overturning appears to be a radical confirmation. The state, under threat, reproposes itself as a substance of the ethical idea, a solution of the particularity in the general nexus of the spirit. Certainly, it is a *spirit* that 'labours'. But did not *Philosophy of Right* seek to be, right from the beginning, a 'hard labour of the highest liberation'?

3.3

Is this ultimate solution of the insurgent and subordinated particularity, within the schema of Hegelian statist conciliation, really capable of closing the problem? Or is it not rather the case that the unresolved opposition finds here – after this last attempt at conclusion – its own ground on which to go deeper? No longer, then, against right, no longer solely against the state, but against labour, which the ultimate solution has revealed as a universally comprehensive substance and as the key to the relationship between cooperation and subordination?

The impetuous advance of the movement of the subordinated particularity, well beyond the limits imposed by the Hegelian prison of socialism, shows that the path of liberation is precisely that of the struggle against work – and it shows its uncontainability in the Hegelian project of the absolute. As practice and as science, the revolution frees itself from Hegelianism: the productivity of spirit reveals itself to be a prison in the same way as the productivity of labour – this latest contemporary deity of the composition of exploitation with development, and of labour with the Enlightenment's utopia of capitalist progress. The refusal of work as a mass condition, a general condition of subordinated behaviour, attacks the Hegelian composition of cooperation and subordination at its roots (both in its capitalist and in its socialist figure). For the first time, cooperation dissociates itself, turns against subordination, discovering itself in subordination, *as object, as absolute poverty*, and reflects instead on itself as cooperation – as 'the *general possibility* of wealth as subject and as activity'. It is '[l]abour not as an object, but as activity; not as itself *value*, but as the *living source* of value. [Namely it is] general wealth (in contrast to capital in which it exists objectively, as reality) as the *general possibility* of the same, which proves itself as such in action' (Marx 1973, p. 296). For the first time, labour breaks the substantial definition that tied it to the state. In the refusal of itself, it presents itself as refusal of the state and proposes itself, simultaneously, as a collective undertaking of liberty. The organisation of social living labour is thus entrusted to the general human proposal of happiness and wealth and develops accordingly, in opposition to every moment of subordination.

3.4

The breaking of the nexus between cooperation and subordination embodied in the social practice of refusal of work recovers the unyieldingness of the particularity; it materialises it as an acting particularity, as a subject. An alternative world, a 'second nature' truly constructed, opens as a very rich possibility, starting from the activity of the particular. But, critically, this has to be stressed: that the refusal of work, the enactment of the 'unyieldingness' of the particularity, is maximally inherent, as a negation, in the most radical dimension of the Hegelian process of the absolute. The shattering of the universe of *Philosophy of Right* occurs at its sources: it goes beyond the necessity of right and of the state, which are not originary, to arrive at the true nucleus of the necessity of the process of objectification – which is the necessity of the capitalist organisation of labour. Here what is brought into question is not some particular content of the dialectic; and there is no repetition of the formalistic story of neo-Hegelian reforms of dialectics. Here it is the dialectical process itself that is rejected as a form adequate to a specific content, namely the capitalist organisation of labour. The refusal of work goes deeper, until it appears as a refusal of dialectic, as a radical dissolution of the composition of the labouring subject with the necessity of subordination, as a radical affirmation of the irreducibility of the collective reality of that particular unyieldingness.

From here on the process is given only as a capacity of rupture, as a series of struggles: the particularity reveals how it is – in itself, as an activity, as a permanent struggle – more general than any possible absolute. There is no need of recomposition because the unyielding-ness of the particular does not recognise others to be exploited, to be included in unities of opposites: there is only a deepening of the particular into itself, the discovery of a new universe through refold-ing onto oneself and an excavation, within oneself, of the collective particular. Reality is not dialectical but partial, autonomous, singu-lar; reality is not universal but radically unilateral; it is a practice that anticipates itself and endangers itself in the construction of itself as a particular *potere*.

We are finally outside dialectic, outside any compositional process that is merely a process of mystification, outside labour as a synthesis of opposites – outside philosophy as a terrain of ideal usurpation of the real, of the particular. Thus the refusal of work draws the conse-quences of the revelation of *Philosophy of Right* as the supreme index of bourgeois ideology and of the capitalist practice of organisation of exploitation. Here the thought of the particular, freeing itself from the dialectic of labour, also frees itself from philosophy as the night-time apparition of an apologetic comprehension of the real. The owl of Minerva disappears from our evening.

3.5

On the two hundredth anniversary of his birth, my homage to Hegel, to the great thinker of *Philosophy of Right*, is bitter – as is fitting when one recognises in his thinking the massive, constantly renewed base of an ideology that wishes for the exploitation of humans by humans and imprisons – albeit identifying it – the hope of liberation. The historical awareness of the necessity of that thought, at the dawn of the nineteenth century and of mature capitalism, pales and changes its sign in front of the mystifying importance, the burden, and the suffocating impact of Hegelian philosophy on a century and a half in the history of thought. The mystification, the political overturn-ing of revolutionary instances: all of this can be laid at Hegel's door. Let us shift this formidable obstacle out of our way! Let us liberate our practice and our thought from his charm! Perhaps only hatred, as an expression of the insubordinate particularity within which our thinking grows, is the adequately defining quality of a relationship with Hegel.

And yet precisely this feeling, in all its intensity, contradictorily binds us to him.

13

Problems of the historiography of the modern state*

France, 1610–1650

1 Machine-state and civil society

In an important conference presentation in June 1956, summing up the results of a century of historiographical work, Federico Chabod asked the question: *Y at-il un état de la Renaissance?* ['Is there such a thing as a Renaissance state?'] (Chabod 1956). He began by listing a series of traditional characteristics that he said were inadequate for defining the specificity of what, from the Renaissance onwards, has been handed down to us as the figure of the modern state: certainly not the lucky analogy with Renaissance works of art, which today nobody would feel comfortable reproposing; not the idea of nation; not that of patriotism, which gets attached to the idea of state only at a later stage; and the concept of absolutism is not adequate either for defining the modern state in its genesis – since even at that point European history had known absolutism for centuries, in the many forms of its development. What characterises the modern state at its birth – or so Chabod concluded – is rather a particular realisation of absolutism: the machine-state [*lo stato macchina*], that is, a new structural organisation, internal to the state, whereby the state makes its action permanent where previously it was intermittent and that is stable and rational by comparison with the precarious operations of medieval absolutism. On the one hand, the creation of practices of professional diplomacy makes it possible to maintain

---

* SOURCE: Antonio Negri, 1967. 'Problemi di storia dello stato moderno: Francia, 1610–1650'. *Rivista critica di storia della filosofia* 2: 182–220.

many-sided and ongoing relationships in the world; and on the other hand, there is the organisation of a centralised system of government, control and repression that enables the state to convey its will to its subjects and to impose it in a uniform manner. The power of the sovereign and the mechanical and rational articulation of the expression of his will through an apparatus of power – this is what characterises the modern state. Two consequences follow from this: on the one hand, a strengthening of absolutism; but also, on the other, an emancipation of the state as apparatus, precisely as a corps of officers, as a permanent mechanism for the expression of sovereign will. The state comes to be emancipated from the person of the sovereign.

Chabod's point remains fundamental. There is no doubt that this definition of the process of formation of the modern state is confirmed by the evolution of European states from the sixteenth to the seventeenth century: the sociology of his depiction is filled with real content. Whether republics or monarchies, and regardless of their evolution through crises of varying intensity, France, Spain, England, the Netherlands and Venice present a structural framework that is homogeneous.

At this point, however, a further set of problems arises, and at least one of these is immediately of great importance. What is the position of civil society in relation to this new and specific emergence of state power? Because, if it is true that the distinctive element in this development is the emancipation of state power from the person of the sovereign, what follows intrinsically is the problem of the social and political legitimation of this abstract figure, which becomes the state. We move away from a relationship of 'fidelity' to a lord, a relationship of being in the 'service' of the most powerful, in a structure based on an uninterrupted series of reciprocal personal relationships; we see rather the triumph of a 'functional' relationship within the ambit of the state apparatus, an affirmation of the independence of civil society as a counterpart to the independence of sovereign power – and thus a total modification and a growing abstraction of the criteria for the social and political legitimation of power. Indeed, this is a recurrent theme of debate in the seventeenth century – a debate that highlights the problem, indicating that attempts to avoid it are pointless. Those who seek to assert the new absolutism of the state cannot refuse to discuss the new criteria for its legitimation. For some, this is an exhilarating opportunity, for others it is an unavoidable evil, but for all concerned there can be no turning back.[1]

But let me approach the problem from another angle. The dissolution of feudal relations in the new structure of the state corresponds to the dissolution of feudal relations in society as a whole. What begins to form the fabric of the new society is an intricate network of contractual relationships. The bourgeoisie is constituted as a class, both social and political, in the same period that sees the formation of the modern state. Civil society assumes, in relation to the state and within it, a position adequate to its new nature; and, reciprocally, the state tends to configure itself as a specific form of the new social order. Of course, none of this happens without long and hard-fought struggles; it all takes place over a period of time – three centuries and more – that sees the completion of the social and political development of the bourgeoisie and of the whole arc of its revolution. It is here, however, in addressing the problems that the first configuration of the modern state raises, that it is possible to grasp the elements of self-awareness – sometimes confused, but all present – that civil society presents. One can also see them prefigured and verified in the first instance, albeit in projects of historical realisation that extend over the long term and then are modified in the stops and alternative paths that the first experience of struggle imposes. The very definition of civil society, of the bourgeoisie as a social and political class, derives from this initial trial.

So, how does civil society define itself in relation to that emergence of the state?

The problem is that precisely the historiography that opened my discussion now fails us. It set out to define the figure of the modern state, it was attracted by it, and it defined its characteristics and its periodisations. But beyond that limit, beyond that description, it had little to offer. Like a powerful breaker, it attacks and defines the shape of a rock, but then dissolves into a thousand rivulets. The perspective that, operating around the figure of the state, had created a unified historical horizon was not, then, able to open itself to the realities and social movements that constituted that horizon. Between state and society there emerged a no-man's land, where, in the best of cases, the problems of society were addressed separately, in parallel with the central and defining problems of the development of the modern state. Was there perhaps a suspicion that, by bringing civil society and state together, this figure of the state might end up being challenged? Or, vice versa, was it only when faced with the crisis of the modern state that historiography would become capable of taking a path that led to self-critical reflection? Anyway, we need to ask how and why this all came about.

2   The historiographic tradition and its limits

Let me simplify the analysis and offer a few examples. Historiography is always a historical construct; so only the answer to a series of historical problems can offer the key to solving the enigmas of historiography.

So let me go back to the genesis of the modern state – France during the period 1610–50. The choice of period is very significant – 1610, the assassination of Henri IV, defeater of the Catholic League; 1614–15, the Estates General; 1624, Richelieu and the struggle over the reorganisation of the state; and then Mazzarino, La Fronde, Louis XIV and, together with absolutism, the triumph of the machine-state. Alongside all this there is the development of civil society; Descartes and Corneille, Gassendi and Mersenne, libertinism and Jansenism, the birth of modern science and that of manufacturing; and then Pascal, Racine and Molière. It is no coincidence that Voltaire praises the *siècle de Louis XIV* as one of the greatest manifestations of the human spirit! And it is a typifying period: all the elements that were brought into play, whether positively or negatively, by the birth of the modern state are present there. The alternatives are radical: anarchy or absolutism, a state of the elites [*ceti*] or a machine-state. There is Reform and counter-Reform along the way and, in the background, the baroque, standing midway between Renaissance and Enlightenment.[2]

But it is above all a privileged period for analysis. The intensity with which the revolution takes place is matched by the depth of how it is perceived. Franz Borkenau noted this in an important book that was published in 1934 but was then forgotten in the tragic events of German culture;[3] he took up Lucien Febvre's call for a renewal of studies on the topic.[4] In this respect too, the state of historiography left much to be desired. Certainly there was no denying the significance of the period. However, it was either underestimated or hypersimplified, and in any case it was dissolved in its own significance, which was the possibility of seeing the great century in development, as a moment – not as a conclusion – in the evolution of the European.

I say underestimated. This is the case with classical historiography, from Voltaire to Thierry, through to traditional literary history. Just as, for Voltaire, the exaltation of the great century is directly equivalent to an apologetics for the bourgeoisie, for its civilising work, and is polemical towards the degradation of the civil and political climate during the reign of Louis XV,[5] so for Thierry the great century reveals for the first time the national mindset of the bourgeoisie and legitimises its development, which leads to the 'great revolution'. It is the bourgeoisie that, choosing not to fight for its own immediate interests after the tragic end of Henri, imposes on the other classes a development that represents the condition of the century in the cultural and political manifestations that make it great.[6] On these premises, the mythical greatness of the great century is a *fait accompli*. The historiographic pragmatism of Voltaire, who has no idea of evolution, equates to Thierry's Saint-Simonian evolutionism, which sees this century as the triumph of the industrial age over the metaphysical age. The historical products of the great century are abstract, anyway: the machine-state and the *esprit philosophique* are regarded as the fruit of French genius, as models to be traced everywhere and to be used, according to Voltaire, as a function of the Enlightenment and of the Revolution and, according to Thierry, as an instrument of apologetics, for the historical support of the political fortunes of the bourgeoisie. Historiography becomes a liturgy of the bourgeois national spirit. And then the fact that the great century, to use a euphemism, was in reality far more varied in dramatic events or, to be candid, had been driven by a profound revolutionary crisis, in the cities and in the countryside, or the fact that the rise of the bourgeoisie had expressed itself in the bloody forms of the processes of primitive accumulation of capital and that the strengthening of absolutism had found its first justification in a consequent, uninterrupted action of repression, carried out in a permanent climate of civil war:[7] it is right that all these facts were passed over in silence by the authors of the enlightened bourgeoisie, aware as they were of the necessarily political function that historiography fulfils!

However, the significance of the great century can be cancelled out in another way: by hypersimplifying the complex thread of historical problems around which it evolves. This is what happens, for example, when one decides against pursuing the problem in the totality of its articulations and seeks rather to simplify it – presuming to abide by the rules of specialisation and interdisciplinary integration – and thus to develop its analysis within the systematics of particular empirical sciences. Therefore, within a given and sometimes prevalent historiography, with the help of statistical methods and models of the sociology of power, the process of formation of the modern state comes to be placed and described in terms of the conflict that, in the question of corruption of offices, opposes parliamentary bourgeoisie to absolutist government.[8] The intuition of a theme that increases and articulates the complexity of the historical problem is adopted with the effect of impoverishing that problem. And then things take a turn for the worse when the excessive simplification turns out to be a transitional phase in the research as a whole, when one moves from there to recognising the possibility and the opportuneness of returning to the general, of representing the whole development as an extension, a proof of that particular point of view. Then the magic word 'structure' intervenes. The problem configured in this way alludes to a 'structure', to a 'self-sufficient meaningful structure'. And then we see how the social, religious and political ideologies, the philosophical systems and the poetics of the great century come to be located in this structure. They are significant figures and resolutive indices of the problem that defines the structure, in this case of the conflict that opposes the parliamentary bourgeoisie to absolutism in the matter of corruption of offices.[9] No methodological caution can hide the brutal extrapolation that this historiographical tendency works from a series of facts described in their sociological dimension to their use in the abstract and to the configuration of a number of permanent models of conflict expression and resolution. In fact the eternity of the French spirit comes to be replaced by the eternity of the dramatic situation! One anti-historical attitude equals the other. It would be easy to point out the ideological presuppositions of this conception.[10]

So this is the current state of historiography. Is there nothing else? It would be unfair to say so. In reality, alongside the historiographical currents mentioned above, slowly but surely, a younger and more attentive school is emerging. It is on this school that I shall focus: in this review I shall limit myself almost exclusively to gathering the new research hypotheses it has developed. This school has taken on board the indications of Lucien Febvre, which constitute a specialist approach to the historical problem. It is an interdisciplinary approach, yes, but it involves awareness that this level of investigation does not permit extrapolation and that it means not conclusion but successive approximation of the totality of the historical problem. The particular techniques – economic, statistical, sociological, and so forth – are useful to the extent that they open up new perspectives and widen the possibilities of defining the problem. And the great century and its first five-hundredth anniversary have become one of the main objects of investigation, perhaps in inverse proportion to the mystifications that have been loaded onto it or, better, in direct proportion to the objective relevance that their problem presents. Of course, as I said, having lost the unifying centre that bourgeois apologetics had seen in the state, the research dispersed in a thousand rivulets. This does not detract from the debt we owe to these studies, which today broadly address the problem of the great century, of the genesis of the machine-state, and especially of the relationship between its formation and the behaviours, the struggles and (in short) the overall figure of civil society. These studies are specialised, partial, sometimes unique, but never peculiar or mystifying. It is thanks to these studies that it becomes possible today to restate the problem of the great century in its entirety.

3   The civil crisis of the Renaissance, premise of the seventeenth century

How does civil society relate to the birth of the machine-state?

If there is one lesson to be drawn from the comments offered thus far on the historiography of the great century, it is that the greatest danger consists in isolating the period under study. This is so not only for reasons of method, but also because the problem itself forces us to transcend the limits of the century. The fact is that at the beginning of the seventeenth century the bourgeoisie has already established itself as a class, and its bow for revolution is already drawn. At the conference mentioned earlier, Chabod pointed out to a scandalised objector that the process that sees the parallel and autonomous developments of the modern state and of civil society respectively began in the fourteenth century in Italy and between the fifteenth and the sixteenth centuries in other European countries.[11] It is in fact humanism that raises those values of freedom and independence around which the bourgeois revolution defines itself.[12]

Independence and freedom: in society, in politics, in religion. From the Italian cities, that revolutionary movement extends to Europe. It was the merchant, the hero of the birth of our civilisation, who came to be the bearer of new values: he was soldier and cleric at the same time, as shown by Lucien Febvre in a memorable article (Febvre 1962b), and also inventor and speculator, avidly and heroically intent on making money bear fruit – that money that was a sign of equality and virtue. As for the state, he wanted it to be open to that equality and virtue, as a community of free people. As for God, he felt him to be close to his innovatory action and a guarantor of his love of freedom – God as 'master of merchandising' [*maestro di un trafico*]. Inasmuch as the medieval image of the world gets dissolved, state and divinity find themselves at the level of individuals, as if to complete their work and at the same time to guarantee hope in the world. State and church arrive at a resolution in the tension that emanates from civil society; they are degrees, forms and moments of its expression. The new naturalism of the Renaissance, in art as in philosophy, wherever one considers it, provides the framework within which the new vision of the world defines itself.[13] As for the world, it is an immense but safe projection of the microcosm, itself animated by the tension that flows from the individual. As for the state, it too is a macrocosm parallel to the individual. All the hierarchical degrees, the static bonds that shaped both the state and nature in the medieval vision collapse; the relationship between individual and totality is direct and immediate; there is continuity between humans and heaven.[14] Freedom is all positive, it is a matter of doing, of struggling. The individual is, like nature, essentially productive. 'Virtue' corresponds to 'fortune': virtue produces or wins over fortune. Yes, it is a world that does not know the impossible, has no sense of limitation.[15] But when does a revolution ever admit the impossible? But some will say that this is illusory – mythical. Never mind. There is a whole society living on this illusion; a class in the process of constituting itself depicts itself in this myth. The golden age is near.[16]

Nevertheless, illusion and myth remain precisely that. And the aporias that the realisation of freedom involves do not take long to reveal themselves – at the social level, at the religious level and at the political level.[17] At the first, the accumulation of wealth breaks the unitary development of society or, better, dissipates yearnings for it: the virtue of many is soon countered by the fortune of the few. A just, balanced, peaceful social relationship: this is a myth, and it reveals itself as such. In reality, what starts to develop here is capitalist economy, and it sets in place those problems that centuries of European history will fail to unravel.[18] So let us look at the subjective resonances of this development, at the time of the first profound crisis, at the moment when huge fortunes were amassed and lost, when a monetary economy discovered its social impact and, in this dangerous game, a class emancipated itself. By emancipating itself it acquires self-awareness, recognises itself, and separates itself. It separates itself from the old feudal classes, but also from the new social strata that capitalist development is forming or restructuring and that reject this development and the new subordination. Social struggle between the classes is accentuated and renewed. What are the subjective resonances of this process? Here we have our protagonist, a bourgeois merchant, questioning himself about the legitimacy of his actions in the world. What right have I to innovate society by breaking every balance, to oppose my virtue to the fortune of others, or to defend my fortune against the virtue of others? The medieval world was a world that was certain about the fixity and objectivity of the ethical and religious criteria it offered for human action. Now this assurance is undermined. It is a crisis of certainty, a bitter moment of reflection that sometimes stands in the way of the bourgeois engaged in his traffic, in his peaceful (but peaceful until when?) and decisive revolution; a crisis of certainty that shifts to the religious horizon, in search of a theodicy of freedom, of subjective will, of the capitalist revolution. If the long-standing debate on the relationship between the genesis of capitalism and the development of reform, and in particular of Calvinism, has left us with one useful idea, it is this: that Protestantism establishes its own vigour as a social ideology, and with it its own successful expansion, in response to this uncertainty, in relating security back to the soul of the free individual regardless of the historical travail, of the social crisis that the development of individuality brings about – as has been said, in giving certainty to freedom.[19]

Yet the historical effects of a social myth or of a religious ideology rarely operate unilaterally – and even less at this turning point in the Renaissance. In fact the impact of the economic and religious upheaval is so profound that it affects the whole society. It is not only the old order that is upset, but order *tout court* – or at least this is the great fear that afflicts European society. 'New order' is a widespread phrase, a hope that soon overwhelms the operating limits that the bourgeoisie had placed on it. The new order now comes to stand for the aspiration of the oppressed classes, the old and always renewed claims of those who are subordinated and exploited.[20] Class revolts follow one another in succession, and sectarian thought sustains them; anarchy seems to extend over the whole of Europe. And it is in the light of these facts that the crisis of bourgeois liberty discloses its most complete meaning: it is certainly a crisis of order: of social, of religious and, finally, of political order. The sorcerer's apprentice has unleashed forces he is unable to control. The nascent bourgeoisie discovers in the necessity of social order the guarantee of the freedom it has won. It cannot solve its crisis unless at the same time it solves the crisis of social order. Now freedom has to be 'defended' against the general upheaval that class struggle generates. The problem is by now entirely political: it means measuring, in given situations, one's own strength and that of one's adversaries and verifying the possibility of making alliances at the lowest possible cost and to the greatest advantage... The great hope of being able to unify the whole of society in the plan for the development of bourgeois liberty has now entirely disappeared.[21] Often there is no other way but an alliance with the old classes and a more blatant compromise of revolutionary standards. Better tyranny than anarchy: Luther and Erasmus, reformers and humanists alike say as much (Adams 1962). As protagonist of bourgeois fortunes, the merchant begins to be replaced by the politician or, worse, by the courtier (Albertini 1955; Berengo 1965). So from now on the problem of the bourgeoisie, pressed as it is by class struggle, seems to be reduced to that of grounding a correct relationship between the development of freedom and the maintenance of order, between progress and security. And this is also the real problem of the placement of the bourgeoisie within the modern state, of the relationship between civil society and the absolutist state.

What becomes of the revolutionary content of humanist ideology? What about pride and confidence in the new values, what about the industrious proposal for a new society? Bourgeois culture takes care to keep this ideological heritage alive. Of course, often all that is left for the bourgeoisie will be the possibility of wrapping its own self-awareness as a class in the forms of utopia. Sometimes humanist nostalgia will try to place itself in a positive relationship with the awareness of the blockage encountered by the revolutionary uprising, and thus to condition subsequent development, to direct it towards desired ends. Finally, at other times a dark and desperate protest will regenerate subversive outbursts.[22]

But this is, in all its articulations, the development that has to be followed, if we want to give an answer to the question about the relationship between the new state and the new civil society. To solve it for the time being: the bourgeoisie presents itself under two aspects – of nostalgia for the humanist ideal and of awareness of the blockage of its own revolutionary will.[23]

4   Libertinism and a nostalgia for the humanist ideal

France in 1610 – the assassination of Henri IV. Ravaillac's action threatens to destabilise the entire political equilibrium, so painstakingly rebuilt after the crisis that reached its peak in the War of the League. Emotions run high. Lamentations are heard in parliament when the news arrives. But had not Henri's policy, after victory, been one of slow, yet continuous detachment from the bourgeoisie that had supported him and made his triumph possible? So, when it seems that the entire range of possibilities for the free development of the bourgeoisie just reopened, why is it that we see instead a run for cover, a very determined assumption, by parliament, of responsibility for the continuation of the monarchy? If a *jeune noblesse française* rushes into the streets of Paris, praising the death of the tyrant and creating disorder, it can be silenced; and the works of the monarchomach Jesuits can be burned. But why is it that parliament and the Sorbonne are the first to lash out at any theoretical trace of contractualism, denouncing its responsibility in the killing of the king? Why is it that, a few years later, the third estate proposes to the Estates General that first article of its *Cahier* that constitutes the most complete definition of royal absolutism?[24] No answer is possible except this: peace and, with peace, the order and security that only a strong monarchy can guarantee are the greatest assets. Everything can be sacrificed to this end. The teaching of Bodin and Charron gains traction, in continuation of a crisis that produced it and now reoffers it as topical.[25]

The failure of the Renaissance ideal of the bourgeois revolution is perceived here in dramatic terms. It is not true that there are alternatives. On the contrary, the more the monarchic power weakens, the higher the price that will have to be paid for its rebuilding. This is what happens in 1614–15 to the Estates General. To raise the monarchy again, to curb the arrogance of the other estates, the third estate is left with no choice but to impose abandonment of the very principle of royal consultation of the estates. The kingdom of France ceases to be a state of elites.[26]

The ideology reflects this conviction fully, and the emotion turns into myth: Henri IV represents security, peace, the happy age that was about to arrive.[27] And on that myth is built the definitive theoretical configuration of absolutism. If humanism had destroyed the hierarchical image of a world in which royalty, nobility and executioners corresponded respectively to God, angels and demons and had imagined a society of equals articulated by virtue, now, on that cosmos flattened by the rule of immanence, the myth erects the sovereign, unique and absolute. Neither is his action hampered by mediations nor are social hierarchies more than expressions of his will. Here the figure of sovereignty becomes abstract in its impersonal absoluteness; its control is impossible, yet its legitimacy is only political.[28]

But the myth leaves reason exposed. Yes, peace must be sought – it is the precondition of civil life, a fundamental defence. But it is a good that is not a value. It is a good, so to speak – an unproductive one, imposed by the failure of revolutionary action, by the realist acceptance of indisputable facts; but it is unproductive, simply has nothing to offer for the *renovatio* [renewal] of this world. It is a situation of stability, not one of development. So let us accept this situation realistically; but let us not identify with it, not mystify it by turning it into a value. The value still lies entirely in the memory of the revolutionary growth of the bourgeoisie – an unrepeatable situation and a dangerous myth, if it is reoffered to the masses. But let us keep that value for ourselves, let us return (individually, nostalgically) to that freedom. It is not something that everyone can do; it is something for those few among whom that freedom is guaranteed by the fact that it doesn't turn again into a terrible instrument of subversion. The revolution has used us in order to destroy us; fine. Let us use this situation to live free lives.[29]

Scepticism? No; *libertinism* – that is, Pyrrhonism, probabilistic and dialogical scepticism, built on the rediscovery of Sextus Empiricus but renewed and nourished by the historical experience of the previous century, by Montaigne and by Charron:[30] a worldly, scholarly and literary libertinism. Making the otherwise due distinctions is not important here;[31] what matters is to underline its specific ideological character in the relationship it expresses with the situation on the ground. The Renaissance myth lives again, jealously guarded, protected against the possibility that the contradictions it was carrying might develop socially. There is nothing aggressive, then, in the libertine stance – rather Epicurean ascesis in the belief of the superiority of conscience, of the inner freedom of the spirit. Many are the world's impostures: positive religion, metaphysics, political absolutism; but these impostures are also necessary for social life. As regards the humanist myth, let us purify it, internalising it – they say. And indeed it comes out isolated and sterilised. But those who refuse pay with their lives: Théophile de Viau, Vanini; and quite rightly, too, says Naudé. His Machiavellianism is as radical as it is unanchored in any ideal other than that of social peace;[32] and so is the deism of La Mothe le Vayer, of course, when libertinism does not become just a proposal for an Epicurean way of living.[33] They live at the French court, immune from the kingdom's passions, and gradually impose a sense of decorum, of politeness, of *honnêteté* [honesty] that represents only the ethical refinement of a substantive civil and political conformism.[34] There would be no point in looking among the libertines for the starting point of a development that leads to the Enlightenment![35] Such intellectual genealogies – from La Mothe to Bayle to Voltaire – risk being twisted. In reality, libertine scepticism is unarmed, a temptation rather than a vocation, caught between acceptance of reality and a nostalgic longing for some unattainable ideal.

And soon the tension breaks down. Nostalgia admits its impotence, and utopia comes on the scene to conclude the plot of the intellectual development of libertinage in the second half of the century. This is a definitive demonstration of a crisis that does not know how to resolve itself and that becomes in fact more acute as the cultural and political situation is stabilised. We find it in the highly vigorous and positive utopianism of Cyrano de Bergerac or in the strong naturalistic polemic and atheistic radicalism of *Theophrastus redivivus*.[36] In any event, a pessimism that declares beforehand that any path of renewal is impracticable dominates all these works. Instead of going in search for Enlightenment's forerunners, we would perhaps do better to see in this pessimism tinged with scepticism an attitude that recurs throughout the centuries of bourgeois culture, almost as if that defeat in the Renaissance were an indelible original sin.

So now I have defined a first, fundamental attitude of the new civil society in relation to the state. It is an attitude of resistance – I pay for the privilege of a bourgeois life by delegating the defence of social peace to absolutism, even though that life is free only within the limits of a sort of individual segregation. But the solitary reminiscence of humanist values is not sufficient: here the dissociation is maximal and the very assumptions of the existence of the bourgeoisie as a political class seem to have failed.

5   Mechanicism and the awareness of crisis

Political dissociation, for sure. But in the meantime the bourgeoisie consolidates itself as a capitalist bourgeoisie and affirms its independence as a social class, through economic growth. That the seventeenth century experienced a profound economic crisis is now commonplace. But that the new society develops even in this crisis, right in the middle of that refeudalisation of the mode of production; that the necessary basis for the structural transformation of the eighteenth century is established precisely in that crisis and in the forced agricultural accumulation; and that the bourgeoisie protects itself in this way from the setback suffered by the sixteenth-century development – all this, too, begins to impose itself,[37] despite the monetary crises and independently of the chaos of state finance (both of which are undeniable). Does this not give even greater emphasis, perhaps, to the autonomy of civil society, free in its economic development? Is it not the case that here too we have to reject that statualist prejudice, already denounced in some historiography, that focused everything on the analysis of royal finance and deduced from its crisis the general characteristics of the conjuncture?[38]

So we have an independent economic development of the bourgeoisie, which may take place through forms of underground accumulation, in a temporary delimitation of the field of activity. But while this social growth cannot be immediately supported by the state, it must at least be offered protection and guarantees. The dissociation of the bourgeoisie from the management of political power has been accepted as a necessary condition in order to ward off the threats posed by the struggle of the oppressed classes. However, this cannot mean that the spontaneity of the economic development of the bourgeoisie is not to be defended. It is precisely around this spontaneity that the true and decisive bourgeois battle is fought. As for peace, it cannot be considered solely and negatively as a foundation for mere social existence – because, for the bourgeoisie, to exist means freedom and accumulated labour, in other words development. Peace has to be positively understood as an element on the basis of which development is guaranteed. And what about the state? It is absolute, yes, and at the service of social peace, therefore of bourgeois development. But it is clear that political absolutism cannot be transformed into an economic absolutism and cannot consolidate itself into forms of patrimonial state. The interest of the bourgeoisie is entirely within civil society; the state is outside it. The bourgeoisie knows to stay in its place; the state should do the same. Of course: when it is realised that accumulation can be facilitated through an appropriate state intervention, then we have the development of the theory and practice of mercantilism, in the period between the economic operations of Richelieu and the Colbertian restoration of finances. However, this instrumentalisation of the state is also characteristic of the sense of autonomy that civil society has of itself.[39]

This recognition of the new position of the bourgeoisie in the state requires, however, a profound reform of civil society itself. If the acceptance of dissociation from political power really ends by exalting the social role and spontaneous development of the bourgeoisie, we cannot accept positions that interpret the awareness of revolutionary defeat as disengagement. In particular, it is not acceptable that nostalgia for the past and the libertines' Epicurean and utopian longing remove from the world groups of 'the elect', however small. This is the meaning of the great wave of antilibertine discourse that develops in the years around 1620.[40] Père Garasse is much more progressive than Voltaire could imagine – Voltaire, who made him the champion of Jesuit obscurantism! Yes, because his 'ballistic apologetics', his

'insults in order better to convert',[41] and the work of his contemporary apologists are, paradoxically, the temporal hand of the spiritual
power of the bourgeoisie. What it wants is not so much to destroy
all residual revolutionary nostalgia along with libertinism, and not
just to impose upon inveterate practitioners of the Renaissance vice a
sense of the impossible; it is rather to impose a sense of the possible.
As if to say, we have wept enough, let us now transform the awareness of defeat into a condition of renewal; we are separated from a
political existence but we live in the world of economics. All right, let
us justify ourselves in this separate world, let us find again sufficient
indications for operating in the world: again, a quest for a theodicy
of freedom.

It is not surprising that civil polemic during this period expresses
itself in the forms of religious polemics, in this case Catholic apologetics. Seventeenth-century life is entirely pervaded, and sometimes
tyrannically dominated, by religious sentiment. On the other hand,
let us try to grasp the positive aspect of this generalisation of religion, which allows us to see a confluence and consolidation of all
the problems of civil society into a unitary ideological horizon – as if
they were gathering together around a paradigm that, within a unity,
assigns every element its specific and distinct positions. So, if we dig
around a little in this amalgam of experiences, we note the productive
value of this extreme moment of polemic against Renaissance naturalism. What the Christian tradition rediscovers here and offers to
civil life is an unsuppressible dualism of experience: exorcised – but
until when? – against any monist reflux; yet fortunately paradoxical insofar as, fixing itself precisely as an irrepressible dualism, as a
'metaphysical' horizon of experience, it still exalts human action in
the field thus defined – so says Mersenne.[42] In this space the world
can be reconstructed scientifically – so says Gassendi.[43] And the
metaphysics of the century, that of the schools and that diffused in
cultured society, soon configures itself on these assumptions.[44] But
everyone insists: away with the myth! It is a race to make a virtue out
of necessity. But on this condition it is possible to reconstruct a free
life in our separate experience. Away with the myth! Which means
away with every possibility of and nostalgia for the revolution, as we
accept the dualism between the socioeconomic reality of the bourgeoisie and political power. It is no coincidence that the scientific
aspect the reconstruction of experience assumes within the limits set
by the metaphysical dualism is based on the socioeconomic structure
of bourgeois existence. Mechanism – that is, the dissociation of
quality, only quantitative reproduction, and rationality in production

– in short, the philosophy and practice of capitalist manufacture (see Borkenau 1934, Nef 1958, etc.).

This is also the structure of modern science. Only in this situation – on the basis of a dualistic metaphysics that would distance science from the immediate possibility of adding strength to the Prometheanism of Renaissance individuals and to their revolution, which is, however, linked to the life of a social class that derives wealth and dignity from the use of technologies – only in this situation could modern science assume its definitive characteristics and secure for itself the possibility of free development. The many discourses on method that the century produced reveal these dimensions (see Lenoble 1958). Certainly there is no shortage of people who repeat the dangerous mistake of wanting to see science as a revolutionary tool. One finds here the *Saggiatore* [*The Assayist*], those Galilean *Dialogues* that repackage the Renaissance myth of a science made to measure for the bourgeois revolutionary. They depict research in the image of an intellectual and political adventure of the Renaissance individual; and they depict the scientist as a merchant – soldier-cleric of a new universe who lives 'in the great world of nature', 'more out in the open than in a room or sitting at a fire'![45] Let the Holy Office intervene to put an end to such archaic hopes! New people such as Mersenne and Descartes, people of an age already severely folded in on itself, people of a wisdom cautiously measured, constructed around the closed space of the *poêle* [stove] – such people cannot help looking at all this with annoyance.[46] Remember Galileo who was not willing to recognise the separation of the bourgeoisie from political power! Those writings that still express the illusion of humanist freedom!

But, it will be asked, how can a complex phenomenon like the birth of modern science – which is precisely the core of mechanicism – be reduced to simple economic and political requirements of bourgeois development? This is precisely what I am *not* doing here. Here I stress the connectedness of these phenomena, relating their explanation back to the general social context in which the struggle between classes is developing – in all its implications. Outside this context there is only the most unproductive specialisation, only history 'in boxes', only idealism, and, above all, an inability to explain; and this should be the touchstone of all methodological approaches. Outside the framework proposed here, the Scientific Revolution remains a mystery. What is it that actually brings about the qualitative leap in quality in the continuous, uninterrupted process that develops over the course of centuries, through new discoveries and technological

improvements, through astrology and astronomy, through alchemy
and chemistry, up until the new method, mechanics – a prelude and
introduction to the new science? Either the history of science is itself
social history, or it is nothing.[47]

And the state? It constructs itself as a machine as well. This is
the moment when the awareness of the new reality of the state – an
awareness that Chabod considers necessary for the full modern configuration of the state – is given in its entirety. And the ideological
foundation of that awareness has to be traced back to the philosophical atmosphere that I have described here. Between 1630 and
1640, between Mersenne, Gassendi and Hobbes on the one hand – a
unique group of individuals, if there ever was one – and Richelieu on
the other, runs the thread of an uninterrupted continuity. For all of
them, *ius naturae primarium* [the primary law of nature] constitutes
a feral state: the social pact, on the other hand, articulates, within
order, the possibility of inclining towards the common utility. In
short, order is not simply an anchor of salvation; it also opens up a
prospect of reconstruction. The transition from the feral state to the
ordered state is radical: nothing preexists order except anarchy. But
it is precisely this radical nature of the transition that allows us to
consider the new state mechanically and to construct it radically[48]
– and with the very method of natural science, because in fact the
mechanist definition of absolutism configures the state as a 'second
nature'. A rational calculation of political operations and behaviours
begins to become a possibility.[49] This is why peace regained is no
longer simply a condition of survival; it is also a value that the state
reconstructs positively within its own organisational structure. That
absolutism presents itself in the form of monarchy and not in a
form of government more open to bourgeois participation; that at
this stage the dissociation of the bourgeoisie from political power is
accentuated through the two parallel phenomena of feudalisation
of parliaments and creation of intendants;[50] and that all this does
happen, triumphing over the deepest crises – none of this should
cause astonishment, because – one cannot forget this now – the
political conditions for the reconstruction of the state are dominated
by awareness of the failure of the Renaissance revolution. So there
is always an underlying *Schuldfrage* [question of guilt] that the bourgeois has deeply suffered.[51] Like it or not, it gets reiterated: this is the
only way to avoid anarchy after the revolutionary crisis and positively
to guarantee order and development. And, anyway, is it not the case
that the separation of the figure of the state from the person of the
monarch, which is affirmed here, and this abstraction, which is the

positive residue of the Renaissance socialisation of political power, are sufficient guarantees and proofs – unspoken but undeniable – of the imposed hegemony of the bourgeoisie as a social class?

So here we are, now in a position to address a final question, one that sums up the problems addressed thus far and argues for the reconstruction not only of absolutism, but of that specific form of it, the machine-state, that was the starting point of our research. In short, if the reconstruction of the state, in the form of monarchical absolutism, registers the temporary failure of the bourgeoisie as a political class and sanctions the dissociation of the social class from the direct management of the state, then why the machine-state? Why does absolutism assume the form of the social mode of production? As I have said, the bourgeoisie emerged from the Renaissance crisis as a socially hegemonic class. But here I have to underline the importance of that statement: although it did not have the possibility of conquering the state politically, the bourgeoisie, with its simple, massive and decisive social presence, configures it in its own image and likeness. The state is a machine for the maintenance of order: social, economic and religious.[52] But society, economy and religion are now dominated by bourgeois feeling and action. If everything is then ordered by the state, this is in the name of a complex relationship of content and form: a state form with bourgeois social content. It brings order of a negative form: everything in its place.[53] On the other hand it brings monetary reorganisation and support for industry and acts as peacemaker in religious matters. The machine-state of monarchical absolutism is mercantilist and Gallican: paradoxically, in the content of the exercise of its power, it is a bourgeois state.[54]

6 Cartesian reasonable ideology

Let me look back for a moment to consider this development. Because what I have traced here is a development: certainly not uninterrupted along a flat evolutionary line, but jagged with struggles, victorious or lost, with moments of bitter awareness of the impossible, with moments of confident expectation of progress. Nor is it a dialectical development: the antitheses cannot be manipulated by a logic that justifies, rebuilds and relaunches everything. Nonetheless, it is a continuous development, and one dominated by the emergence of a fundamental problem, which is the problem of the development of the bourgeoisie as a social and political class and of the emergence, there and then, of modern absolutism. And a chain of people, events and ideas gives focus to the problem.

The chain of people goes from Erasmus, Lefèbvre d'Étaples, Calvin, Etienne Dolet and Rabelais to Montaigne and Charron. And I should add those whom my investigation has encountered, from Theophile de Viau, La Mothe le Vayer, Naudé and Cyrano to Mersenne, Gassendi and Hobbes (Febvre 1951); and Descartes[55] – because the metaphysics of Descartes comes to life and develops within this circle of ideas and problems. The *Discourse on Method* is the work of a century.

But this is not possible! Descartes is the founder of modern philosophy, he is the absolute beginning, he is the father par excellence: that's the response that I would get from a long-standing tradition of philosophical historiography that is rooted in the Enlightenment and finds its definitive expression in Hegel and his school.[56] In this way Descartes comes to be isolated from his century. But his century, too, had been isolated – and we have seen why. The ideology of the enlightened and liberal bourgeoisie required it, to justify its political task historically. Will not Descartes have suffered the same fate?[57]

Certainly, in Descartes there is much that is new. There is above all an original response to the problems of his time – a response preceded and sustained by eye-witness evidence of the crisis of his class: Descartes lives through this crisis with a sense of restless participation as he – himself a knight of fortune in the Europe of the Thirty Years' War, during the baroque period, among the fading echoes of Renaissance culture (his youthful writings tell us enough about it) – completes his extraordinary philosophical apprenticeship.[58] But it is a radical response, and one that captures the problem of the times in its deepest essence, foregrounding it in a hyperbole of doubt and exalting the need for a solution in the renewed concern for a theodicy of freedom.[59] This response nevertheless moves within a problematic that centuries of bourgeois history had raised and therefore the bourgeoisie deeply appreciated, to the extent of mythologising it.[60] For what could be seen as new in it was the refusal to consider as definitive the fracture between civil society and state and the dissociation of the social class from political administration. In this perspective, the philosophy of Descartes offers itself as a reasonable ideology that willingly consents to rebuild unity.

Let us be clear: there is nothing revolutionary about Descartes. The awareness of the Renaissance setback of the bourgeois revolution is no less strong in him than in the libertines or in the mechanists. Indeed, in his thought doubt and metaphysical dualism reach a level of clarity never achieved before. What plays a different role is the nostalgia for the humanist myth that, far from resulting in longing or utopia, expands here into the metaphysical design of a reconstitution of the relationship between humans and God, a reconstitution that is foundational for the truth of human action. Renaissance philosophy had naturalised this relationship, flattening it on the human horizon; and thus it had related history back to humankind, extolling time as an essential place and dimension of the divinisation of humans. There is none of this in Descartes: the relationship he posits develops indefinitely.[61] Yet it is a real relationship, based on two indestructible certainties: the emergence of the thinking individual; and the guarantee of the validity of such individuals' thinking and working, via the proof of divinity.[62] The human being is not god; the human horizon and the divine horizon are essentially distinct. But this undefined space that opens up between the world and divinity is marked by a twofold tension: one divine – insofar as divine freedom weaves and bases the worldly horizon on an infinite number of creative moments; and one human – insofar as, through this divine guarantee, humans discover their destiny as rebuilders of the world, in science, in technology, in the associative work that these demand.[63] Of course, the world cannot be rendered divine; an infinite metaphysical distance exists between humankind and god. But along the eternal thread of the divine creation of instants of truth it is possible for human beings, too, to attain truth and to base on it their work and reconquest of the world.

One could say that Descartes' metaphysical discourse is articulated between a before and an after that are historically fixed: the one configured – in doubt – by the memory of the setback; the other nourished – in the confident proposal of Descartes' method and in ethics – by the nostalgia of the humanist, now reactivated. These two situations intersect. Paradoxically, the certainty arises here from the split, and the truth of human action arises from absolute divine transcendence. (It is in the interpretation offered by Ferdinand Alquié that one finds the most comprehensive definition of this process.) The path indicated by mechanicism – taking a realistic acceptance of the world as the starting point of its new valorisation – becomes a possibility. Dualism is not resolved here either – no more than it was in mechanicism. But on the tension that occurs in it is founded the possibility – ethically, the obligation – of a work of reconstruction, between soul and body, between humankind and nature, between individual and divinity. But is this not the answer that the bourgeois – pressed by those same historical conditions within which the discourse of Descartes is articulated – was seeking as the foundation of the validity of his personal activities? With Descartes, the seventeenth-century individual and, next, the eighteenth-century individual will be able to nurture a hope of reunification on the basis of an awareness of the split. And is this not the perspective from which the destiny of civil society shows itself – no longer separate, as if cut out from the whole life of the state, but open, expanding indefinitely, just as the expansion of freedom in civil society is indefinite? Is it not the case that, once it attains an ideological level, Cartesian philosophy gives strength to the request of civil society to become state?

Let me consider this point more closely. As we have seen, the ideological horizon in which mechanicism was moving was not much different from this one. There, too, the perspective of reconquest of the world passed through the realistic acceptance of the Renaissance defeat, and it was from the starting point of this awareness that it sought a relaunch. It was almost a dialectical sublimation of the negative into the positive. But then is Descartes' philosophy really a simple 'metaphysical accident' in the history of mechanicism (Lenoble 1943, p. 614)? One well-established brand of philosophical historiography, not liberal this time but democratic (starting from Feuerbach 1906), would willingly accept this notion. It rids Descartes of a development that sees itself as being continuous all the way from the Renaissance to the great revolution, not without serious crises but homogeneous around the progress of science from naturalism to modern empiricism. Mechanicism is an important stage along this empiricist path to the bourgeois revolution; and Descartes is a marginal episode that acquires meaning only against the backdrop of the development of empiricism. But all this falls through: the historical truth of Cartesianism, whatever its premises, is irreducible to mechanicism just as the power to dominate the crisis is irreducible to awareness of the crisis, and just as indicating a path of reconstruction is irreducible to the capacity to follow it. It is no accident that, when it directs its gaze beyond the terrain of denunciation and wants to set itself to work, too, mechanicism ends up again in utopia. In the years after 1640 we find the peace movement for reconciliaton among the Christians becoming stronger (see Vivanti 1963, 1964; Lecler 1955; also Saitta 1951), and we find the same 'minimalist' Mersenne in correspondence with heretics all over Europe, reselling the noble ideal of reunification, of a *respublica christiana* (Mersenne 1943, pp. 532–80)! But nobility does not pay: the demands of civil society are quite other. Here utopia is only a sign of failure, because it remains extraneous to the requirements of development. The fact is that mechanicism has made the bourgeoisie aware of its separation from the state, has heightened its freedom in that separation, and has destroyed all residual, impotent longing for the humanist myth. Further than that it did not go.

And this is precisely the point where I see the greatness of Descartes and the specific role played by his philosophy in the development of civil society. On the rejection of all revolutionary radicalism and of both historical despair and utopia, he founds a reasonable ideology and indicates a path that can be pursued in the long term, as a payback entrusted to civil society, which makes it its task. God is restored to humankind and freedom is justified. Freedom is defined again as expansion, as a possibility of conquering the world. Descartes restores confidence to the seventeenth-century individual: this is no small thing, when confidence is conjoined with the social industriousness of a hegemonic class. Of course, the indication is metaphysical; but will it not still be adequate for the efforts of a class that wants to draw from separation a reason for its own universality?[64]

7   Jansenism, or the theology of refusal

Finally, there are those who do not accept all this: the aristocratic libertine longings, the mechanist realism, Descartes' reasonable ideology. Yet the political dissociation of the bourgeoisie from the state is not something that one can be unaware of. It is an incontestable fact: so how can one refuse to see it, while at the same time having to recognise the lack of any possible alternative? Here we have Jansenism[65] at the heart of an ideology that affirms 'the radical impossibility of leading a valid life in the world' (Goldmann 1955, p. 117) and that reacts with a radical rejection of the development of the modern state towards its definitive machinic structure.

For we should remember that, while it is true that this psychology of the rejection of the world is characteristic of a millennial Christian tradition, here it presents itself in a very specific way, as a moment internal to the life of civil society in its relationship with the machine-state. Who are these Jansenists? They come from the highest ranks of the parliamentary bourgeoisie, that is, from the elite that, during the sixteenth century, had functioned directly as the political brain of the social revolution effected by the nascent bourgeoisie. But when the bourgeois victory over the old ruling classes finds itself exposed to the threat of popular revolt, it is these same *robins* who impose that sudden reversal [*révirement*] that pushes the bourgeoisie to take a decisive gamble on the restoration of absolutism. Without too much scruple, they associate with the king and with the nobility in order to stifle the struggle of the oppressed classes (see, again, Porshnev 1963). Hence it is not absolutism that they reject, nor is it the class restructuring that their own revolution has provoked. What they reject – to the point of expressing their will in the most radical way – is the separation of civil society from the political management of power, that is, the dissociation of the bourgeoisie as a political class: it is the machine-state. And yet is not the bourgeoisie's staying in its place the condition for all the classes to stay in theirs? Is this not the price paid for the development of the bourgeoisie as a social class, free from the threats of a turbulent nobility and yet protected as it develops that process of primitive accumulation that creates and at the same time oppresses new classes, with terrible consequences? Is not the self-restructuring of the state as a machine the paradoxical effect of the hegemony of the capitalist mode of production, and thus of the bourgeoisie, which dominates the century as a social class?

It would be easy to reply that the Jansenist breakup of the relationship that civil society, intent on accumulation, maintains with the state, which is simultaneously its adversary and its instrument, is founded on purely political terms and is – putting it brutally – a matter of price. There are indeed those who make it a question of price. In the development of seventeenth-century Jansenism there is an active opposition that aims at compromise – and this not among the lesser figures of Jansenism.[66] There are countless episodes along this path; the occasions and their associated tactics are many. But all this sediments in the chronicle of the historical development of Jansenism. This chronicle is, rather, in its truest nature, an extremist and radical ideology, because what is at stake here is not a more or less satisfactory collocation of the bourgeoisie in the machine-state, but the very destiny of the bourgeoisie as a revolutionary class. Here humanist nostalgia gets the upper hand over awareness of the real political conditions.

Yet the de facto situation is not such as to allow illusions or to leave alternatives. It would be madness to refuse to face the facts. Indeed it is madness – raging nostalgia, acute denial. For instance, in 1637 we have Antoine Le Maistre's withdrawal from the world – ideologically motivated not so much in the traditional terms of Christian asceticism, but rather as a desire to escape from any function at all, whether social, civil or monastic. It is not a search for a higher sociality, but a rejection of this society. All this becomes plain when the rejection of society, in an extreme version of Jansenist asceticism, is brought 'in' the world (Namer 1964). It is a theology of the rejection of the world 'in' the world. This develops largely around the 1650s, and then continues in the second half of the century: a historical despair that permits no religious tranquility, imposes its rejection through struggle, and develops into metaphysical despair. A theology of rejection – of rejection 'in' the world, of what the world concretely presents; a theology of rejection supported by bourgeois who do not forget that they are bourgeois, and thus an operative asceticism, a refusal that wishes to become defeat after having proved itself in the world. A theology of defeat:

> The world is a place of eternal combat and of the eternal victory of God. God is present, certainly, lived in his truth by those who proclaim him until the human defeat; his victory is hidden only to the eyes of those who do not participate in the struggle, refusing to act in the world or betraying it through compromises with the enemy. (Namer 1964, p. 163)

Of course, let me repeat, Jansenism cannot be reduced solely to this current of extremism about the world, of radicalism in struggle and in refusal, of search for defeat. Yet, whichever way you look at it, all these elements are in play to a greater or lesser degree. Others have described this as a dramatic situation; and, when the analysis is purged of a series of equivocal methodological elements, such a description is acceptable and the definition can be extended to the movement as a whole – as long as we know how to see in intramundane extremism its most noteworthy manifestation. ('Equivocal methodological elements': these are the ones that Lucien Goldmann scatters far and wide in his 'structuralist' works!)

Let me now return to the second level at which our inquiry proceeds and say what Jansenism reveals about the attitude of civil society to the machine-state. For it may not even be enough to speak of rejection any more, given the high degree of radicalism by which this is motivated. Indeed, we witness a tragic reversal of themes and perspectives. Until this point, nostalgia for the revolutionary myth had served, at the social or the political level, to cement the bourgeoisie; now the radicalism in which this nostalgia is couched seems to want to destroy the actual determinations of the existence of the bourgeoisie as a class – and, among these, the specific machinic structure that the social emergence of the bourgeoisie had imposed on the state. The relationship with the machine-state, far from configuring itself in positive form, is rejected. Here, in short, the awareness of the political dissociation of the bourgeoisie from the state and the sense of defeat of the Renaissance revolution of the bourgeoisie combine to bring about a radical rejection of the system in its entirety. It is no coincidence that the ideology of rejection extends far beyond the bourgeois groups that conceived it, involving large sections of the working classes: it becomes a mass ideology and a constitutive element of democratic thought in its troubled genesis, finding new intense expressions throughout the eighteenth century.

However, if our focus is on the seventeenth-century determination of this position, we have to address the refusal and the metaphysical dimension it assumes, rather than stressing the later manifestations of the ideology. For the refusal, precisely because of the intensity with which it is expressed, reveals in exemplary fashion both motifs – awareness of setback and nostalgia for revolution – around which the other positions of the seventeenth-century bourgeoisie are also expressed, in their different articulations. Pressing this point confirms that the series of hypotheses of historical understanding assumed in this investigation have real value and can be applied homogeneously.

8   On the use of certain historiographical categories

With this reference to Jansenism I have gone slightly beyond the chronological limits in which my examples were intended to remain, but I did so with a view to verifying the hypothesis initially proposed. This hypothesis is as follows. The modern absolutist state, in its specific figure as a machine-state, was formed and consolidated through a total transformation, an upheaval, one might say, in its relations with civil society; on the other hand, the historical necessity of this development was founded on the crisis of the revolutionary project of the Renaissance bourgeoisie. But my extension is legitimate, if it is true that at the base of Jansenistic ideology stands the same problem that the other positions had assumed, in thought and in politics. The picture of seventeenth-century responses to the crisis of the bourgeois revolution thus seems to be complete. And it is this completeness of development, between the intensity of the oppositions that one discovers in it and the unity of the inspiring motifs from which each position emanates, that allows us not to treat the observations made thus far as if they were merely archaeological. A bourgeois measure, so to speak, shows up in all of them, and it is capable of extending or emerging, as *potenza* [power] or act, throughout the whole historical development of that class. This is a further demonstration, if indeed such was needed, of the significance of the period under consideration.

Except that precisely this completeness can also put us in a difficult spot: four positions, well placed between maximum awareness of the Renaissance setback and maximum humanist nostalgia. Is my analysis not vitiated by schematism? Does it not risk imposing onto the historical material categories that are too tidy? Would it not be safer and more productive to frame my inquiry in more familiar sets of ideas, such as *raison d'état* [reason of state] and natural law?

But is it really safer and more productive to resort to such working hypotheses instead of confronting the problem in the full range of social relations in which it arises? I think not. In fact, the kind of results that one might achieve would not be able to conceal the historical disarticulation of the materials on which they are built.

Let me now take a closer look at things, starting with *raison d'état*. Generally, research results would be as follows: *raison d'état* is a concept that, when viewed in its proper dimensions, lies at the heart of those positions that suffer most acutely from crisis but that, with bitterness and awareness of the lack of an alternative, accept its outcomes. It is a way of making a virtue out of necessity. The theorists of *raison d'état* are to be found among libertines and mechanists. Gabriel Naude is the best known of them, but in general – as we have seen – the reception of Machiavellianism in France is entirely modelled along these lines.[67] A survey focused on the concept of *raison d'état* would thus give results similar to the ones I have arrived at from another angle. But how much less possible would it then be to penetrate historical phenomena in their different realities and to proceed to further analytical subdivisions! The idea of *raison d'état* risks becoming simply a label. But equally it might not. And then, to the extent that it does not, will not a concept of state be introduced into the inquiry – a concept characterised in 'demonic' terms of sheer *potenza* that is totally inadequate to the reality of our problem?[68] Indeed this concept of *Staatsräson* [reason of state] is alien not only to our authors but to the whole thematic of the century. The century is rather characterised by an uninterrupted tension between two formidable thrusts, which Werner Näf[69] saw developing already at the end of the Middle Ages: one towards the unification of political power, the other towards its social and juridical legitimation. *Machtorgan* [ruling body, organ of power] and *Rechtsstaat* [constitutional state]: two forces that the French bourgeoisie is unable for a long time to unify – until the triumph of the great revolution. Yet the one is founded on the other, in the indissoluble dialectical relationship between monarchical absolutism and bourgeois existence, between the mechanical consolidation of power and its social legitimation.

The situation is not much different when we approach the problem in the name of the category of 'natural law'. It seems that, by a long tradition, any attention paid to the social elements in which the category is embodied (and only to those) must here be irrelevant. But things become more complicated when, going to the heart of my argument, I note that the tradition of natural law studies is rarely able to grasp the humanist and radically revolutionary elements that natural law takes on board from the sixteenth century onwards, or in any case to underline the continuity between those of its first onset and its subsequent development.[70] But in fact it is the humanist myth that constitutes the natural law: an eagerness for the construction of a rational world, and then, after the defeat, a burning nostalgia or an angry reproposal. Yes, natural law gets consolidated in very elaborate academic forms as well; it dissolves, in part, into the natural law of the Christian tradition through the mediation of the new scholasticisms, both Catholic and Reformed. It becomes a doctrine of state. But not now: now it is still a theory of civil society; it reproduces itself with the same radicalness that founded its revolutionary use by monarcomachs, where nostalgia for the humanist world and for the heroic genesis of the bourgeois world is at its strongest. Here, then, we have the radical affirmation of the ego and of its irreducible reality, which 'natural light' guarantees to Descartes; and it is certainly a natural law perspective, or anyway an affirmation that can be used for its foundation. On the other hand, the religious extremism of the Jansenists flows towards positions of revolutionary political radicalism; thus sublimated we find it in Jean-Jacques Rousseau and the Enragés of 1789.[71]

9   The age of humanism as a historical period of the machine-state

So then, does this leave us with a radical impossibility of using the categories *raison d'état* and natural law to address the seventeenth-century problems of the genesis of the machine-state in its relations with the bourgeoisie? I would say not. However, these categories can be applied only in the context of a more general view of the seventeenth-century problem of the modern state, which is one of splitting, not of unity. But, then, does the concept of *raison d'état* risk ending up with only a generic validity? We have seen how this might come about. And if natural law fares better in a confrontation with the historical material, this is only because of the ambiguity of its concept – which oscillates between signifying a specific positive science of the state and representing an ideology of civil society (or more often an efficacious myth). Certainly, there is a moment in the history of bourgeois culture in which both these terms consolidate and become specific ideological functions in the life of the state: *raison d'état* defines the autonomy of sovereign will in its unconditioned efficacy; natural law, through the travail of codification, changes into a science of positive right, into a theory of the validity of state action. But by then we are in a different era: when the bourgeoisie has won back the state, has covered the painful distance between social existence and political existence, it has transformed itself from a socially hegemonic class into a politically dominant class. At this point, all its problems change, because the general social and political relationship of the classes has changed. Now the bourgeoisie no longer has the state ahead of it: it is the state. And ahead of the bourgeoisie there emerges, bit by bit, a new class, generated by that same historical necessity: the industrial proletariat, itself in search of social hegemony and political dominion.

These pages have brought me to a strange outcome. I began by arguing against those who isolate the seventeenth century from the centuries that came before and after it, and I conclude by stipulating that it is necessary to isolate the seventeenth century – and the preceding and following centuries – from the more recent thematic of the state. However, the two affirmations are complementary. For we have seen that the seventeenth century was a moment of development, a crossroads if you like, or the most significant point – but always in a continuity – of an era that opened with the revolutionary rise of the bourgeoisie, a process characterised by stops and starts and by alternatives and possibilities around which the history of the bourgeoisie as a class develops; and, we can now say, an era that closed with the definitive triumph of this class and with the reduction of the state to its dimensions, in the context of a new set of conflictual relationships – those between the bourgeoisie and the working class. So my analysis has brought me to an initial overview that seems to offer a more adequate periodisation for the history of the modern state. Recently, prompted by similar problems, Cantimori has defined as the 'humanist age' the period that 'goes, in literature, from Petrarch to Goethe; in church history, from the western schism to processes of secularisation; in socioeconomic history, from the communes and from mercantile precapitalism to the industrial revolution; and, in political history, from the death of Emperor Charles IV to the French revolution'.[72] I cannot but share this point of view, for reasons that I have outlined above. But I also need to add, in the history of philosophy, from Cusano to Hegel; in law history, from the glossators to the historical school and the nineteenth-century Pandectist school. Perhaps it really is only 1848 that sees the birth of the contemporary world – as opposed to the modern age and the humanist age – when the 'humanism' of the bourgeoisie, having attained the greatest splendour of its political triumph, finds itself – if not for the first time, at least for the first time dangerously – radically challenged by the working class.

But this conclusion would be rather general, and already familiar, if it did not allow me to highlight a second and more congruent result of this investigation. It is this: one cannot write the history of the modern state – and, in my case, a history of the state during the humanist age – that is not at the same time a history of civil society. Nor, analogously, can one write a history of civil society in the humanist age – philosophical and juridical history, and so on – that is not a history of the ongoing relationship with the state. Everything is characterised by this relationship.

One last remaining doubt, then. Is the definition of the machine-state that I took as my starting point valid? Is it permissible to make a fixed point of Chabod's representation of the modern state? Is it not rather the case that this state, which, as I said, has thoroughly spelled out the nature of absolutism, making its activity permanent, stable and rational, in reality reveals a life that is continuously open to an articulate social relationship, such that its own structural features seem to be negated? We have to recognise a positive foundation to such doubts. But, however paradoxical it may seem, all of this is far from meaning that the structure of the machine-state does not end up in self-assertion. Rather it means that it asserts itself only in struggle, in a relationship with civil society that is, however, determined; my exemplification, relating to its seventeenth-century history, has amply demonstrated this. And it also means that in the end the machine-state will only be able to establish itself, without further qualms, shocks or alternatives, when the bourgeoisie will have resolved the struggle in its favour, definitively appropriating the state to itself.

Other problems to address, and an exciting road to travel! Let us not think about it for now; rather let us return and examine the problems raised by this limited investigation, which should certainly not be taken as closed. Here I have simply tried to suggest some working hypotheses and discuss some bibliographic contributions in the context of ongoing research.

Notes

1 On this point it is sufficient to see the point of view expressed by Charles Loyseau (1610) as regards the third estate and, for the nobility, by Cardinal de Richelieu in his political testament (Richelieu 1947). For a general treatment there is also the fine volume of Albertini 1951 (little used in Italy). Albertini's inquiry, expressly intent on examining 'the image of man in relation to the absolutist state' (p. 3), forefronts the theme of the legitimacy of power and follows the thinking around this problem in pamphlets of the time. See also Clark 1961 and the articles collected in Lubasz 1964.

2 At the time of this writing in the 1970s, the most up-to-date bibliographic introduction to the study of the period is Edelmann 1961. For the study of political and economic history, this volume can be supplemented with Mousnier 1965. See also Heinz Otto Sieburg's useful review, published in 1965 in volume 200, issue 2 (April) of *Historische Zeitschrift* (pp. 303ff.). For a critical introduction to the literary history of the period (and not only for this), see Tortel 1952. In fruitful controversy with some of the essays contained here is Bonfantini 1964 (esp. pp. 17–59 and 89–102). Starting from the many materials that criticise the traditional interpretation of the 'great century' elaborated up to its time, Bonfantini's volume expresses the need to move to a new general mapping of the literary development of that century. The extensive literature cited above, both Italian and French, is particularly relevant to the problem of the French baroque.

3 Borkenau 1934. The work was published in German, as volume 4 in the Frankfurt Institute's series Schriften des Instituts für Sozialforschung, after the emigration of the institute to Paris, and it had a very limited circulation. However, see the 1935 review by H. Grossmann in *Zeitschrift für Sozialforschung* 4, pp. 161–4. Some observations can also be found in Lefebvre, Procacci and Soboul 1956.

4 First of all in the review of Borkenau's book, which would not have escaped Lucien Febvre's attention and can now be found in Febvre 1962b. But there is also another insistent and timely reference to Borkenau in an earlier collection of Febvre's writings (Febvre 1957a, pp. 345–6). The amicable discussion with Borkenau did not arise in a void; similar needs were fundamental to the entire work of Febvre, who was the founder of the *Annales*.

5 See Ernesto Sestan's introduction to the Italian translation of Voltaire (Sestan 1951). Equally valuable is Brumfitt 1958, pp. 46–61. To these elements, which he shares, Furio Diaz adds a number of convincing notes on the important function exerted by the myth of Henri IV on the formation of Voltaire historiography (Diaz 1958, pp. 15–16, 19–23, 25–6, 43–9, 129–34). We also find this myth of King Henri in Voltaire;

and, as we shall see shortly, it is essential to the bourgeois historiography of the seventeenth century.

6 Thierry 1856, vol. 1, ch. 8. On the lack of foundation to Thierry's thesis, see Mastellone 1962, pp. 4–8; for Thierry's ideological antecedents, see Mellon 1958, pp. 9–12.

7 It is to the credit of Boris Porshnev, whose monumental research has at last been translated from the Russian under the title *Les Soulèvements populaires en France de 1623 à 1648* (Porshnev 1963), to have highlighted, beyond the traditional mystifications of bourgeois historiography (which he identifies and denounces – see pp. 31ff. and 505ff.), the huge development of the class struggle in the first half of the century. From now on it does not seem possible to address the study of the evolution of the modern state without taking this powerful investigation into account. Around his work there has developed a controversy that is not always fruitful: Mousnier 1958 and Mandrou 1959 opened the way. For further development, see Vivanti 1964 and, once again, Mandrou 1965.

8 This is an old hypothesis, and it was perhaps first outlined in full by Jules Caillet (Caillet 1863); it was then renewed in the classic Pagès 1928 and especially in Pagès with Tapié 1948 – as well as in Mousnier 1946. A less extreme and more balanced statement of the problem can be found in Vicens Vives 1960.

9 The most explicit and radical application of structuralist method to the history of the seventeenth-century bourgeoisie is certainly the well-known Goldmann 1955. Let us be clear that here I discuss and reject the structuralist method precisely in its methodological underpinnings. Goldmann's work, to which I shall return, often manages to break free of the shackles of the method adopted and arrives at some useful historiographical results.

10 Which, on the other hand, are not concealed by the authors of structuralism. The particular form of their historicism is clear, the political presuppositions of their research are expressly declared, and neither is it denied that the research tends to 'eternalise' certain situations, well beyond the concrete dimensions in which they are defined. See especially Goldmann 1964, and also Goldmann's contribution in Bastide 1962.

11 Chabod 1956, p. 77.

12 In this paragraph I am referring to the 'civil' interpretation of humanism that has as its principal author Eugenio Garin: *L'umanesimo italiano*, *Medioevo e Rinascimento*, and *La cultura filosofica del rinascimento italiano* are necessary reading for any inquiry into the culture of the Renaissance. My only concern is that, in spite of the consonance of themes, of interpretations, and often of problems, such a reading still knocks at the door of philosophy of right, doctrine of state, and historiography that is produced around both. For a preliminary view of the various currents in the interpretation of the Renaissance, Ferguson 1948 remains useful. See also the recent volume *Il Rinascimento* (1953).

13 Cassirer 1963 (which is a second reprint of the Italian translation). Despite the passing of the years, the volume maintains its validity.

14 It is perhaps above all among the Paduans that this vision of the continuity between the human and heaven – a continuity that rests on and blurs into astrology – finds its utmost clarity. As for the bibliography, one can feel embarrassed about it, not for want of works that illustrate the thought of the Paduan school – indeed, the renewal of studies in this field is proceeding rapidly and with remarkable results – but for want of works that tackle the problem by highlighting its wider social, political, and generally ideological ramifications. How much longer must we continue to consult the excellent but necessarily ageing Charbonel 1919? There are some good ideas in Mattingly 1959.

15 Who does not recall Lucien Febvre's perceptive reflections on this theme in Febvre 1962e?

16 With respect to the consolidation of myth – especially the social myths of the 'golden age' and the 'good society' – among the cultural themes of humanism, it is important to see what Robert R. Adams (1962) writes in *The Better Part of Valor*. This is an accurate analysis of the discussions that developed in the humanist circle in London; and it also offers a precise account of the antecedents of More's *Utopia*.

17 There is general effort in historiography to specify, through the connection of the various elements that compose it, the nature of the sixteenth-century crisis of the revolutionary bourgeoisie – an internal crisis, engendered by the same elements that made strong that same bourgeoisie whose critical downturn forced them... Among the best recent surveys, albeit limited in scope, are Albertini 1955 and Berengo 1965.

18 See Mollat's (1956) contribution on the topic; also Nef 1958 (translated into French in 1964).

19 As was said by Febvre 1962e. Also, on the social contents of reformed teaching in general, see Bieler 1959 and 1961.

20 Bloch 1962, otherwise impossible to find, is now finally available to us in a new edition. I recommend this work as fundamental for the understanding of the movement of social subversion that developed from the Reformation onwards. For the social effects of early capitalist development in the sixteenth century, see the fine pages in Braudel 1996, especially Part II, ch. 6 (and see note 3 there).

21 Corrado Vivanti (1963) has tried, with excellent results, to describe this crisis in French society. See also E. Rambaldi's review, published in the January–March issue of *Rivista critica di storia della filosofia* 1967.

22 This dualism between social development (with its specific cultural contents) on the one hand and, on the other, the longing and transfiguration of the revolutionary experience has been the basis of some questionable statements regarding the duality of the concept of Renaissance; see Haydn 1950 and Van Gelder 1961. A more correct approach can

be found in Weise 1961. Here too, in effect, there is a quest for two antithetical directions in humanist culture, directions that can already be grasped at the twilight of the Middle Ages. And it is perhaps in this premise, which has a very sociological ring, that we find the main limitation of the investigation. But when the author arrives at the final phase of the Renaissance, when he describes how the passage to the baroque continued through a consolidation of the heroic vision of the world, the book offers propositions that are entirely convincing and that reappear in a second volume devoted to this problem, namely Weise 1965 (esp. the first two chapters, 'Il Rinascimento visto da oltre le Alpi' and 'Il concetto dell'eroico nella letteratura francese del Rinascimento e del Seicento', pp. 1–184).

23 It is this dual nature – nostalgia, but also awareness of defeat – that renders doubtful the hypothesis cautiously advanced by Firpo 1957, who argues for a substantial continuity between sixteenth-century and seventeenth-century utopias. Firpo's position is certainly tenable if one sticks to the literary typology of utopias, but becomes doubtful – and we shall see more closely why – when one shifts the analysis towards the relationship that pins the ideological form of the utopia to the development of the bourgeoisie as a class.

24 Mousnier 1964. One will find here an anthology of documents, the article on the third estate, and a substantial bibliography. See also Mastellone 1962. It is true that, at this point, one should a priori reject the thesis of those who (as an example of all, see Mandrou 1965, especially pp. 9–29 and 49–62, and also Mandrou 1961) are not not prepared to concede to the third estate 'class consciousness', and thus existence as a class. From this point of view, the disorientation that followed Henri's death is perfectly understandable. The negation derives from the report of a certain heterogeneity in the social composition of the 'third estate', a heterogeneity supposed to preclude the possibility of homogeneous social and political behaviours. Furthermore, the social and political 'promotion' of the bourgeoisie would have been blocked by the unfavourable economic and political conjuncture of the seventeenth century. On this point, see note 41 in this chapter. But not even Mandrou's underlying thesis seems convincing. He points to an undoubted heterogeneity of behaviours, but are these not rather indicative of a differentiation of strategies, rendered necessary not so much by the disarticulation of the bourgeoisie as a class as by the difficult conditions in which the bourgeoisie as a class is obliged to move? My own treatment adopts this second position as a fundamental hypothesis. It seems to me that it overcomes the difficulties that derive both from spontaneism – typical, for instance, of many pages in Porshnev, where the bourgeoisie seems to constitute a 'political bloc' through the spontaneity of its behaviours – and from mechanicism, as in Mandrou: if there were a unity of the bourgeoisie as a class, there should also be a singleness of political behaviour; but what if, instead, the unity

of a political project were to articulate itself in a plurality of 'movements', in a multiplicity of 'strategies'?

25 This is covered in some detail in Vivanti 1963. On the ideology of the *robins*, see Bütler 1948. On the significance of Bodin's work, see Caprariis 1959 and Franklin 1963 (the latter reviewed by F. De Michelis in the second issue of *Rivista critica di storia della filosofia* for 1964). On the cultural climate in which Bodin's work developed, the most recent contribution at the time of this writing was Tenenti 1963. And further, for the rehabilitation of Bodin's thesis in the learned journals of the seventeenth century, see Albertini 1951, pp. 35–6 and 85–6. On Charron as a politician, see Dagens 1952b (extract), Battista 1964, and Julien Eymard d'Angers 1951, which is a fundamental study of Stoicism in seventeenth-century France. A complementary account could be Saunders 1955.

26 This is indicated clearly in Mousnier 1964. See also the 1955 volume *Comment les Français voyaient la France au XVII siècle*, special issue of *Dixseptième siècle* 26–26, with articles by R. Mousnier, V. Tapié, J. Meuvret, A. G. Martimort and G. Livret.

27 On the genesis of the myth of Henri IV, see Raumer 1947, Reinhard 1936 and Vivanti 1963, pp. 74–131. On the transfer of characteristics of mystical imperialism to national monarchies, see the fundamental work done by Frances A. Yates: Yates 1947, 1960 and 1964, which deals broadly with the Renaissance theoretical premises of these phenomena in their European dimension. Of course, the writings of Georg Weise should also be consulted. We have already seen, in the genesis of the historiography on Voltaire, for how long the myth of Henri IV endured in the consciousness of the French bourgeoisie.

28 For the intensity with which the work of strengthening and defining absolute monarchy developed during this period, see Mousnier 1946, 1958, 1964 and 1965 and Mastellone 1962. See also Picot 1948 – an important contribution. For sixteenth-century antecedents, see Dumont 1955, Doucet 1948 and Church 1941.

29 Febvre 1957c. This is a review of two books that are fundamental for an understanding of the period discussed here, and both were published in the same dark year: Pintard 1943 and Lenoble 1943. It would be incorrect to say that these volumes have not been appreciated in Italian historical and philosophical culture. However, it is certainly the case that in Italy they are not regarded as classics of seventeenth-century historiography, although they deserve to be.

30 On the fundamental characteristics of French scepticism, see Popkin 1964. As for the fortunes of Montaigne in France in the seventeenth century – a necessary topic for the present study – Boase 1935 is still pertinent.

31 See, however, the works of Antoine Adam on the subject: Adam 1935, 1948–56 (esp. vol. 2, published in 1951) and 1964. There are some

acute observations in Vittorio de Caprariis 1951. Spink 1960 should be included in any bibliography on libertinism. See also Tenenti 1962.

32 One should bear in mind the extremely precise chapter dedicated to the 'politics of the libertines' in Pintard 1943 (vol. 1, pp. 539–63). However, this – Machiavellianism in France in the seventeenth century – is a topic still awaiting its author. Neither Meinecke's idea of reason of state (Meinecke 1924) nor the scanty pages in Cherel 1935 provide an adequate picture (although for opposite reasons). However, there are (as always) pertinent observations in Albertini 1951, pp. 175ff.

33 See Adam 1964, pp. 216–17. On the relative isolation of some libertine experiences, see J. S. Spink 1960, pp. 45–7 and Popkin 1964, pp. 89–90.

34 Barrière 1961, Mongredien 1948, Burckhardt 1961. However, the fundamental work on the subject remains Magendie 1925. Related to this topic is an interesting note in Spink 1960, p. 135, further developed on p. 251, on the possibility of tracing a continuous development between the libertine idea of *decorum* and Montesquieu's notion of convenience as an element in a purely rational definition of justice. Should not this note be taken further, in a discussion of the development of the idea of legality?

35 This claim forms the entire basis of Spinks (1960). Spink begins by proclaiming that 'French free thought was social at all times' (p. v), which is correct. But there is sociality and sociality; in particular, there is sociality in the libertine defeat and in the Enlightenment revolution, but only in the name of a totally disembodied history of ideas can this 'sociality' be considered even analogous.

36 On Cyrano, see Spink 1960, pp. 48–66 ('Cyrano de Bergerac ... was one of the most daring speculative thinkers of his generation') and Mounin 1952. On *Theophrastus redivivus*, see again Spink 1960, pp. 67ff.

37 I have reservations about this, too, but it is certainly the framework that emerges from the most recent studies in economics historiography, and in particular from the important and polemical Baehrel 1961 (esp. pp. 29–30, 41–2, 395–6, 439–40, 445–6, and 495–6 and 495). See also Vénard 1957. These are highly specialised works, but how can one begin to dismantle the centuries-long misunderstandings of the economic crisis of the seventeenth-century bourgeoisie if not by starting from these strongholds of specialisation? That there was an economic crisis does not appear to be disputed; indeed, despite Baerhel's claims, many economic indicators appear to bear it out (see Sapori 1953, Lopez 1953, Chaunu 1960, Goubert 1960 and, recently, Romano 1962). But to go from this to stating that the seventeenth century is *l'époque d'une crise qui affecte tout l'homme, dans toutes ses activités* ('the epoch of a crisis that affects the whole of man, in all his activities', Mousnier 1965, p. 143), or that the whole development of the seventeeth century has, if anything, 'dark' shadings (Goubert 1960, p. 356), won't do. For the problem – if we accept, as it generally is, that we are dealing with an

economic crisis – is to understand the use that the bourgeoisie made of that crisis. Some commentators (for instance Mousnier, or Mandrou 1961) have claimed that the third estate was radically shaken by it; others have spoken of 'refeudalisation' or 'betrayal of the bourgeoisie', and suchlike. Still others have asked, more accurately: 'To what extent were the "reaction" or the "feudal restoration", or even the "betrayal of the bougeoisie" in the seventeenth century necessary for laying the base of that capitalist accumulation that the sixteenth-century economy had not been able to create?' (Vivanti 1964 (a work dedicated to popular uprisings), p. 965, with reference to Baehrel 1961 (see also p. 980) and to the theses elegantly advanced in Hobsbawm 1965; see also Labrousse 1955 and Braudel 1963). Putting the matter in these terms not only helps to clarify important moments in the ideological evolution of the third estate; it also sheds light on the whole question of its position within the state structures of absolutism. The third estate conceals a permanent tension between state and civil society, a tension that the crisis accentuates and through which a series of possibilities opens – in this case, both the possibility of reformism (in places like France, where the political state structure still exhibits a certain elasticity, particularly thanks to the mechanism of selling offices and the bourgeois 'promotion' it stimulates) and the possibility of revolution (in places like England, where such margins of manoeuvre do not exist). H. R. Trevor-Roper has described these alternatives with particular brilliance in Trevor-Roper 1965.

38 For a typical example of this attitude, it is sufficient to recall the works of Henri Hauser or Prosper Boissonade (see the fierce attack in Febvre 1962d against both). However, those authors deserve credit for having reintroduced an economic dimension into discussions of the great century – a dimension that, however mystified, is still present. Hauser 1944 is extremely suggestive, in its own way.

39 Porshnev 1963 has perceptively observed how, from Richelieu on, the imperialist action of the French monarchy was determined by the failure of all attempts to block the independent development of the bourgeoisie and to close the margins of free initiative (sometimes also political) that it takes independently of the operations of the monarchical state; see Pagès 1949. As for the transformation of the idea of social peace that takes place during this period (peace becomes a value in itself and the quest for peace has to be dissociated from ends external to the development of civil society – for example, the time-honoured functional dependence of peace on crusades is contested, although such archaic ideas are still alive even among Richelieu's advisors: see Lafue 1946), on these issues, see the extensive documentation in Albertini 1951, pp. 76, 159ff. and 196ff., and also in Souleymann 1941.

40 On the wave of apologetics in the 1920s, see Busson 1933 and 1948, in addition to Pintard 1943 and Lenoble 1943; also Chesneau 1946, Dagens 1952a and Willaert 1960.

41 Lenoble 1943, p. 203. See large samples of the apologetic writings of Père Garasse in Adam 1964, pp. 33–50.

42 On the reconstructive function of the radical mechanist dualism in Mersenne, there are explicit chapters (6, 7, 10) in Lenoble 1943. See also his fine intervention at the Descartes conference in Royaumont (Lenoble 1957).

43 On Gassendi, see the updated Gregory 1961, as well as Centre National de Synthèse 1955, with articles by B. Rochot, A. Koyré, G. Mongrédien and A. Adam. A large number of bibliographic references, too, can be drawn from these volumes.

44 On the metaphysics – pre-Cartesian – of the century, see the observations in Spink 1960, esp. pp. 75ff. 108ff. and 188ff.; also the fundamental Dibon 1954, which is a very careful analysis of an extremely significant period and place: the universities of the reformed new bourgeoisie, which was intent on building its own world. It is no coincidence that, precisely during these years, the Dutch universities become the reference point of the most active European bourgeoisie. For the French youth, see the still valid Cohen 1921. For the influence of Dutch political publications and the political example of the new institutions, see Mousnier 1955.

45 Quoted from vol. 10 of Galileo Galilei 1968, p. 302. For a digital version of the *editio princeps* of *Il saggiatore*, see Galileo Galilei 1623. On the figure of Galileo, see Geymonat 1962. And remember that 'the assayer' is the one who weighs gold with the *esquisita*, the high-precision scale of your typical sixteenth-century merchant! Who does not remember Quentin Metsys' portrait of the merchant?

46 On the repercussions of the Galileo affair in France, see the balanced pages (and the related bibliography) in Lenoble 1943, pp. 391–408, and Gregory 1961, pp. 170–2.

47 Obviously it is not possible to offer here even an indicative idea, let alone a full one, of the huge bibliography that now extends around the problem of the origin of modern science; or even, more simply, to point out the most important alternatives, in both substance and method, that this literature offers. Carugo 1964 (an essay on the scientific revolution that also discusses the relevant bibliography) is useful in this respect. Here it is enough to mention a few of the more or less reliable attempts at a social history of the scientific revolution: Merton 1938; Kocher 1953; the articles by Giorgio de Santillana and Rupert Hall in Marsak 1964; and finally Zambelli 1965. For the particular period that interests me here, there is a substantial bibliography in Boas 1962. A specific break of the intellectual, scientific and philosophical horizon took place during this period, above all in matters of method; this is proved – negatively, through emphasis on differences from the scientific method of the Renaissance, and also positively – in Gilbert 1960, Randall Jr 1961, and Crombie 1952. And allow me a last reference to Febvre 1957b.

48 The relationship with Hobbes is fundamental for the elaboration of

this doctrine, both in Gassendi (see Gregory 1961, pp. 236–7) and in
Mersenne (see Lenoble 1943, pp. 308, 576–8).

49 Nef 1957; Prestwich 1957. It has been correctly observed that mechanist
rationalism was already fully operative in the government of Louis XIV.
See King 1949.

50 This is the process that leads to the Fronde. In general, one should
consult all the bibliography of political history cited so far, and above all
Porshnev 1963, which is, broadly, a study of the literature on the Fronde
(see pp. 11–15, 17–18, 505–37, 574–82), and the important Kossmann
1954.

51 One could roughly exemplify this by looking at a figure such as Guez de
Balzac, in whom many of the motifs recorded so far could be identified
– and in many others beside him… Concerning this particular figure, see
Sutcliffe 1959.

52 See Hartung and Mousnier 1955. For problems related to the establishment of the religious order, see – for France – Lecler 1955, vol. 2,
pp. 130–5 and 159–60; and there is an updated bibliography in vol. 1,
pp. 11–39. For the latest developments, see instead Préclin and Jarry
1955–6. An interesting research topic, which would make it possible to
deepen the links between scientific reform through mechanicism and the
foundation of the machine-state, is that which could develop around the
figure of Thomas Erastus, whose work enjoyed considerable popular-
ity in France, both in the field of scientific methodology and in terms
of Erastianism – that is, the theory of the extreme extension of the
state's *ius circa sacra* ['right over sacred matters']; see in this regard
Wesel-Roth 1954. Then, generally on the absolute state, see Palm 1942,
Hubatsch 1962, Just 1961, Skalweit 1961, Kraus 1957 and Hartung
1949.

53 I should also recall the countless passages that can be found in the writings of Loyseau and Richelieu, Mersenne and Descartes, from which
an essentially homogeneous attitude emerges: one of reaffirming the
need – the imperative – for everyone to be in the right place. Just like
the famous *je ne saurais aucunement approuver ces humeurs brouillonnes et
inquiètes* ['I could in no way sanction these messy and troubled moods']
of the second part of Descartes' *Discours de la method* [2.3], which is
reiterated by so many other authors in almost the same words! On the
other hand, it should be noted that the Catholic renewal associated with
the likes of Sales, Paoli and Bérulle positively supports the same point
of view: sanctification is possible starting from one's own condition,
in one's own condition! But these ideas find their maximum clarity in
Richelieu's thought. See Skalweit 1951, Hassinger 1952, Andreas 1958
and Dickmann 1963.

54 But then is Mousnier right when he talks about a bourgeoisification of
the French monarchy? It seems not: because these bourgeois contents
can be taken on board by the state only to the extent that its figure stands

over them. We should remember that in the past few years Mousnier himself has substantially moderated his thesis.

55 Sebba 1964. The existence of this excellent bibliographic tool, indispensable for any research into Descartes, enables me to avoid superfluous references to the literature.

56 Hagmann 1955. Hagman's book, albeit modest overall, gives useful information in this direction.

57 The stages in the formation and discussion of the legend of Descartes are closely surveyed in Vartanian 1953.

58 See the fundamental Gouhier 1958.

59 One should bear in mind the two crucial interpretations of the most recent school, developed respectively by Ferdinand Alquié and by Martial Gueroult (Alquié 1950 and Gueroult 1953).

60 A mythologisation that reaches its peak after Hegel and, in the footsteps of Hegel, in Erdmann 1932 [1834]: the continual referencing of Erdmann's outline has played a role in generating the nineteenth century's interpretations. Useful reading in this regard is Biscione 1962.

61 Especially Koyré 1962 insists on this indefiniteness of the relationship. His interpretation is worth remembering out of many similar ones, because in it the scientific aspect of this indefiniteness of the dualistic tension appears with particular clarity.

62 On the relationship between these two certainties, one can look at the controversy that has opposed Henri Gouhier and Martial Gueroult (see Gouhier 1954 and 1957; Gueroult 1955 and 1957). For an overall view of this controversy one can consult two successive interventions in the *Revue philosophique de France et de l'étranger* (Brunschwig 1960 and Rochot 1961). A contemporary reading of the lively and youthful Wahl 1953 may not be unprofitable either.

63 Febvre 1957d. On the ethics of Descartes, see Sebba 1964 and most of Geneviève Rodis-Lewis's oeuvre.

64 Here it might be useful to recall Sartre 1947.

65 The movement for the renewal of the study of Jansenism is a postwar phenomenon and has already made considerable advances. On the one hand, it has enabled the publication of many materials that are useful for the history of Jansenism; on the other it has enabled us to arrive at a new overall historical representation of the movement – its genesis, its articulations, and so on. For this one has to credit Orcibal 1948, 1951 and 1957 and Goldmann 1955. Fortunately the revisionism that has assailed the historiography of the great century has neglected Jansenism. A special role in this literature is played by the fortunate Bénichou 1948. The chapters that Bénichou dedicates to Jansenism (pp. 77–130) are a rare example of understanding the social character of the 'ideology' behind the movement. But the basic thesis of the book, which sees in the heroic element of the seventeenth-century a revival of the aristocratic ideology of the Middle Ages (a thesis expounded especially in the

chapters dedicated to Corneille, pp. 13–76, and rightly refuted in Weise 1965, pp. 118–42), prevails in the end over the elements of analysis of the Jansenistic movement and distorts its interpretation: Port-Royal contributed to the disintegration of the ideals inherited from the Middle Ages, putting into conflict, in an open way, aristocratic idealism and religion. Other useful literature includes Cognet 1949 and Laporte 1952.

66 We owe the best and most recent analysis of the internal articulation of the currents in Jansenism to Namer 1964. Namer's work is also important because it represents an attempt to move from what has been described as a 'static', simply classificatory analysis of the various currents of Jansenism to a 'dynamic' study of their development.

67 See also the chapter on the 'politics of the libertines' in Pintard 1943; more generally, Skalweit 1957 and von Raumer 1953.

68 As regards that definition of *raison d'état*, which here is completely unacceptable, the reader may wish to consult Negri 1959. See also Maspétiol 1965 and, for subsequent developments, Gallouedec-Genuys 1963.

69 Näf 1935 and 1949. If recirculated, these very important works, also mentioned by Chabod and Braudel in the discussion of the Renaissance state that constituted my starting point, could prove very useful for a revision of the traditional specialist historiography on the origins of the modern state.

70 A fortunate exception is Mesnard 1952. For the developments, see Hazard 1935.

71 Namer 1964, pp. 165–6 explains this well. But, on these Jansenistic positions, see also Groethuysen 1977. Finally, see Mornet 1954.

72 Cantimori 1959 [1955], p. 361.

14

Considerations on Macpherson*

The author of this book, C. B. Macpherson, is a Hobbesian. Of course, he is not in the thick of things, like the master, nor – as far as we know – has he experienced persecution and exile. He lives in tranquil Toronto, where he is an academic professor of political science. He also lacks the darker side of Hobbes, the quality that excited the late romanticism of the likes of Tonnies and Brandt, the first contemporary interpreters of the great Englishman. However, all his work – and particularly this volume, which represents its highest point – is typically Hobbesian in the particular way in which it seeks to define the dramatic story of the contemporary world by means of analytic categories, and also to recompose the irrationality of the real into the rule of scientific method and political order. The economic crisis of the 1930s, the Second World War, the political crisis and collapse of the reformist hypotheses in the 1950s, the tragedy of the third world, the permanent civil war between workers and capital all over the world – all this is registered in Macpherson's essays in Hobbesian fashion, as a fabric on which to exercise the historiographic question, which is basically the same as that of the theoretical problem of political science. The equal condition of insecurity registered by Hobbes as the foundation of his theoretical question, albeit at a different level, is also the condition in which we move today. The science of politics and philosophical historiography need to give an answer on this front.

In *The Political Theory of Possessive Individualism*, the direct encoun-

---

* SOURCE: Antonio Negri's Preface to Crawford B. Macpherson, 1973. *Libertà e proprietà alle origini del pensiero borghese: la teoria dell'individualismo possessivo da Hobbes a Locke.* Milan: ISEDI. (Macpherson 1973 is an Italian version of Macpherson 1962.)

ter between Macpherson's thinking and that of Hobbes is fascinating, because it is charged with this dramatic actuality. This is all the more so as the unitary design of the book gradually came into being during the period of the 1950s, and the various essays that feed into the project as a whole lose nothing of the psychological intensity of the historical document. But there is something else. In this work of Macpherson's one finds not only a repetition of Hobbes' awareness of crisis in its generality but also the specificity of a contradiction that has reached the height of its *potenza* [power]. This is, namely, the contradiction between the mode of production (the market society, bourgeois society, possessive individualism – terms that are synonymous in this book) and the social conditions of production: *ex ante*, in Hobbes, when the new way of producing clashes with the need to form a matching order; *ex post*, in Macpherson, when the social forces produced by capitalist development require, again, not only a substantial modification of the mechanism of development but also a political system to match. On this limit the continuity of the liberal–democratic tradition inevitably has to break; it evidences the close functional relationship between its presuppositions and developments and the very emergence of the capitalist mode of production. Of course, in Macpherson there is, so to speak, a sort of intellectual nostalgia for individualism, and it shows up in some of his pages of bitter pessimism. But alongside those there is a lucid awareness of the limit, the urgency of a new definition. How can one arrive there? How can one raise the question about the destiny of the political individual within the crisis of bourgeois society?

Macpherson thinks that we have to return to Hobbes; he believes that his method cannot be bettered; and he believes that the premises of his thought ought to constitute a permanent foundation for the science of politics. Thus the return to Hobbes becomes, first of all, a need for method. But not only that: reconquering the foundations of Hobbes' thought allows one to conquer the essential scheme around which the bourgeois debate about society takes place, on the basis of which a scientific theory of society becomes the ideology of bourgeois society. To raise the question of the destiny of the political individual within the crisis of bourgeois society is therefore both to dig in search for the revolutionary idea that, through Hobbes, supports its development and to grasp the succession of classist determinations that the political thinking of the seventeenth century exercises on the Hobbesian scheme of things.

In his approach to Hobbes' thought, while not ruling out an encounter with the extensive (and some might say excessive) critical literature, Macpherson adopts and privileges essentially two criteria: the first is that of a literary reading based on an incomparable familiarity with the texts; the second is that of the immersion of Hobbes' thought into the contradictory history of class struggle in the seventeenth century and, from this perspective, into a history of political thought of his time. *The Political Theory of Possessive Individualism* is thus formed as a true and proper history of political thought during the bourgeois revolution and sees Hobbes as developing a scientific scheme for the grasp of his time. This scheme is founded on a physiological theory of human beings, on a coherent model of society that follows from it, and finally on a criterion for the understanding of institutions that bases its necessity on preceding levels.

But this science is not enough. We witness Hobbes' isolation even as we recognise the indispensability of his discourse – what that world finds itself in need of is of a class determination, an ideology. Gradually, from the Levellers through Harrington to Locke, the foundation of a classist society – classist in the bourgeois sense – is implanted within the scheme of logical necessity discovered by Hobbes. The appropriative instinct, which is physiologically the same in all people and which Hobbes had placed at the centre of his historical (as well as natural law-based) understanding of development, is now distinguished and differentiated. A differentiated rationality is used to define ideologically the direction of development and the quality of the institutions in bourgeois society. Beyond the Levellers' contradictions and those of Harrington, Locke definitively operates this passage by introducing into natural law a classist theory of the 'work–property–political obligation–law–institutions' nexus that is now entirely determined in the direction of the ideology of modern liberalism.

It is starting from Locke, therefore, that the mystified tradition of bourgeois ideology arises as a theory of division between classes, and it is within this continuity that the contemporary crisis of political thought occurs. To ask the question of the destiny of the political individual within the current crisis of society will thus mean first of all developing this discriminating operation in the very field of political science, going beyond mystification to reconquer the scientific foundation of Hobbes' intuition. It is not much more than a restart operation, the new fulfilment of a methodological urgency: from here on all the problems remain to be resolved, but it is still an essential operation, especially since, as we have said, the methodological instance of the return to Hobbes coincides with the substance of the situation in which we find ourselves today: the state of equal insecurity of all is immediately the only terrain from which the question about the possibility of political community can repropose itself.

Among scholars of Hobbes and of seventeenth-century political thought, Macpherson passes for a Marxist – or rather he has been labeled as one. That this is just a label is clear from what I have just said. Macpherson is in fact Hobbesian in his theory of science, not Marxist, unless by Marxism we mean simply the self-evident observation of the contemporary emergence of the working class and the urgent need of taking that fact into account, and the consequent perception that the liberal model of society is insufficient. Macpherson is not a Marxist, first of all because his concept of political science, which is based on and rehearses the psychological and individualistic conception of Hobbes' science, lacks a class determination. Neutrality is not a sign of Marxist science; it can be a sign of Hobbesian science only insofar as individualism constitutes the latter's root and form. Neither is Macpherson's excellent historical methodology (which leads him, positivistically, to reconstruct the class conditions of English society in the seventeenth century, to verify political thought on these conditions, and to propose this as a method for today) sufficient, by itself, to describe his approach as Marxist. One might almost say, were it not a paradox, that Macpherson is too good an analyst to be a historicist, and in that sense Marxist: in fact the continuity of the scientific categories – both methodological and substantive – that he assumes is misleading. At the centre of Macpherson's entire investigation and giving meaning to his entire historiographical and political problematic is the concept of political obligation. But the problem of political obligation only repeats the individualistic assumptions of liberalism and bourgeois society. It is true that the problem of obedience to the law and of the justification of this obligation is, and will continue to be, at the centre of any political theory, but this attention is misleading, or rather it becomes, again, a purely formal problem when the development of the capitalist mode of production has removed the very possibility of an individual relationship between worker and state.

The lack of relevant political results, the simple expression of the need to start over again, which is the concluding statement of Macpherson's book, is therefore natural. He is too good a historian to mystify the outcomes of his research, which is historical research pure and simple; he is too honestly bound to the positivity of the historical method to think of forcing the results in a theoretical sense.

And even when he mentions – after having argued for the urgency of uncovering and eradicating the contamination that bourgeois ideology has worked on the thinking of both Hobbes and Locke – the possibility in our times of contaminating the thought of Hobbes with that of the Levellers (which is as if saying, with the demands of contemporary socialism), it is obvious that this hypothesis is a limit of hope, a worry that remains formal, from a historian who sees himself as a living person.

And yet, if Macpherson is Hobbesian and not directly Marxist, it must be said that in the Marxist science of society there are some Hobbesian elements on which Macpherson's work helps to shed light. First, the sharp sense of the relationship between institutions and the mode of production, between state and market; then the sense that only the crisis of this relationship can lay the foundation for science and revolution. Of course, these are formal elements, but they are nonetheless important for the foundation of political science. And this is all the more commendable in Macpherson as this series of links is programmatically evaded and mystified precisely in the Anglo-Saxon environment in which he lives and where his scientific language was formed, precisely in that field of political science that is his profession. Macpherson alludes to Marxism insofar as he places dramatically at the centre of his work not so much the problem of the crisis of liberalism as the nexus between science and crisis. In this he succeeds in recovering and expressing how much of Hobbes there is in the Marxist experience.

One last point to consider. In terms of bourgeois ideology, Macpherson's survey reintroduces to the attention of historians of political ideas and to political scientists a term that has been forgotten for too long: the term 'appropriation'. This is not the place to give a history of the use of that word (although an investigation would be useful and of immediate applicability). We need only recall that, from natural law thinkers through to idealists, through to Hegel and the young Marx, the term 'appropriation' is the positive and complementary counterpart of the term 'alienation'. It is no accident that this term has been expelled from use: by a (frightened) bourgeois science that 'had to' understand appropriation only in terms of the ideological matrix and theoretical support of property, and therefore limited the scope of its application and exorcised its aggressive potential; and by the (impotent) socialist science that excluded all notions of appropriation, inasmuch as it own perspective exalted only the possibility of replacing a political class in the management of the mechanism of accumulation and reproduction of capital. Socialist science thus lost sight of the direct struggle designed to hit alienation, of the material contents of this struggle, and of the proletarian will for an immediate satisfaction of needs and for the reappropriation of wealth in the here and now. Nor did the reintroduction of the term 'alienation' into contemporary political debate serve to provide an incentive for a resumption of the use of 'appropriation'. In fact onto 'alienation' there has been tipped such a pile of psychological, philosophical idealistic, behaviourist, and often even theological hypotheses as to render pointless any attempt to tie this term to a material substrate, when that would have been the only way to restore its class function. Whereas 'appropriation' is a term that only with difficulty (or anyway with greater difficulty than 'alienation') can be stripped of material overtones, of a present density that refuses to accept any kind of idealistic translation.

Now, in Macpherson's investigation (and this serves not only as a critique of the contemporary ideologisms of alienation, but also as a critique of all non-materialistic interpretations of Hobbes' thought and of the origins of liberalism) the raw meaning of the question of appropriation is restored. And here I should stress one of the most important aspects of Macpherson's Hobbesian viewpoint – not only in relation to the problem of liberalism, and not only as a possibility of restoring a correct materialist dimension for the categorial pair alienation–appropriation, but above all in the perspective of a correct methodology for writing the history of political doctrines and the science of politics. Where it is not possible to relate the direct reference of ideology to the material interest of the struggling classes – whatever criterion of interests one may assume – there the history of doctrines and the science of politics breathe only the dead atmosphere of philological swamps. Or, as Hegel would have said, they sacrifice in temples from which the god has disappeared. They revive science only in relation to the interests and needs of humans, and that is why Macpherson's is such a fine effort.

Certainly, in Macpherson again, the capacity to read liberal individualism as 'possessive individualism' (and whether 'possessive' should not rather be rendered in Italian as 'appropriative' was in doubt for a long time) does not turn into a capacity to critique it in terms open to the immediate needs of class struggle in the postliberal era or into a capacity to identify the new collective subject, both of alienation and of appropriation. That unique texture of wealth and poverty that constitutes market society in liberalism's theory and practice does not reconfigure itself dialectically as a possibility to have a material impact on liberalism, to revolutionise it from within the equally solid and material perspective of working-class movements. Rather the theme of 'obligation' (that very special topos of political philosophy) imposes on Macpherson almost a devaluation of his own historiographical assumptions. The bourgeois philosophical theme of obligation shuts him into an enclosure of meanings dominated by the categorial continuity of individualism, as if obligation were not, today, a faded and distorted image of the real relations of domination and servitude, as if an effective consideration of these relationships in terms of alienation and appropriation (materially founded) would not lead to the image of a future society much more deeply revolutionised, insofar as it does not derive from any mystified and reductive conception. Macpherson implants a new criterion of obligation into a complex of human relationships from which 'differential rationality' is removed – that is, from which the inequality between the subjects is removed; thus he reproduces individualism, if only in equality. The scope of revolutionary thematics, of revolutionary reappropriation in opposition to the alienation effected by capitalist development is quite another matter: it is the thematics of the construction of a new world by the overall proletarian individual, moulded in alienation by capitalist development, which is contradictorily defined both as overall labour power and as collective power for the founding of a new universe.

Bearing these limitations in mind, let me address, nevertheless, what seems to me one of the greatest merits of Macpherson's book: that of having reintroduced a model of historiography of political thought that has not only undoubted scientific efficacy but also a greater human significance.

* * *

I have referred to the connection between the crisis of a culture and the innovative capacity of science. Such a connection loses any irrational overtone when by 'culture' we mean mode of production and when by 'the innovative capacity of science' we mean the theoretical reflection of the revolutionary development of new social classes. The connection is determined and articulated by interests and social needs within which are organised on the one hand the misery of the revolutionary class as an oppressed class and on the other hand its wealth, its creative potentiality as a revolutionary class. Contemporary historiography revolves with increasing interest around these issues, around the creative and simultaneously destructive ambiguity of revolutionary periods; and, in highlighting the themes of transformation, historiography tends, with success, to merge with political science.

The arena of seventeenth-century politics – English, French and

Italian – has become a privileged field for these historiographical operations. Preceded by a long period of studies on the Renaissance – these, too, intent on identifying the fundamental traits of the bourgeois transformation of the vision of the world – the study of the seventeenth century has the advantage of grasping the mass social characteristics of this revolution rather than the striking prediction or singular prefiguration of the new world (as often happens in the studies on the sixteenth century). For this reason, aesthetics is replaced by sociology and the science of politics. The fact is that the thematic interest of historiography in the seventeenth century has an immediate bearing on the living history of class transformations in the twentieth century: the world that appeared there, here decomposes; the hegemony of the bourgeoisie develops and is destroyed within this arc of time; throughout this period, the dimensions of the process are general and in mass.

But the fascination with the study of the seventeenth century as a subject of relevance for our own times risks having negative effects. Simplification and schematicism in historical–political readings, repetition as a mode of interpretation – these are ever present dangers. Understanding what is different and what is unique and specific to the seventeenth century permits us to relive as much of it as is topical without squeezing the interpretation into a model of mere analogy. This is a very hard thing to achieve, and we have many examples of books, even quite attractive works, that end up being trivial, obvious and beside the point. Macpherson solves the problem with an elegance that is not formal but relates closely to his capacity for positive historiography. The demonstration starts from a rigorous reconstruction of the fabric of English society, an analysis that we might call an investigation into the social and political composition of the classes. Then he examines individual theoretical positions as they arise in this context, more careful to locate the conformity between political thought and reality than eager to find some internal continuity, coherent or dialectical, from one author to another. The ideological horizon thus snaps when it collides with reality, from which Macpherson gathers often contradictory and sometimes inconsequential moments – yet real ones nonetheless (and he chooses among them). Within the nascent thought of the bourgeoisie, he is able to identify not only the moment of continuity – of strategy, so to speak – but also the tactical variants, the choices between opportunities, the temporary alternatives. He is able to describe the vivid interweaving of these various opportunities and to grasp, within this tangle, moments of ideological foundation and moments of broader

cultural change, from class analysis to the understanding of political ideas – which is almost to say, to the destruction of ideology as
a body separate from class struggle; and this could be regarded as
Macpherson's watchword.

It is within this methodological framework that a reassessment of
the work of the Levellers and an overall re-evaluation of Harrington's
utopia become possible, and it also becomes plausible to detect both
the contradictions and the solution to those contradictions in John
Locke's thought – a thought governed by the practical intention
of providing a moral foundation for a class society on the basis of
the new system of grounding political obligation in the concept of
labour. But in particular this framework offers the possibility of a
new reading of Hobbes. Just when, unlike so many other authors
past and present, Macpherson refuses to say that there is a split in
Hobbes' thought, just when he unifies naturalistic, physiological and
ethical–political moments in Hobbes and defines their continuity,
he draws Hobbes' amazing work outside any stale and purely cultural allusion – medieval, traditional, natural law. The function of
Hobbesian theory within the struggle of the classes, this solid determination, which pervades all parts of it, to highlight the necessity of
power in relation to class struggle and to the new figure of a political
subject that emerges from it – the free and materially creative individual: it is, then, the recognition of the function of his theory that
renders this solid Hobbes modern. And it is a Hobbes whom contemporary political science, whatever the field in which it operates, has
to recognise, realistically, as a theoretical reference point, especially
if this terrible world that we inhabit is destined to produce and to
recognise itself in the hard and powerful reality of Leviathan far more
than in the fabulous enterprise of a Prince.

15

Reflections on Grossmann and Borkenau*

1

In a review of my *Descartes politico* (Negri 1970) that was published a few years ago, a friend of mine raised a number of objections that I found rather hard to decipher and sometimes, I have to say, entirely unfounded (see Cacciari 1970). On the basis of an overview of political thought in France in the first half of the seventeenth century (Negri 1967: Ch. 13 in this volume), I had tried to show – drawing on the work of Borkenau (1934) and on some suggestions of Lucien Febvre (1957a, pp. 345–6, and 1962d, pp. 743–51) – that the 'philosophy of manufacture' was anything but a unitary bloc; the structural elements of the transformation of world production, the revolutionary forces that freed themselves in Italy and Flanders from the fourteenth century onwards and elsewhere in Europe from the Renaissance onwards, found a vast field of ideological alternatives, in a definitive manner, in the seventeenth century.

These alternatives represent themselves politically above all; they also appear in the methodology of the new science and of the new philosophy. They often constitute the basis of tendencies in bourgeois ideology that are lived with some historical efficacy throughout the period of bourgeois domination. I also showed how class struggle was the engine of these alternatives, which I did by examining both the mechanisms of the relationship between the bourgeoisie and the ancien régime state and the terribly bitter class struggle that

---

* SOURCE: Antonio Negri, 1978. 'Manifattura e ideologia', in *Manifattura, società borghese, ideologia*, ed. Pierangelo Schiera. Rome: Savelli. The volume contains chapters by Franz Borkenau, Henryk Grossmann and Antonio Negri.

developed during the same period against the emerging proletariat (the manufacturing proletariat, or at any rate the proletariat located within the effects produced by the advance of the new mode of production on class composition).[1]

My basic position was, and remains, that one cannot speak in general terms of a bourgeois 'revolution'; one must speak of a *capitalist revolution* (in the four phases of accumulation – primary, manufacturing, industrial, and then socialist); and that the category of the 'bourgeoisie as a class' is extremely ambiguous. As the study of the seventeenth century demonstrates (in other words, as the analysis of that crucial period between the phase of primary accumulation and the rise of early manufacturing demonstrates), the limited amount of class 'theory' that the variants of bourgeois ideology present is largely dominated, qualitatively, by the 'metaphysical' affirmation of separation, splitting and dualism. Furthermore, the theory is determined, so to speak, from the outside – that is, by the complex structure of class relations to which the variants of bourgeois ideology are subjected.

These are the various models of 'differential rationality' to which 'possessive idealism' becomes subject, a topic on which Macpherson has written well.[2] In other words, they are the theoretical and political articulations of the process of appropriation of the 'average social value' that was being set in motion at that time.[3]

The capitalist functions of the determination of value immediately collide (after an initial 'mythological' humanist and Renaissance illusion) with the antagonistic realities of the process, and it is in the continuous attempt to dominate this antagonism that separation becomes inherent in bourgeois thought. It interprets capitalist domination and the antagonism of the mode of production; it moves continuously from the mode of production to the multiplication of its antinomies in the sphere of political relations and ideological representations.

In this context, the fact that the bourgeoisie, as a political class, as an ideological class, may have tended to represent itself as a universal class should not be as difficult as it seems to have been for my reviewer (Cacciari 1970). On the contrary, it seems to me quite natural and obvious: the fact that the universal and magical sense of the Renaissance goes hand in hand with the establishment of manufacturing operations and with the genesis of mechanical science has to be the specific element that defines the political and ideological project of the bourgeoisie.

The rise and the internalisation of a consciousness of separation, the definitive metaphysical qualification of the problem of separation, will have to be imposed by the class struggle. As has been widely emphasised, and not only in the case of France,[4] this happens mainly in the crisis of the first half of the seventeenth century. In historiography it is always dangerous to establish critical and epoch-making break points, but what happens in the early part of this century is so dramatic that, whichever way you look at it, you have to see it as the moment when the accumulation of critical elements that constitute the ideological 'consciousness' of the bourgeoisie (which, of course, had many forerunners) consolidates and fixes itself, in a qualitative leap.

This is not, then, about contrasting a luminous and satisfied century with a dark and dramatic century. It is rather about grasping the qualitative change, the reversal of revolutionary hope into a sense of defeat. However, those who do not accept this interpretation can turn for information in the first place to the likes of Giordano Bruno and Lucilio Vanini, and above all to the dozens of witches who were burned at the stake in that period.

Today, some ten years since I began my research on Descartes, I feel that I should restate this position, not only in relation to my deepening pursuit of that research, but most of all – paradoxically, though not too much – in relation to the study I am currently engaged in on Spinoza and political society in his contemporaneous Netherlands. At that time Dutch capitalism had emerged victorious from the critical test of the first decades of the century. Spinoza lives the triumph of a bourgeois oligarchy in which the capitalist revolution and the political project seem to go hand in hand.[5] This is an anomaly vis-à-vis the parallel development of contemporary philosophical thought, an anomaly that seems to become a characteristic of Spinoza's thought. Here the Renaissance ideology of spontaneity and wealth is also organised formally, in the perspective of mechanism; it is, all in one, classic thought and savage thought.[6]

It is therefore no coincidence that, in recent times, the socialism of poverty has taken as its ideal the enlightened mythology of Spinoza (Kline 1952). But on the other hand it is precisely the intensity of this anomaly that reveals how deep the break was in the first half of the seventeenth century: when it comes to settling the accounts, the Dutch bourgeois oligarchy will be decapitated, commercial accumulation will show itself to be in contradiction with the progress of manufacturing production (Mantoux 1928), and Spinoza will come down to us through the centuries as *Iudaicus et atheista, atheorum princeps, primi systematis inter atheos subtiliores architectus* ['a Jew and a non-believer, leader of the godless and architect of the first system among the more subtle of the godless'] (Vernière 1954, vol. 1, p. 35). The consciousness of the law of value, of the law of separation, is imposed on the savage anomaly: bourgeois mythology will become bourgeois consciousness of the split, and that split will constitute the content of the 'class consciousness' of the bourgeoisie.

2

But my reviewer presses the point (or perhaps he will forgive me for putting words into his mouth, just as I have excused him for the silly things that he has ascribed to me): the consciousness of separation is the fabric of philosophical speculation, but bourgeois philosophy is theory (not simply ideology) to the extent that this separation is mastered.

But by whom? That the separation should be mastered is fundamental to accumulation. Capitalist consciousness has no doubts on this terrain. And Spinoza has no doubts either. But before this awareness of domination penetrates philosophy, before the bourgeoisie becomes a participant in the capitalist revolution, we have to wait a bit: only classical economics and Hegel will address the problem (see especially Bodei 1975). Only a grand reformism, under attack from the struggle of the working class and from the communist revolution in its first stages, will succeed in defining the terms of this travail (see the essays in Bologna, Rawick, Gobbini et al. 1972). But wanting to see the problem formulated and resolved in the seventeenth century is absurd – even without using that bad philosophical methodology of 'filiation' that narrow-minded Italian Croceanism handed down to us in nineteenth-century forms (and in this it exhibited an incredible backwardness, even by the standard of other, equally conservative and backward-looking cultures) – unless we impoverish the ideological thickness of a drama in several acts (struggle of the bourgeoisie with the state; struggle with the proletariat; conflict over its class nature) with a short comic finale: mechanicism.

Now, this is exactly the point of view that Grossmann (1935) opposes to Borkenau. He denies, in a tone that is often both learned and angry, that the seventeenth century, the early 1600s, was the original starting point of the 'philosophy of manufacture'. This because the seventeenth century was neither the place of origin of mechanist philosophy nor the place of origin of capitalist manufacturing.

On the first point, Grossmann has no difficulty in showing that the methodology of mechanicism is already widely present in the productions of late humanism, and specifically in the work of Leonardo (ibid., pp. 176–7). As for the second point, Grossmann easily shows that it is difficult to speak of 'organic manufacture' in the first half of the seventeenth century (ibid., pp. 183–4). In consequence, this is a frontal attack on the fundamental theses that sustain both Borkenau's periodisation – and thus the assessment of the seventeenth century as marking the *essor* [take-off] of bourgeois philosophy – and his definition of manufacture – namely that the philosophy of the seventeenth century was both a registration of and a mystification of the *essor* of manufacturing labour as mechanical labour reducible, through the division of labour, to an average social value.

Both of Grossmann's claims are one-sided and thereby false. The first presupposes an extremely poor conception of mechanicism: contrary to what Grossmann thinks, mechanicism always presents itself instead as a 'philosophy' of mechanicism. There is no mechanist theory that is not part of a philosophy – not in the seventeenth century, and even less in the fifteenth – if only because mechanicism is certainly part of a plan to destroy traditional metaphysical physics. But above all there is none in the seventeenth century, when the relationship between mechanicism and labour becomes integrated and internalises, as separation, the contradictory nature of the function of the law of value as a law of exploitation.

Grossmann writes: 'the impulse to theoretical mechanics thus does not derive from human labour but from the objectivity of the instruments of labour, of machines; in other words, it is exercised only to the extent that the subjective limits of human labour are overcome!' (ibid., p. 191). As if the overcoming of the subjective limits of human labour did not constitute a dialectical process, as if the machine did not exist and were not in opposition, as objectified labour! But objectifying labour is a *political operation*, it is certainly not only – as Grossmann infelicitously tries to prove (ibid., pp. 210–11) – the production of highly articulated mechanical devices.

Here Grossmann seems to forget that the fundamental point of primary accumulation consists in this political operation. The heavy insistence with which Marx stresses this point has found support from contemporary historians (on behalf of the working class: Dobb 1958, esp. pp. 103ff., 143ff., 243ff.) and matching mystifications (on behalf of employers, as broadly shown in Coldagelli 1969). Furthermore, this political operation for primary accumulation undergoes a structural shift in the critical conjuncture of the first half of the seventeenth century: a fundamental restructuring crisis, and also one of political restructuring of the state (of the big continental states) for this purpose. The continuity of mechanist ideology bends to this rupture and finds in this qualitative turn some long-term determinations, in other words it articulates itself around the new structure that the dialectic of the historical process has brought about.[7]

Secondly, as regards manufacture, it exists, and very much so. Certainly we still do not have, except minimally, a factory system – that productive structure in which the transition from manufacturing to industry takes place in an organic manner, with capital hiring labour in one single place and under homogeneous conditions of production. But the heterogeneous and cooperative manufacturing system, to be precise, the 'putting-out system' or *Verlagssystem*, is very widespread and tendentially dominant, and – to be clear – in it the average value of labour is already broadly the reference point for the capitalist revolution. As old Marsilio said, in this way it was possible *mundum universum capere et metiri* ['to understand and fear the whole world', Ficino, *De vita* 3.110][8] – but how much water has passed under the bridges! Of course, the demonstration of Borkenau (who no doubt counts Boissonade among his sources) is not at all conclusive in this regard: but Borkenau's indications, immediately picked up by Lucien Febvre (who certainly does not sympathise with the methods of writers such as Boissonade, as he stresses several times), are nevertheless correct.

3

The critique that Grossmann makes of Borkenau is the immediate reversal of his version of the Marxist theory of capital. It is a projection of it, so much so that in Grossmann's fundamental work of 1929 we find reference to the hegemony of commercial and financial capital throughout the period of primitive accumulation, and in any case up to the time of the full triumph of the factory system.[9] The limitations of Grossmann's historical explanation are the same as the ones we find in his economic theory: they are limitations that pertain to his endogenous conception of crisis, development and collapse. Whatever the formidable antireformist impulse that animates the work of Grossmann – and we turn to it as a continuous source of nourishment (Rosdolsky 1971, p. 441) – one cannot hide the fact that the Grossmannian interpretation of the period from the sixteenth century to the eighteenth is just as fallacious as his critique of political economy – and insofar as the latter is so on the whole.

The essence of the concept of capital as a relationship and the conception of capitalist development as an outcome of struggles are actually the fundamental polemical targets of Grossmann's methodology: restoring validity to materialist objectivism and expunging subjectivism from Marxism seemed to him the most efficacious theoretical weapons in the fight against reformism. How wrong this political line was has been amply demonstrated by the history of both workers' struggles and Marxist theory.[10] However, Grossmann's theory of 'collapse' – which, more than any other element of his theory, is what he is known for – is the most explicit point of his political programme. But these digressions and historiographic projections are not far behind! It's just that one does not understand their utility.

In any case, in his review of Borkenau, Grossmann reaffirms his basic hypothesis (which is characteristic of all of his writing) of a very high rationalising power (completely linked to the machine system) of capitalist development, and thus about a very strong underestimation of the political components of the process of primary accumulation, and in particular of that fundamental political fact that is the formation of the proletariat. He must have found the 'exogeneity' of this 'fact' hostile, about as much as he found alien to the explanation of contemporary economic crises all the elements that allegedly repressed the 'endogenous' fall of the rate of profit and corrected the supposed 'underconsumerist' tendencies of capitalist development (see Moszkowska 1974, pp. 37ff.) – elements that, on the whole, proposed alternative policies within capitalist development, in terms not only of technical rationalisation of machinism but rather of rationalisation of the political control of the cycle of class struggle.

Not by chance, in the American propagator of Grossmann's work – not so much à propos the theory of 'collapse', which in fact is strongly criticised (see Sweezy 1951, pp. 271ff.), as à propos underconsumerist tendencies and therefore a basic underestimation of the action of the working class as a driving force of the capitalist system – in the work of Paul M. Sweezy, then, there reappears the tendency to fix the central point of accumulation in the formation of a 'scientific' bourgeoisie, urban and mercantile, rather than in the action of the dialectical laws of the separation between town and country and of the forced formation of a labour market.[11]

Along this line, for all the elegance and measure with which this research may be carried out, there is a risk of introducing mystifications regarding the independence of scientific development and the prevalence of parameters of circulation and trade in the definition of capitalist development (and of the capitalist class), and especially mystifications regarding the independence and autonomy of the bourgeoisie as a class.

This should not happen, if we want to define, around this pivotal point in the seventeenth century that is so important for the history of the political economy of capital and for the critique of bourgeois ideology, both a substantive transition of accumulation and of the state and a correct approach and valid methodology for the historiography of the bourgeoisie.

In the first half of the seventeenth century only the opening of the range of alternative political solutions for the explosive class conflict that had built up explains the logic of the formation of this social stratum, dramatically stretched between a past nostalgically wished for as a place of absence of struggles and an uncertain and dangerous future; between pressure from above, for the old ruling classes and for the state as a moment that offers guarantees, and an uprising from below, a necessary effect of the upheaval in the social structures for development.

Furthermore, no history of bourgeois ideology can avoid raising the problem not only of the formal character of the separation (as a defining element of the bourgeoisie) but especially of the material characteristics, the historically relevant and effective elements on which that separation is established.

When Grossmann accuses Borkenau of giving these political elements too much importance and of forgetting the structural framework of the process as a result (Grossmann 1935, pp. 216ff.), he is mistaken, because it is only in this way that bourgeois ideology – not only then but always, yet at that time with extreme effectiveness – constitutes itself, becomes visible, becomes identifiable. The bourgeoisie does not have and has never had a scientific theory of development and revolution; its so-called progressive function has never been more than a mediation in relation to the forces of capital (and state) and of class; its structure is always an outcome of the dialectical process of class struggle, all the way back to the phase of primitive accumulation. The category 'bourgeois spirit' is always apologetic, anyway. The same goes for any historical conception of the continuity of bourgeois ideology, a position that, in contradiction with the theoretical assumptions that inspired its beginnings and the historical contributions published then, was perhaps not understood by the editors of *Contropiano*, who, not accidentally, have ended up today as high priests of the 'political' and of the 'intellectual', on the rhythm of the continuity of bourgeois ideology.[12]

4

The bourgeoisie has only one continuity: that of the function of money [*denaro*]. Of money as currency [*moneta*], not as capital. It lives the relative independence that money lived in the process of circulation of capital, in the face of directly productive movements. In primary accumulation, during the period of manufacture, the function of the mercantile bourgeoisie is anyway secondary. Grossmann is correct on this matter when he points to the importance of financial capital in the period under consideration and stresses this precisely in order to exclude its function of control over the development of manufacturing (Grossman 1935, p. 176 and passim).

But something else is useful in Grossmann's argument: he introduces us to an appreciation of the real situation, and thus to the fact that it is *not* financial and commercial capital, and it is *not* the function of money – prominent as they both were during the period under consideration – that are fundamental to accumulation, but the contemporary, factual and indisputable emergence of an entrepreneurial capitalist class (of humble origins, not directly linked to financial capital), and its confrontation with the parallel emergence of the first proletarian strata (see the analyses carried out in Dobb 1946 and Coldagelli 1969).

In this process the bourgeoisie mediates its existence in relation to the state in order to guarantee the certainty of its own fortunes and the stability of its own position. It would like to conquer the state but the relations of forces escapes it. What endures and becomes stronger is the bourgeois capacity for mediation. The emerging capitalist class, for its part, needs the state as a political force rather than as an agent in any intermediation of the process of accumulation and realisation. Or rather the state has to establish the labour market; it has to intervene as 'concentrated and organised violence of society, artificially to foment the process of transforming the mode of feudal production into a capitalist mode of production, and to shorten the passages',[13] but for everything else capital is sufficient unto itself.

Money appears and, in the seventeenth century, is chaos. Self-accumulation is sufficient for manufacturing. But the capitalist revolution is not the sum of capitalists' operations (not even if it were the sum of all of everyone's operations); it is a revolution of value, the construction of a new cycle of dirty values. Money, and the independent functions of intermediation, then necessarily begin to abandon their independence, step by step. The relativity of their functions is always strongly affirmed, but tendentially denied. Money turns itself into currency, bends itself to the representation and the measurement of the average social value of labour. The ideology of the bourgeoisie bends to this transformation of the function of money.

From nature to second nature, to the universe produced from scratch by capitalist production, this is the path that – through a meditation on money – the bourgeois ideology of mediation must follow. Alfred Sohn-Rethel (1976) has recently stressed the importance of treading this path and the consequences that taking it might have for an investigation into the transformations of scientific thought in bourgeois ideology.

Proceeding on this terrain means addressing a set of problems that were left unresolved by Borkenau and by the writers who followed him. For there is perhaps to Grossmann's critique a valid element, which is then simply a suggestion to perfect Borkenau's investigation; Grossmann accuses him of not having sufficiently addressed, in theoretical terms, the connection between the rise of abstract manufacturing labour and the ideological determinations that derived from it.

It is true: faced with the unfinished work, the 'torso', of Borkenau, Grossmann goes off at a tangent. But there is no doubt that the dissatisfaction that drives him to critique and to an incorrect interpretative alternative is the sense of insufficient depth in Borkenau's structural investigation. This also applies to my study *Descartes politico*.

In short, it is necessary to readdress the tangle of themes mentioned and developed, above all the dialectical relationship between the philosophical–political process and the structural modifications of the historical frame of reference, to test more deeply the functioning of the Marxian categories of primary accumulation and manufacture.[14] We will have to dialecticise more deeply the thematic of the prerequisites and the thematic specific to accumulation; to grasp class tensions more accurately; to analyse fully the correlations between the development of machinism and the trinity accumulation–market–processes of realisation; and, above all (so far as the bourgeoisie is concerned), to fix the times and the forms in which the exercise of the function of mediation takes place, where money gradually changes its position between mystification of nature and production of a 'second nature'.

That the philosophy of mechanism is related to changes in the function of money is an intuition that we often find in the critique of science – an intuition inspired by the analysis of commodity fetishism.[15] But here it is perhaps possible to turn this intuition into a powerful instrument for defining the ideology of the bourgeoisie as a whole – as indeed was already done by William Petty who, writing in 1687 about Holland in Spinoza's time, could consider 'progress in the knowledge of nature' to be the most important complement of productive industrial labour, at the same time as it was changing labour into 'gold and silver as imperishable wealth', thus establishing an embryonic science–production–capital relationship in the form of money.[16]

To put in another way what I just said, in the early part of the seventeenth century the analysis of classes on the bourgeois side has to grasp the relationship of structural intermediation that some strata (scientists, cultured people, functionaries) determine in the face of development of manufacturing and in the face of the class insurgency – particularly on the side of the state. But the analysis has to grasp this structural intermediation not only in the articulation of political (ideological, functional) alternatives, very important though they are; it must also fix it as a fundamental and synchronic intermediation, as the foundation of a function – relatively independent but nevertheless essential – of capitalist development. Borkenau has set in motion a discourse that has to be deepened by following in the footsteps of his work, by breaking the rhythm of ideology at the theoretical level, and by seeing clearly the function of money, this a priori of money[17] – when it is clear that, in the face of the Cartesian a priori, there begins to come into existence that other a priori: average social labour value.

5

Borkenau's historical materialism is marked in some respects by the limitations of the theoretical elaboration of the 1920s and by the ideological hegemony of the Third International. This means that the development of political alternatives within the philosophy of manufacture takes place along the lines of a kind of historical necessity, too often not sufficiently dialectical. Now, since at one end the usefulness of breaking the progress of this historical reality upwards, in a theoretical function, has been demonstrated, it seems that in this way one can consider the importance of deepening the intensity of the dialectical articulations of the picture that Borkenau traced by following his indications and developing them.

One should note: this is not about going against the methodological concerns of the historiography of science, of recapturing that taste, of historicising memory, for the individuality of historical research in science and political economy as well as in the history of philosophy, and of thus vaccinating (in a Gramscian sense) historical materialism. I leave these concerns to others, in the hope that they will develop them with more than Crocean or Gramscian dignity (Kuhn 1970).

Here instead one has to investigate deeply into the specific thematics of materialism in history, that is, to perceive more intensely and dialectically the nexus between structures and superstructures, not confusing them but revitalising them. In short, historical materialism comes alive historiographically not only when it determines undeniable relations between substructural and superstructural aspects, but especially when, to this formal dialectic, it joins the real dialectic of antagonistic classes in struggle. On the theoretical side, the anatomy of monkeys is explained by the anatomy of humans; on the historical side, it is the full subjectivity of the class forces that explains the structural relationships shown by the relationships of force, by the processes of accumulation, by the institutional levels.

When we enter the period of maturity in the development of the Industrial Revolution, this truth jumps to the eye in such a way that the overall picture can be illuminated only starting from the 'making of the working class' (see the now classic Thompson 1968). But is there not a certain emptiness in Borkenau in this respect? Is there not some need to make historical materialism capable of sustaining this approach also in the phase of primitive accumulation and manufacture?

The contributions of historians who have studied class struggle in the seventeenth century[18] undoubtedly increased our knowledge of the contradictions of the century. But are we not dealing, in this case too, with a too general conception of the antagonistic relationship between 'popular' struggles and the state – a conception that ultimately broadens the picture of an all-too-familiar framework of political relations (the crisis of the seventeenth century in all its aspects) without making significant innovations? Without adding that *quid* [something] proper to historical materialism – namely the insistence on (proletarian) class struggle within the 'social' processes of primary accumulation and within the formation, through manufacture, of the average social value of labour? This seems to me to be the specific terrain on which Borkenau's analysis should be continued, bearing in mind that, for sure, the deepening of the materialist analysis of class subjectivity is not done exclusively through the deployment of the means of economic–political research. Rather – at least for the seventeenth century – it is very important to recognise religious ideology and minor ideologies as powerful media and bearers of attitudes (also) of revolt, or at least of political recognition of the subaltern classes and of the proletariat.

But if we take a further look at the work of Borkenau and that of the other writers who have been active until now in the field of historical materialism, in particular Porshnev, we have to admit that perhaps the limit is a little deeper. Once again, the concept of bourgeois class – as it also appears, incidentally, in the less rigorous writings of Marx[19] – lies at the root of the rigidity of the historical picture. For, when one takes this category of 'intermediation' – this referent of 'ideology' – as an object of analysis, then, inevitably, the conflict that begins to define the historical process *in reality* and that figures in the story of the bourgeoisie *only ideologically*, hence the conflict – incipient, but tendentially winning and already defining – between capital and proletariat, is necessarily fading away.

We have to move beyond this impasse. The concept of bourgeois class is an apologetic concept, entirely tied to a particular phase of capitalist development: the phase in which civil society and the state established a specific alliance. But not even in that phase did the bourgeoisie merge with capital, with the class of capitalists. This categorial and apologetic confusion, which we owe to classical economics and to the Hegelian school, has to be be resolved: it is the bearer of confusion, always ideological, both at the historiographic and at the political level.

At the political level, it prevents us from seeing the intermediary role of the bourgeoisie in relation to capital; it creates illusions about the fact that the defeat of the bourgeoisie is equivalent to a defeat of capital; it excludes the possibility that, in the management of capital, equally importantly when it comes to exploitation, other social classes may be set in place against proletarian productive labour. At the historiographic level, the use of the category 'bourgeois class' unifies a process of continuous formation and reform of a simple function of social control, always subordinated, always constructed exogenously. It gives an existence of its own to something that exists only in mediation. It creates illusions about the continuity of an ideology that is instead a mediation and mystification of the struggle between the particular interests of the two classes in struggle. It is no coincidence that the history of the bourgeoisie is always the history of ideology, of the 'autonomy' of the mediation of the political[20] – or rather *ideological history, not real history*, of the state, of law, of its officials and priests. University departments are full of lectures and courses on the subject. But why not rather ask yourself, after Sieyès and with him: What might the bourgeoisie be? And, particularly, what substance might there be in concepts such as 'bourgeois revolution', 'civil society' and the rest?[21] There is no shortage of fraud here.

But, to return to the core of my argument, the fundamental problem now reappears with clarity. The only true meaning that we can give to the category of bourgeoisie in the seventeenth century is that of mediation (philosophical, scientific, political, at any rate ideological) of the conflict that develops in the sphere of manufacturing. There is no continuity in conceptualisation, not even just ideological, for the bourgeoisie; it has a parasitic existence within sharply defined antagonisms. Borkenau, writing from within the traditions of the Second and Third Internationals, where the term 'bourgeois' at least had a reference to struggle, has laid too much stress on continuous functions in his analysis of the relationship between structure and superstructure. Today, when the term 'bourgeoisie' becomes secondary and the relations of domination rightly appear to be more directly implanted on the fundamental antagonism, Borkenau's political justifications fall as well. Therefore an analysis that develops by way of deepening his thematic should in all probability look for the subjective poles of class antagonism in primary accumulation and in manufacturing.[22]

6

It is perhaps worth pausing on one last element, to complete my analysis of the limitations of Borkenau's work. This element is the insufficient sense of 'conjuncture' that runs through his excellent book. Obviously Borkenau did not have at his disposal the impressive amount of materials on conjunctural movements in the first half of the seventeenth century that more recent historians have dug out and systematised.[23] But the problem is not this.

In Borkenau, in certain theoretical rigidities of his historical materialism, in his adoption of the concept of bourgeois class, it is impossible to grasp conjuncture as a relevant and sometimes fundamental aspect of how the ideological alternatives of the century defined themselves. But if the function of ideological mediation – which repeats aspects of the relative autonomy of money [denaro] in capitalist circulation, and these aspects are all the more intense in their relativity and all the more fragile as the level of production and reproduction of capitalist social relations is more backward – if, then, this function of ideological mediation constitutes the central point of the existence of the bourgeoisie, then the conjunctural aspects become central in the historical narrative of the bourgeoisie.

In his essay 'Montaigne and the function of scepticism', Max Horkheimer highlights this very effectively (see Horkheimer 1974, vol. 2, pp. 196ff.): the separation of society presents itself to consciousness and here creates a tendency towards transcendental unification; but what is conjunctural is the entirety of social relationships that bourgeois daily consciousness records, and what remains conjunctural, too, is the mediation of the separation, which is always pushed beyond the horizon of the everyday. The form of the essay and of the biography registers, in an unfulfilled tension towards an essence of reunification, the dispersion and the conjunctural fragmentation of the everyday.

Money [*moneta*] presents itself in the same way, with a degree of mobility and ungraspability, a violent alternation of cycles and leaps: capital, already in its first manufacturing configuration, does not like money, turns to self-accumulation and stakes its growth on the large-scale dimensions and conditions of the social processes of exploitation.

The bourgeoisie has no alternative: it is condemned to this mobility and structured by the conjuncture. The emotions of the century consolidate in it with all the characteristics of uncertainty and fleetingness. Even the Cartesian 'revolution', in its radical intensity, far from consolidating itself, disintegrates between nostalgia and hope. In the face of the laborious but assured strategy of capitalist development, the bourgeoisie articulates a tactic, a withdrawal, continuous and endured, into the conjuncture. Thus it is crucial that we grasp these conjunctural aspects of seventeenth-century thought; and on the terrain already defined by Borkenau the research has progressed and can progress still further.

I repeat: this happens, however, on the terrain defined by Borkenau. For he is entirely correct and fundamental beyond the limitations stated – and, paradoxically, also with respect to the limitations stated, since the definition of the fields of inquiry that I have invoked to complete the research of Borkenau and to deepen the methodology of historical materialism is *implicitly* developed by our author, too – obviously around the point that interests him most, where his analysis probes deeper – and it is the point where, objectively, the analysis needs to go deeper because the material requires it dialectically. This point is the theory of the state and the analysis of the relationship between the bourgeoisie and the state.[24] Here then, on this screen, we read the highest characterisation of the bourgeoisie itself: not only does it want to mediate the projection of the form of relations of production onto the state, it also wants to conquer the state for itself. And yet it is constrained to the mediation of juridical individualism, to the function of juridical categories and relations, and to the continuous rationalisation of irrational contents in the theory of sovereignty and of the state. The effects of bourgeois action, in their continuous heteronomy, reveal in the background the nature of the contradictory relations that define the bourgeoisie.

Far from mediating in linear fashion with the theory of the state, the 'philosophy of manufacture' approaches it on contradictory terms; and, in the relationship with the practice of command, the theory of the social value of labour reveals its antagonistic content and immediately subjects the bourgeoisie to it. The whole history of the bourgeoisie is marked, defined, unsettled by this antagonism. But the emergence of the leitmotiv is here, in these early years of the seventeenth century.

To conclude: there is a concept – the concept of political class composition – that was introduced in Italian Marxism's theoretical and political debate in the 1960s (Tronti 1966). It offers the possibility of defining the levels of the working class with (antagonistic) reference to the levels of development of capital and to articulate the interrelations that the general course of the struggle between classes brings about. But its hermeneutic capacity is not limited to this. All the articulations that seem to me to be flawed in Borkenau's development of historical materialism can be addressed on the basis of the category of class composition. Furthermore, the historiographic scope of this concept can make it possible to break certain rigidities of traditional historical materialism, while remaining fully and thoroughly on the terrain of historical materialism and avoiding the false non-dialectical paths of organicism (whether positivist, historicist or Gramscian).[25]

In dealing with a work such as that of Borkenau, I believe that the scope of a methodology articulated on the category of class composition can allow us to proceed on a broad front: on the plane of historiography, to the confirmation of some important results of Borkenau's research and towards their intersection with conjunctural analysis; and, on a theoretical plane, to a more thorough definition of bourgeois ideology and of the ideological existence of the bourgeoisie. In this case we would combine a historiographical approach and a structural and category-based approach (bourgeoisie, money, circulation, and so on – state).

To date there have been a few attempts to tackle current problems in historiography, from the point of view of class. It is now time to study the tension of research in greater depth, also in relation to the major themes raised in *Capital*.[26] The essay by Coldagelli cited in this chapter is already a remarkable example of the efficacy of our methodology; we need to concentrate our efforts on attacking past history with the weapons of historiography – the history of the bourgeoisie in particular. The seventeenth century is undoubtedly a privileged terrain for this endeavour.[27]

Notes

1 In addition to the fundamental research in Porshnev 1963, see the more recent bibliography used in Negri 1967.

2 I have sought to clarify some of these points in my Preface to Macpherson 1973 = Ch. 14 in the present volume.

3 For a bibliographic summary and a very sharp review of the economic history aspect, see Coldagelli 1969.

4 Here I make another reference to Negri 1967 = Ch. 13 in this volume.

5 Huizinga 1968 and Thalheimer 1928 reached similar conclusions.

6 Deleuze 1968 arrives at such conclusions, through an accurate internal analysis of Spinozian thought, bringing influential innovations to the interpretative tradition.

7 On the definition of the integration of historical dialectics and structure in terms that seem well founded from a Marxian angle, see Schmidt 1971.

8 As quoted in Cacciari 1970.

9 Grossmann 1929, p. 48 (but see the 1967 reprint by Verlag Neue Kritik in Frankfurt 1967). See also Grossmann 1971, a collection with important insights that touch on my subject.

10 See in particular Sergio Bologna's notes in the Introduction to the Italian translation of Moszkowska 1974.

11 This is how those who sided with Sweezy in the debate, carried out in *Past and Present*, on the crisis of the seventeenth century expressed themselves, in opposition to the historiographical line taken by Maurice Dobb (see Negri 1967 = ch. 13 in this volume).

12 See my notes on the 'school' of 'the autonomy of the political' in Negri 1976.

13 From *Capital*'s 'unpublished chapter six' (Marx 1976), translated here from the Italian version (Marx 1969a, p. 7).

14 I am of course referring to the categories developed in Sections 3 and 4 of *Capital*.

15 Not only in G. Lukács's *Geschichte und Klassenbewusstsein* but in the whole tradition – which might be worth reconstructing today – that arises in the Soviet Russia of the 1920s. See now Rubin 1972.

16 In addition to the references in Tahlheimer 1920, see Marx 1961b, pp. 296–97, 307 [Italian translation of *Theories of Surplus Value*].

17 Of special interest are Sohn-Rethel's (1976) attempt to redeem Koyré's work and his very positive evaluation of it.

18 Beside Porshnev 1963, see all the works cited in Negri 1967 (= ch. 13 in the present volume).

19 It should be made clear that in Marx the term 'bourgeois class' or 'bourgeoisie' bears the two senses of economic class of capital and ideological class of intermediation. The first sense generally gets the upper hand as Marx's study of the critique of political economy deepens.

20 It seems possible to read a coherent use of this conceptualisation in Asor Rosa 1975.
21 The problem is posed with great clarity in Zapperi 1974. But see also Bobbio 1967–8.
22 Lucien Goldmann's work on Jansenism would deserve a separate discussion. He has the merit of having identified some fundamental moments in the culture of the French bourgeoisie and in its crisis – but, simultaneously, of having produced a 'methodologically' mystified reading of it.
23 On the crisis of the seventeenth century, and particularly on its first phase, see the bibliography examined in Negri 1967 (= ch. 13 in this volume).
24 The best part of Borkenau's (1934) study – even better than the section on Descartes – is the section dedicated to Hobbes (from p. 439 on). These pages on the philosophy of Hobbes represent indeed the peak of Borkenau's research and are indisputably the most convincing pages in the book. Strange that, in his radical critique, Grossmann does not seem to take them into account.
25 These difficulties, characteristic of Gramscianism, are still to be found in the recent methodological revisions in Luporini 1974 – not to mention the contributions of Badaloni 1975.
26 Apart from Gaspare de Caro's important work (Caro 1970), also worthy of mention here is the kind of research that developed around the journal *Primo Maggio* and the kind of research that appears periodically in the series Materiali Marxisti at Feltrinelli.
27 Any reprise of Borkenau's work should, however, be integrated with the viewpoint expressed in Horkheimer 1932.

16

Notes on the history of politics in Tronti

Many things come to mind as you read the two parts of volume 1 of the anthology edited by Mario Tronti and titled *The Political: From Machiavelli to Cromwell* (Tronti 1979). For Tronti goes, as usual, to the heart of the problem. It is true: the labour movement always hovers around the edge of a void of knowledge about politics: about the political element – statal, functional, material – that constitutes the state-machine. How can we work together to redress this short-coming? One way is by studying the history of politics: this is a useful way of proceeding, if it is true that the historical critique of theories of surplus value comes before the systematic definition of the critique of the concept of value; this is how Marx has it. But Tronti insists that the history of the political [*il politico*] must be current history – a political theory of a given social formation that today, at the present level of capitalist crisis, points to the political as a problem. Politics appears in its modern guise as a politics of the bourgeoisie: the crisis of the bourgeoisie and of its foundational power–capital relation-ship turns on its head the very concept of politics. Big programmes, reformist and conservative alike, have failed. So what is politics today? Did politics die with the end of its bourgeois definition? Or should we today, building upon that historical experience, establish a class politics by uncovering autonomous forms of political power, fix in them the anticipated expression of anti-institutional movements, and grasp the new levels of class struggle that seek power? To paraphrase Tronti, a rise in the maturity of the class movement through a crisis in the rationality of the bourgeois autonomy of the political – this is what it takes to ground and build the research; this is both the hope and the theoretical programme.

So much for Tronti. But the programme laid out in these two

volumes, is it adequate to the proposal? Frankly, I would say not. In great part, what we are offered here is a (rather old-fashioned) 'history of political doctrines' manual – a strange discipline with ill-defined boundaries whose confused definition has been for years the subject of delectable academic diatribes and foreclosures consequent upon them. But then, why is it that a programme that was so lucidly expounded fritters out into a final product that is so traditional? Because, by the end, this anthology becomes just another of the familiar histories of *raison d'état* – ouch, Professor Meinecke, why has the Sozialistischer Deutscher Studentenbund given you such a hard time?

To answer this question – and to confirm the objective difficulty raised by the problem – I probably need to begin by highlighting a number of facts. These are objective conditions with a direct influence on research, conditions perhaps too much neglected by a tradition to which this history is also subject. The first point to note is that, in the given social formation that we define as capitalist–bourgeois, politics presents itself predominantly in the form of metaphysics, and therefore any attempt to isolate politics as such becomes pointless, that is, fails to reveal that intertwining between power and capital, between the state and the movement of social classes that the research addresses programmatically, as its object. It is only by passing through metaphysics – the most abstract and the most random of all forms of knowledge – that politics and the political come to be revealed. There is not, in the specific historical formation of the bourgeoisie, in its genesis, in its maturity, and in its decline, there is no other true politics except metaphysics. The political form of thought is not separable from the metaphysical. Only the history of metaphysics allows us to construct, piece by piece, the concept of sovereignty and the concept of general will. Renaissance Platonism and baroque dualism say more about the concept of sovereignty than does any political tract by Machiavelli. Malebranche tells us infinitely more about the seventeenth century than does [Richelieu's] *Testament Politique*. The *Critique of Practical Reason* tells us infinitely more about the eighteenth century than does the *Social Contract*, even if the latter is also a treatise of metaphysics.

But there is more. Only the history of metaphysics prevents us from viewing the history of politics as a linear affair, as a functional development. The history of metaphysics (and of its alternatives) shows in fact a relationship, (always) dialectical and (often) antagonistic, between the development of forces of production and the development of relations of production. Borkenau has written powerfully about this relationship – specifically in relation to the seventeenth-century state.

More recently, Jon Elster has written about the development of the capitalist spirit and, using the methodological tools elaborated by the English historical materialism of the 1930s (Needham, Merton, etc.), has compared it with Leibnizian metaphysics. Many other attempts are under way, in both the French and the Anglo-Saxon schools of history, and the results are precious, especially when the materialistic method is applied to complex contents and to the global and articulated assumptions of modern methodologies. Interesting, for example, is Grosrichard's study of the structure of the seraglio, where the relationship between the machinery of administration and the machinery of mystification becomes absolutely clear. Here the abstract linearity of the history of *raison d'état* is cancelled out.

I agree, then, that we have to write the history of politics – but in the dimensions in which it is possible to do that, and always remembering that the political entails the dominance of a class relationship: of a relationship, hence of alternatives. Does this mean alternatives that are all the more radical as the form of domination develops? In all probability, yes. So, returning to my discussion of the history of politics during the centuries of the bourgeoisie's ascent, we have to ask ourselves again: Will there not also be a history of alternative proposals contemporary with, parallel to and antagonistic to the history of *raison d'état*? And shall we not find that the connection between the two is such that the history of one is impossible to address without the history of the other? Will there not be, alongside and against the metaphysics of bourgeois domination, of the capitalist relationship of production, both a development of thought and a theoretical planning that connect with each other around the emergence of the new force of production and attempt to make it into an alternative political force?

By way of example, it seems to me that, in the centuries from the seventeenth to the beginning of the nineteenth, on the terrain of the metaphysics of power, there are at least two antagonistic lines: one, blessed, which goes from Hobbes to Rousseau to Kant to Hegel; and the other, cursed, which runs from Machiavelli via Spinoza to Marx. One builds the theoretical basis of bourgeois domination and its right (the transcendence of normativity); the other raises the concept of force of production from republicanism to constitutionalism and to class struggle. This historical alternative is certainly not linear. It reacts point by point to the events of class struggle. In its abstraction, metaphysics is sensible. In its lack of historicity, metaphysics is historical. In its inconclusiveness and randomness, metaphysics is chronotopic. *Qua* metaphysics it may open to the alternatives in the class struggle, precisely because it is mystification, appearance – even if efficacious appearance. This example functions as symbol of a possibility of theoretical analysis that, while accepting the importance of metaphysics, also locates it within the history of class struggle.

So a history of bourgeois politics during the centuries covered in Tronti's anthology can develop only on the terrain of metaphysics. In these centuries, metaphysics alone anticipates the movements of extra-institutional forces and grasps the dynamics of class struggle as a positive motor of liberation and as a negative engine of the continuous restructuring of the ideology and machine of capitalist power. The historical form of metaphysics is quite specific: this means that the only history of metaphysics consists in reflecting the individual historical emergences of class struggle. Its continuity and its discontinuities have to be filtered through the density of real movements. Metaphysics takes place through chronotopical units. When capital builds its politics as the rule of a class relationship, metaphysics suffers in consequence from both ends of the relationship: it is the forces in struggle that ascribe themselves the meaning of a metaphysical tradition and oppose it to another. Only within the concreteness of this relationship can we arrive at a reading of the political. One metaphysics, several metaphysics: their alternatives are the most concrete of historical objects – concrete because crammed with antagonism and possibility.

Machiavelli, Bodin, Botero, Boccalini, Bellarmino, Suarez, Calvino, Althusius, Junius Brutus, Campanella, Grotius, Barclay, Mun – all missing from the anthology... No, really, this will not do! The justifications for these omissions, which Tronti appends at the end of the first two volumes, are not acceptable, because this – the omission of other possible subjects of anthologising – is not the problem!

The thing is all the more infuriating as Tronti clearly grasps the real problem, not only in the Introduction but also in the planning of his anthology, quite obviously. Indeed, one part of the second volume is devoted to 'political practice'. The birth of the modern state is thus seen in the formation of its functions: the pages from Piazzi on functionaries and officials, and the following pages, also by Piazzi, and by Rizzardi, Tibruzzi and Segatori, on the great creators of the modern state (Charles V, James I, Richelieu, Cromwell), are emblematic in this regard – apart from often being very fine. Here the contradictions explode, they are visible, and history is almost as alive as metaphysics. But this concern with the concrete also ends up by not delivering: in the framework previously defined, it risks either pure juxtaposition or pure functionalisation, when it comes to elucidating the theory of politics. It is instead the metaphysical interweaving of theory and practice that, once again, reveals those antagonisms that are the engine of the overall process. This is because practice, as the pages just mentioned clearly show, is essentially a resolution of antagonisms – not neutral, not technical, but a solution always charged with bias and knowingly tendential. Thus structural practice cannot be separated from antagonistic practice. Of course, an accurate analysis of the practice of power, especially if carried out on the rhythms of its genesis, allows us to go beyond the level of *Ideengeschichte* [history of ideas], but remains stuck in the false alternative between functional historiography and institutional historiography (the final legacy of the mystifying bourgeois organisation of human sciences). Breaking this cage is important – and it is the same thing as regaining the full significance of the metaphysical horizon as the only one capable of 'simulating', within its chronotopic structures, the complexity of the relations between classes, of the meaning and significance of the specific conditions of domination that resolve those relations.

But, some will say, the incompleteness of the approach taken by Tronti and his colleagues does not negate the validity of the book's analytical segments. This is true; I am simply making the point that the (partly correct) objective is not matched in the execution. So let me now return to my subject, which – as we have seen – is that of grasping the internal dynamics of the organisation of power: the political, as a relationship between power and capital. But this definition is not sufficient for me. So I would ask a further question, adding specificity to the previous, insufficient definition. Is it possible to explain the relationship between power and capital as overdetermination and as a machine of social organisation for the extraction of surplus value? I believe so. And then – if we accept this definitional integration – the political is nothing other than the plot of the competing functions of social exploitation and subordination (hierarchy), within a given historical formation, in the reality of particular conflicts and antagonisms. Unless we take the complexity of this framework into account, the specificity of the mechanisms analysed does not become meaningful. Only when we grasp the maximum of abstraction in the metaphysical alternatives can our gaze extend to the point of identifying the tangle – of microphysics, of antagonisms, of variables – against which and on which the machine of power is formed. The autonomous specificity of its development implies possession of the horizon and of the coordinates of the relationship. The history of this autonomous specificity can be understood materialistically only by following through the determinations that lie between generalities and concrete determinations. To put it another way, the thing that most resembles power and the political is money. Could you imagine a history of money – and of its autonomous functioning – that does not include the relations of production, the proportions of reproduction, the dynamics of the forces of production? Since when does the structure of the Treasury explain how money works? Only the history of struggles can make the history of the general equivalent. By that token, metaphysics is the only science that, in the age of the bourgeoisie, during the period of accumulation, and thus down to the point where science develops into political economy (among the founders of market ideology, the continuity of metaphysics and economics is absolutely indestructible), offers an abstract and interchangeable terrain – a true currency [*moneta*] of pure intellect – where the complexity of social relations and the dimensions of relations of domination unfold. Metaphysics, as Schmitt would say, marks the essential determinants of power in the bourgeois age; where previously it would have been theology, today it is probably the critique of political economy and of administration. This is the only point I want to make.

Why? Because I do not believe in a theory – let alone a history – of the political that can be defined in linear terms. Because I am convinced that a class politics – in other words, what we need to build today – can come about only if it is totally innovatory in relation to the machine that bourgeois practice draws from its mythology and demands for its present as a necessary mystification. And, on the other hand, I believe that not even a metaphysics of the modern age granted it in full form. There is indeed a history of revolutionary uses of metaphysics, too. There is also an 'other' history of the political. Even without succumbing to the lures of Porshnev's school and to its framework of analysis, it is possible to grasp it in revolts, in insubordination and in the desire for liberation. But above all it is possible to grasp it through a close analysis of great metaphysics and of great writers. Machiavelli, first and foremost, if we limit ourselves to the authors studied in these two volumes. Earlier I cited Schmitt. Let me paraphrase another great reactionary author, Leo Strauss. If it is true that every self-respecting culture necessarily posits something one is absolutely forbidden to laugh at, it can be said that the will to transgress this prohibition is inbuilt in Machiavelli's intention. The metaphysics of transgression runs in the opposite direction of the metaphysics of obedience and of normative transcendence. The priestly figure of the political encounters resistance in the popular and active figure of insubordination, of insurrection, of constitution. If political thought formalises war – which pervades the articulations of classist society – as a fundamental problem, then peace, security, the machine constitute one of the solutions, and bourgeois politics is reduced to that. But the reality of politics is not exhausted in this operation. Another strand sees war as a fundamental and insurmountable condition: in that case the question is not to eliminate war, but rather to make it work without hurling oneself into massacre at the same time – to make it work against the relations of production and in favour of the forces of production and their liberated expansion. There is a constitutional politics that underpins the great revolutions of the eighteenth century and cannot be reduced to bourgeois politics, but announces the advent of class politics. Only by tracing the history of metaphysics, only by distinguishing real alternatives within it do we have the possibility of contributing to building, in antagonism, models for the re-establishment of a class politics. And – forgive me – certainly not only by doing historiography!

Bibliography

Adam, Antoine. 1935. *Théophile de Viau et la libre pensée française en 1620*. Lille: Giard/Geneva: Droz.

Adam, Antoine. 1948–56. *Histoire de la littérature française au XVII siècle*, 5 vols. Paris: Domat.

Adam, Antoine, ed. 1964. *Les Libertins au XVII siècle*. Paris: Gallimard.

Adams, Robert R. 1962. *The Better Part of Valor: More, Erasmus, Colet and Vives on Humanism, War and Peace, 1496–1535*. Seattle: University of Washington Press.

Agamben, Giorgio. 2013. *Opus Dei: An Archaeology of Duty*. Stanford, CA: Stanford University Press.

Albertini, Rudolf von. 1951. *Das politische Denken in Frankreich zur Zeit Richelieus*. Marburg: Simons.

Albertini, Rudolf von. 1955. *Das florentinische Staatsbewusstsein im Übergang von der Republik zum Prinzipat*. Bern: Francke Verlag.

Alliez, Éric. 2004. *The Signature of the World: What Is Deleuze and Guattari's Philosophy?* New York: Continuum.

Alquié, Ferdinand. 1950. *La Découverte métaphysique de l'homme chez Descartes*. Paris: PUF.

Andreas, Willy. 1958. *Kardinal Richelieu*. Göttingen: Muster-Schmidt.

Ansaldi, Saverio. 2001. *Spinoza et le Baroque*. Paris: Kimé.

Asor Rosa, Alberto. 1975. *Storia d'Italia: dall'Unità ad oggi*, vol. 2: *La cultura*. Turin: Einaudi.

Badaloni, Nicola. 1975. *Il marxismo di Gramsci*. Turin: Einaudi.

Baehrel, René. 1961. *Une croissance: la Basse-Provence rurale (fin XVIe siècle–1789): essay d'économie historique statistique*. Paris: SEVPEN.

Barrière, Pierre. 1961. *La Vie intellectuelle en France: du XVI siècle à l'époque contemporaine*. Paris: Albin Michel.

Bastide, Roger, ed. 1962. *Sens et usage du terme structure dans les sciences humaines et sociales*. The Hague: Mouton.

Battista, Anna Maria. 1964. *Alle origini del pensiero politico libertino: Montaigne e Charron*. Milan: Giuffrè.

Bénichou, Paul. 1948. *Morales du grand siècle*. Paris: Gallimard.

Berengo, Marino. 1965. *Nobili e mercanti nella Lucca del Cinquecento*. Turin: Einaudi.

Bergson, Henri. 1924 [1900]. *Le Rire: essai sur la signification du comique*, 23rd edn. Paris: Éditions Alcan.

Bieler, André. 1959. *La Pensée économique et sociale de Calvin*. Geneva: Librairie de l'Université.

Bieler, André. 1961. *L'Humanisme social de Calvin*. Geneva: Labor et Fides.

Biscione, Michele. 1962. *Neo-umanesimo e Rinascimento: l'immagine del Rinascimento nella storie della cultura dell'Ottocento*. Rome: Edizioni di Storia e Letteratura.

Bloch, Ernst. 1962. *Thomas Münzer als Theologe der Revolution*. Berlin: Bibliothek Suhrkamp.

Boas, Marie. 1962. *The Scientific Renaissance, 1450–1630*. New York: Harper & Brothers.

Boase, Alan M. 1935. *The Fortunes of Montaigne: A History of Essays in France, 1580–1669*. London: Methuen.

Bobbio, Norberto. 1967–8. 'Sulla nozione di "società civile"'. *De homine* 24–5: 12–36.

Bodei, Remo. 1975. 'Hegel e l'economia politica', in *Hegel e l'economia politica*, ed. S. Veca. Milan: Mazzotta, pp. 29–77.

Bologna, Sergio, George Philip Rawick, Mauro Gobbini, Antonio Negri, Luciano Ferrari Bravo and Ferruccio Gambino. 1972. *Operai e stato: lotte operaie e riforma dello stato capitalistico tra rivoluzione d'Ottobre e New Deal*. Milan: Feltrinelli.

Bonfantini, Mario. 1964. *La letteratura francese del XVII secolo: nuovi problemi ed orientamenti*, 2nd rev. edn. Naples: Edizioni Scientifiche Italiane.

Borkenau, Franz. 1934. *Der Übergang vom feudalen zum bürgerlichen Weltbild: Studien zur Geschichte der Philosophie der Manifakturperiode*, ed. Max Horkheimer. Paris: Félix Alcan.

Bove, Laurent. 1996. *La Stratégie du conatus: affirmation et résistance chez Spinoza*. Paris: Vrin.

Bove, Laurent. 1999. 'Le Réalisme ontologique de la durée chez Spinoza lecteur de Machiavel', in *La recta ratio*, ed. Laurent Bove. Paris: Presses de l'Université Paris-Sorbonne, pp. 47–64.

Braudel, Fernand. 1963. Review of Goubert 1960, in *Annales ESC* 18: 766–78.

Braudel, Fernand. 1996. *The Mediterranean and the Mediterranean World of the Mediterranean in the Age of Philip II*. Berkeley: University of California Press.

Brumfitt, J. H. 1958. *Voltaire Historian*. Oxford: Oxford University Press.

Brunschwig, Jacques. 1960. 'La Preuve ontologique interprétée par M. Guéroult'. *Revue philosophique de la France et de l'étranger* 150: 251–65.

Bütler, R. 1948. *Nationales und universales Denken im Werke Etienne Pasquiers*. Basel: Helbing Lichtenhahn Verlag.

Burckhardt, C. J. 1961. 'Der *honnête homme*, das Eliteproblem im 17. Jahrhundert', in C. J. Burckhardt, *Gestalten und Mächte*. Zurich: Manesse Verlag, pp. 339–70.

Busson, Henri. 1933. *La Pensée réligieuse française de Charron à Pascal*. Paris: Vrin.

Busson, Henri. 1948. *La Religion des classiques (1660–1685)*. Paris: PUF.

Cacciari, Massimo. 1970. Review of Negri 1970. *Contropiano* 2: 375–99.

Caillet, Jules. 1863. *L'Administration en France sous le ministère du Cardinal de Richelieu*, 2 vols. Paris: Didier.

Cantimori, Delio. 1959 [1955]. 'La periodizzazione dell'età del Rinascimento nella storia d'Italia e in quella d'Europa', in Delio Cantimori, *Studi di storia*. Turin: Einaudi, pp. 340–65.

Caprariis, Vittorio de. 1951. 'Libertinage et libertinismo'. *Letterature moderne* 2: 241–61.

Caprariis, Vittorio de. 1959. *Propaganda e pensiero politico in Francia*, vol. 1: *1559–1572*. Naples: Edizioni Scientifiche Italiane.

Caro, Gaspare de. 1970. *Salvemini*. Turin: UTET.

Carugo, Adriano. 1964. 'La nuova scienza: le origini della rivoluzione scientifica e dell'età moderna', in *Nuove questioni di storia moderna*, vol. 1. Milan: Marzorati, pp. 1–165.

Cassirer, Ernst. 1963. *Individuo e cosmo nella filosofia del Rinascimento*. Florence: La nuova Italia.

Centre National de Synthèse, ed. 1955. *Pierre Gassendi: sa vie et son oeuvre, 1592–1655*. Paris: Albin Michel.

Certeau, Michel de. 1986. 'Le Rire de Michel Foucault', *Le Débat* 4.41: 140–52. [Translated into Italian as 'Il riso di Michel Foucault', in Rovatti, P. A., ed. 1986. *Effetto Foucault*. Milan Feltrinelli, pp. 24–9.]

Chabod, Federico. 1956. 'Y-a-t-il un état de la Renaissance?', in *Actes du Colloque sur la Renaissance organisé par la Société d'histoire moderne, Sorbonne 30 juin–1er juillet 1956*. Paris: Vrin, pp. 57–78.

Charbonel, Roger. 1919. *La Pensée italienne au XVIe siècle et le courant libertin*. Paris: É. Champion.

Chaunu, Pierre. 1960. *La Conjoncture* (vol. 8.2 of *Séville et l'Atlantique*), vols 1–2. Paris: SEVPEN.

Chaui, Marilena. 1999. *O nervura do real: imanência e liberdade em Spinoza*. São Paulo: Companhia das Letras.

Cherel, Albert. 1935. 'Machiavel et notre XVIIe siècle', in Albert Cherel, *La Pensée de Machiavel en France*, 2nd edn. Paris: L'Artisan du livre, pp. 71–120.

Chesneau, Charles. 1946. *Le Père Yves de Paris et son temps (1590–1678)*, vols 1–2. Paris: Société d'histoire ecclésiastique de la France.

Chiereghin, F. 1961. *L'influenza dello spinozismo nella formazione della filosofia hegeliana*. Padua: Cedam.

Chomsky, Noam and Michel Foucault, 2011. *Human Nature: Justice versus Power: The Chomsky–Foucault Debate*, ed. with an Introduction by Fons Elders. London: Souvenir Press.

Church, William Farr. 1941. *Constitutional Thought in XVIth Century France: A Study in the Evolution of Ideas*. Cambridge, MA: Harvard University Press.

Clark, G. N. 1961. 'The social foundation of states', in *The New Cambridge Modern History*, vol. 5: *The Ascendancy of France, 1648–88*, ed. F. L. Carsten. Cambridge: Cambridge University Press, pp. 176–97.

Coldagelli, Umberto. 1969. 'Forza lavoro e sviluppo capitalistico: la discussione storiografica sui "prerequisiti" della rivoluzione industriale in Inghilterra'. *Contropiano* 1: 81–127.

Cognet, Louis. 1950. *La Réforme de Port-Royal*. Paris: Flammarion.

Cohen, Gustave. 1921. *Écrivains en Hollande dans la première moitié du XVIIe siècle*. The Hague: Nijhoff.

Cornell, Drucilla, Michel Rosenfeld and David Gray Carlson, eds. 1992. *Deconstruction and the Possibility of Justice*. New York: Routledge.

Crombie, A. C. 1952. *Augustine to Galileo*. London: Falcon Press.

Dagens, Jean. 1952a. *Berulle et les origines de la Restauration catholique*. Paris: Desclée de Brouwer.

Dagens, Jean. 1952b. 'Le machiavélisme de Pierre Charron', in *Studies aangeboden aan Gerard Brom*. Utrecht: Van de Vegt, pp. 56–64.

Del Lucchese, Filippo. 2004. *Tumulti e indignatio: conflitto, diritto e moltitudine in Machiavelli e Spinoza*. Milan: Ghibli.

Deleuze, Gilles. 1922. 'What is a *dispositif?*', in *Michel Foucault, Philosopher*, ed. Timothy J. Armstrong. Hemel Hempstead: Harvester Wheatsheaf, pp. 159–68.

Deleuze, Gilles. 1967. 'L'Éclat de rire de Nietzsche: interview with Guy Dumur', *Le Nouvel Observateur*, 5 April, pp. 40–1. [Translated into Italian as 'Lo scroscio di risa di Nietzsche', in Deleuze, Gilles. 1999. *Divenire molteplice: Nietzsche, Foucault ed altri intercessori*. Verona: Ombrecorte.]

Deleuze, Gilles. 1968. *Spinoza et le problème de l'expression*. Paris: Minuit.

Deleuze, Gilles. 1972. 'Sur capitalisme et schizophrénie'. *L'Arc* 49: 47–55.

Deleuze, Gilles. 1972 [1968]. Expression in Philosophy: Spinoza, trans. Martin Joughin, New York: Zone Books.

Deleuze, Gilles. 1981. *Spinoza: philosophie pratique*. Paris: Minuit.

Deleuze, Gilles. 1988a. *Bergsonism*, trans. Hugh Tomlinson and Barbara Habberjam. New York: Zone Books.

Deleuze, Gilles. 1988b. *Spinoza: Practical Philosophy*, trans. Robert Hurley. San Francisco, CA: City Lights Books.

Deleuze, Gilles. 1995. *Negotiations, 1972–1990*, trans. Martin Joughin. New York: Columbia University Press.

Deleuze, Gilles. 2001. *Pure Immanence: Essays on A Life*, trans. Anne Boyman. York: Zone Books.

Deleuze, Gilles. 2002. *L'Ile déserte et autres textes: textes et entretiens, 1953–1974*, ed. David Lapoujade. Paris: Minuit.

Deleuze, Gilles. 2004. *Desert Islands and Other Texts, 1953–1974*, ed. David Lapoujade, trans. Michael Taormina. Los Angles, CA: Semiotext(e).

Deleuze, Gilles. 2010. *Cosa può un corpo? Lezioni su Spinoza*, trans. A Pardi (from French). Verona: Ombre Corte. (See also the subdirectory 'On Spinoza' in 'Lectures by Gilles Deleuze' at http://deleuzelectures.blogspot.com/2007/02/on-spinoza.html.)

Deleuze, Gilles and Félix Guattari. 1982 [1977]. *Anti-Oedipus: Capitalism and Schizophrenia*, trans. Robert Hurley, Mark Seam and Helen R. Lane. New York: Viking Press.

Deleuze, Gilles and Félix Guattari. 1994. *What Is Philosophy?*, trans. Hugh Tomlinson and Graham Burchell. New York: Columbia University Press.

Deleuze, Gilles and Félix Guattari. 1999 [1972]. *L'anti-Œdipe: capitalisme et schizophrénie*. Paris: Minuit.

Deleuze, Gilles and Félix Guattari. 2004 [1980]. *A Thousand Plateaus: Capitalism and Schizophrenia*, trans. Brian Massumi. London: Continuum.

Derrida, Jacques. 1992. 'Force of law: The metaphysical foundation of authority', in *Deconstruction and the Possibility of Justice*, ed. Drucilla Cornell, Michel Rosenfeld and David Carlson. London: Routledge, pp. 3–67.

Derrida, Jacques. 1994. *Force de loi*. Paris: Galilée.

Diaz, Furio. 1958. *Voltaire storico*. Turin: Einaudi.

Dibon, Paul. 1954. *La Philosophie néerlandaise au siècle d'or*, vol. 1: *L'Enseignment philosophique dans les universités à l'époque precartesienne, 1575–1650*. Amsterdam: Elsevier.

Dickmann, F. 1963. 'Rechtsgedanke und Machtpolitik bei Richelieu: Studien an neu entdeckten Quellen'. *Historische Zeitschrift* 196: 265–319.

Diderot, Denis. 1961. *Le Rêve de D'Alembert*, ed. P. Vernière. Paris: Garnier.

Dobb, Maurice Herbert. 1946. *Studies on the Development of Capitalism*. London: Routledge.

Dobb, Maurice Herbert. 1958. *Problemi di storia del capitalismo*. Rome: Editori Riuniti.

Doucet, R. 1948. *Les Institutions de la France au XVIe siècle*. Paris: Picard.

Dumont, François. 1955. *Histoire du droit public: le déclin et le rétablissement de l'autorité royale au XVIe siècle*. Paris: Cours de droit.

Edelmann, Natan, ed. 1961. *A Critical Bibliography of French Literature*, vol. 3: *The Seventeenth Century* (general eds D. C. Cabeen and Jules Brody). Syracuse, NY: Syracuse University Press.

Erdmann, Johann Eduard. 1932 [1834]. *Versuch einer wissenschaftlichen Darstellung der Geschichte der neuern Philosophie*. Stuttgart: Faksimile-Neudruck.

Febvre, Lucien. 1951. 'De 1566 à 1660: la chaîne des hommes', in *Le Préclassicisme français*, ed. Jean Tortel. Marseille: Cahiers du Sud, opening article.

Febvre, Lucien. 1957a. *Au coeur religieux du XVIIe siècle*. Paris: Apostolat de la Presse.

Febvre, Lucien. 1957b. 'De l'à peu près à la précision en passant par oui-dire', in Lucien Febvre, *Au coeur religieux du XVIe siècle*. Paris: Apostolat de la Presse, pp. 293–300.

Febvre, Lucien. 1957c. 'Libertinisme, Naturalisme, Mécanisme', in Lucien Febvre, *Au coeur religieux du XVIe siècle*. Paris: Apostolat de la Presse, pp. 337–58.

Febvre, Lucien. 1957d. 'Le Tricentenaire de la mort de Descartes: un homme libre', in Lucien Febvre, *Au coeur religieux du XVIe siècle*. Paris: Apostolat de la Presse, pp. 310–20.

Febvre, Lucien. 1962a. 'Capitalisme et Réforme', in Lucien Febvre, *Pour une histoire à part entière*, Paris: SEVPEN, pp. 350–6.

Febvre, Lucien. 1962b. 'Fondations économiques, superstructure philosophique: une synthèse', in Lucien Febvre, *Pour une histoire à part entière*, Paris: SEVPEN, pp. 743–51.

Febvre, Lucien. 1962c. 'Le Marchand du XVIe siècle', in Lucien Febvre, *Pour une histoire à part entière*, Paris: SEVPEN, pp. 428–53.

Febvre, Lucien. 1962d. *Pour une histoire à part entière*. Paris: SEVPEN.

Febvre, Lucien. 1962e. *Le Problème de l'incroyance au XVIe siècle: la religion de Rabelais*. Paris: Albin Michel.

Ferguson, Wallace K. 1948. *The Renaissance in Historical Thought*. Boston, MA: Houghton Mifflin.

Feuerbach, Ludwig. 1906. 'Descartes', in Ludwig Feuerbach, *Geschichte der neueren Philosophie von Bacon von Verulam bis Benedikt Spinoza*', in vol. 3 of *Sämtliche Werke*, ed. F. Jodl. Stuttgart: Frommanns, pp. 108–246.

Firpo, Luigi. 1957. 'L'utopismo del Rinascimento e l'età nuova', in Luigi Firpo, *Lo stato ideale della Controriforma: Ludovico Agostini*. Bari: Laterza, pp. 241–61.

Fish, Stanley. 1999. *Doing What Comes Naturally: Change, Rhetoric and the Practice of Theory in Literary and Legal Study*. Durham, NC: Duke University Press.

Foucault, Michel. 2001. 'De la nature humaine: justice contre pouvoir', in Michel Foucault, *Dits et écrits*, vol. 1: *1954–1975*. Paris: Gallimard, pp. 1339–80. [In English as Chomsky and Foucault 2011.]

Franklin, Julian H. 1963. *Jean Bodin and the Sixteenth Century Revolution in the Methodology of Law and History*. New York: Columbia University Press.

Galileo Galilei. 1623. *Opere di Galileo Galilei*, part 3, vol. 15 [= Astronomy]: *Il Saggiatore*. Rome: Accademia dei Lincei. https://teca.bncf.firenze.sbn.it/ImageViewer/servlet/ImageViewer?idr=BNCF0003623344.

Galileo Galilei. 1968 [1890–1909]. *Le opere*, 20 vols, ed. A. Favaro. Florence: G. Barbèra.

Gallouédec-Genuys, Françoise. 1963. *Le Prince selon Fénelon*. Paris: PUF.

Geymonat, Ludovico. 1962. *Galileo Galilei*. Turin: Einaudi.

Gilbert, Neal W. 1960. *Renaissance Concepts of Method.* New York: Columbia University Press.

Goethe, Johann Wolfgang von. 1822. *Belagerung von Mainz.* Project Gutenberg. http://www.gutenberg.org/ebooks/17657.

Goethe, Johann Wolfgang von. 2003. *Faust,* Part II, trans. A. S. Kline. http://www.poetryintranslation.com/PITBR/German/FaustIIActIScenesItoVII.php.

Goldmann, Lucien. 1955. *Le Dieu caché: étude sur la vision tragique dans les Pensées de Pascal et dans le théatre de Racine.* Paris: Gallimard.

Goldmann, Lucien. 1964. 'La Méthode structuraliste génétique en histoire de la littérature', in Lucien Goldmann, *Pour une sociologie du roman.* Paris: Gallimard, pp. 211–29.

Goubert, Pierre. 1960. *Beauvais et le beauvaisis de 1600 à 1730.* Paris: SEVPEN.

Gouhier, Henri. 1954. 'La Preuve ontologique de Descartes'. *Revue internationale de Philosophie* 8: 295–303.

Gouhier, Henri. 1957. 'L'Ordre des raisons selon Descartes', in *Descartes,* ed. Cahiers de Royaumont. Paris: Minuit, pp. 72–87.

Gouhier, Henri. 1958. *Les premières pensées de Descartes: contribution à l'histoire de l'anti-renaissance.* Paris: Vrin.

Gregory, Tullio. 1961. *Scetticismo e empirismo: studio su Gassendi.* Bari: Laterza.

Groethuysen, Bernard. 1977. *Origines de l' espirit bourgeois en France,* vol. 1: *L'église et la bourgeoisie.* Paris: Gallimard.

Grossmann, H. K. 1929. *Das Akkumulations und Zusammenbruchsgesetz.* Leipzig: C. L. Hirschfeld 1929.

Grossmann, H. K. 1935. 'Die gesellschaftlichen Grundlagen der mechanistischen Philosophie und die Manifaktur'. *Zeitschrift für Sozialforschung* 2: 161–231.

Grossmann, H. K. 1971. *Aufsätze zur Krisentheorie.* Frankfurt-am-Main: Verlag Neue Kritik.

Guattari, Félix. 2008. *Chaosophy: Texts and Interviews, 1972–1977,* ed. Sylvère Lotringer, trans. David L. Sweet, Jarred Becker and Taylor Adkins. Los Angeles, CA: Semiotext(e).

Gueroult, Martial. 1953. *Descartes selon l'ordre des raisons.* Paris: Aubier.

Gueroult, Martial. 1955. *Nouvelles reflexions sur la preuve ontologique de Descartes.* Paris: Vrin,

Gueroult, Martial. 1957. 'La Vérité de la science et la vérité de la chose dans les preuves de l'existence de Dieu', in *Descartes,* ed. Cahiers de Royaumont. Paris: Minuit, pp. 108–20.

Gueroult, Martial. 1968, 1974. *Spinoza,* vol. 1: *Dieu;* vol. 2: *Éthique* II. Paris: Aubier-Montaigne.

Hagmann, Moritz. 1955. *Descartes in der Auffassung durch die Historiker der Philosophie. Zur Geschichte der neuzeitliche Philosophiegeschichte.* Winterthur, Zurich: Keller.

Hartung, F. 1949. L'État c'est moi'. *Historische Zeitschrift* 169: 1–30.

Hartung, H. and R. aMousnier. 1955. 'Quelques problèmes concernant la monarchie absolue', in *Relazioni del X Congresso internazionale di scienze storiche*. Florence: Sansoni, vol. 4, pp. 3–55.

Hassinger, Erich. 1952. 'Das politische Testament Richelieus'. *Historische Zeitschrift* 173 (3): 485–503.

Hauser, H. 1944. *La Pensée et l'action économique du Cardinal de Richelieu*. Paris: PUF.

Haydn, Hiram. 1950. *The Counter-Renaissance*. New York: Charles Scribner's Sons.

Hazard, Paul. 1935. *La Crise de la conscience européenne (1680–1715)*. Paris: Boivin.

Hegel, Georg Wilhelm Friedrich. 1962. *Scritti di filosofia del diritto, 1802–1803*, trans. Antonio Negri. Bari: Laterza.

Hegel, Georg Wilhelm Friedrich. 1965. *La filosofia del diritto*, trans. F. Messineo and A. Plebe. Bari: Laterza.

Hegel, Georg Wilhelm Friedrich. 1967a. *Philosophy of Right*, trans. T. M. Knox. London: Oxford University Press.

Hegel, Georg Wilhelm Friedrich. 1967b. *Phenomenology of Spirit*, trans. A. V. Miller. Oxford: Clarendon.

Hegel, Georg Wilhelm Friedrich. 1975. *Natural Law: The Scientific Ways of Treating Natural Law, Its Place in Moral Philosophy, and Its Relation to the Positive Sciences of Law*, trans. T. M. Knox. Philadelphia: University of Pennsylvania Press.

Hegel, Georg Wilhelm Friedrich. 1979a. *System of Ethical Life and First Philosophy of Spirit*, ed. and trans. H. S. Harris and Thomas M. Knox. Albany: SUNY Press.

Hegel, Georg Wilhelm Friedrich. 1979b. 'Über die wissenschaftlichen Behandlungsarten des Naturrechts: Seine Stelle in der praktsichen Philosophie und sein Verhältnis zu den positiven Rechtswissenschaft', in Georg Wilhelm Friedrich Hegel, *Werke*, vol. 2: *Jenaer Schriften, 1801–1807*. Frankfurt: Suhrkamp, pp. 434–53.

Hobsbawm, E. J. 1965. 'The crisis of the seventeenth century', in E. J. Hobsbawm, *Crisis in Europe, 1560–1660*. London: Routledge & Kegan Paul, pp. 5–58.

Horkheimer, Max. 1932. *Anfänge der bürgerlichen Geschichtsphilosophie*. Stuttgart: Kohlhammer.

Horkheimer, Max. 1974. *Theoria critica*, vol. 2: *Scritti 1932–1941*. Turin: Einaudi.

Horkheimer, Max. 2002. *Critical Theory: Selected Essays*. New York: Continuum.

Hubatsch, Walther. 1962. *Das Zeitalter des Absolutismus*. Brunschwick: Georg Westermann.

Huizinga, Johan. 1968. *Dutch Civilisation in the Seventeenth Century*. London: Collins.

Jacquet, Chantal. 2005. *Les Expressions de la puissance d'agir chez Spinoza*. Paris: Publications de la Sorbonne.

Jacquet, Chantal. 2017. *Spinoza à l'oeuvre*. Paris: Publication de la Sorbonne.

Joyce, James. 1993. *Ulysses*. Oxford: Oxford University Press.

Julien-Eymard d'Angers [Charles Chesneau]. 1951. 'Le Stoïcisme en France dans la première moitié du XVIIe siècle'. *Études Franciscaines* 2: 287–99, 389–410.

Just, Leo. 1961. 'Stufen und Formen des Absolutismus: Ein Blick'. *Historisches Jahrbuch* 80: 143–59.

King, James. 1949. *Science and Rationalism in the Government of Louis XIV, 1661–1683*. Baltimore, MD: Johns Hopkins University Press.

Kline, George Louis. 1952. *Spinoza in Soviet Philosophy*. London: Routledge and Kegan Paul.

Kocher, Paul Harold. 1953. *Science and Religion in Elizabethan England*. S. Marino, CA: Huntingdon Library.

Kossmann, Ernst H. 1954. *La Fronde*. Leiden: Brill.

Koyré, Alexandre. 1962. 'Entretiens sur Descartes', in Alexandre Koyré, *Introduction à la lecture de Platon*. Paris: Gallimard, pp. 163–229.

Kraus, Karl. 1957. 'Die absolute Monarchie und die Grundlegung des modernen Staats'. *Geschichte in Wissenschaft und Unterricht* 8: 257–71.

Kuhn, Thomas S. 1970. *The Structure of Scientific Revolutions: How the Ideas of Science Change*. Chicago, IL: University of Chicago Press.

Labrousse, Ernest C. 1955. 'Voies nouvelles vers une histoire de la bourgeoisie occidentale au XVIIIe et XIXe siècles', in *X Congresso internazionale di scienze storiche*. Florence: Sansoni, pp. 365–96.

Lafue, Pierre. 1946. *Le Père Joseph, capucin et diplomate*. Paris: Hachette.

Laporte, Jean Marie Frédéric. 1952. *La Doctrine de Port Royal*. Paris: Vrin.

Le Goff, Jacques. 1999. *Un autre Moyen Age*. Paris: Gallimard.

Lecler, Joseph. 1955. *Histoire de la tolérance au siècle de la Réforme*. Paris: Aubier.

G. Procacci, G. Lefebvre and A. Soboul. 1956. 'Observations', in 'Du féodalisme au capitalisme', *La Pensée* 65: 11–32.

Lenoble, Robert. 1943. *Mersenne ou la naissance du mécanisme*. Paris: Vrin.

Lenoble, Robert. 1957. 'Liberté cartésienne ou liberté sartrienne?', in *Descartes*, ed. Cahiers de Royaumont. Paris: Minuit, pp. 302–24.

Lenoble, Robert. 1958. 'La Révolution scientifique au XVIIe siècle', in *Histoire générale des sciences*, ed. René Taton, vol. 2. Paris: PUF, pp. 185–208.

Lopez, Robert S. 1953. 'Hard times and investment in culture', in *The Renaissance: A Symposium*, ed. Metropolitan Museum of Art. New York: Metropolitan Museum of Art, pp. 19–33.

Loyseau, Charles. 1610. *Cinq Livres du droit des offices, suivis du Livre des seigneuries et de celui des ordres*. Paris: Abel L'Angelier.

Lubasz, Heinz. 1964. *The Development of the Modern State*. New York: Macmillan.

Luporini, Cesare. 1974. *Dialettica e materialismo*. Rome: Editori Riuniti.

Macherey, Pierre. 1995. *Introduction à l'Éthique de Spinoza: la troisième partie: la vie affective*. Paris: PUF.

Macherey, Pierre. 1997a. *Introduction à l'Éthique de Spinoza: la première partie: la réalité mentale*. Paris: PUF.

Macherey, Pierre. 1997b. *Introduction à l'Éthique de Spinoza: la seconde partie: la condition humaine*. Paris: PUF.

Macpherson, Crawford B. 1962. *The Political Theory of Possessive Individualism: Hobbes to Locke*. Oxford: Clarendon.

Macpherson, Crawford B. 1973. *Libertà e proprietà alle origini del pensiero Borghese: La teoria dell'individualismo possessivo da Hobbes a Locke*. Milan: ISEDI.

Magendie, Maurice. 1925. *La Politesse mondaine et les théories de l'honnêteté en France au XVII siècle, de 1600 à 1660*. Paris: Félix Alcan.

Mandrou, Robert. 1959. 'Pour une histoire de la sensibilité'. *Annales ESC* 14 (3): 531–2.

Mandrou, Robert. 1961. *Introduction à la France moderne: essai de psychologie historique, 1500–1640*. Paris: Albain Michel.

Mandrou, Robert. 1965. *Classes et luttes de classes en France au début du XVIIe siècle*. Messina: G. D'Anna.

Mantoux, Paul. 1928. *La Révolution industrielle au XVIIIe siècle*. Paris: Génin.

Marcherey, Pierre. 1997. *Introduction à l'Éthique de Spinoza, deuxième partie*. Paris: PUF.

Marsak, Leonard, ed. 1964. *The Rise of Science in Relation to Society*. New York: Macmillan.

Marx, Karl. 1969a. *Il Capitale*. Florence: La Nuova Italia.

Marx, Karl. 1969b. *Teorie sul plusvalore*. Rome: Editori Riuniti.

Marx, Karl. 1973. *Grundrisse: Foundations of the Critique of Political Economy (Rough Draft)*, trans. Martin Nicolaus. Harmondsworth: Penguin Books.

Marx, Karl. 1976 [1873]. 'Results of the immediate process of production' [= 'Unpublished Chapter VI'], in *Capital*, vol. 1, trans. Ben Fowkes. Harmondsworth: Penguin and New Left Review, pp. 964–1084.

Marx, Karl. 1987. *Quaderno Spinoza 1841*, ed. Bruno Bongiovanni. Turin: Bollati Boringhieri.

Maspétiol, Roland. 1965. 'Les deux aspects de la "raison d'état" et son apologie au début du XVIIe siècle'. *Archives de Philosophie du Droit* 10, 1965: 209–20.

Mastellone, Salvo. 1962. *La reggenza di Maria de' Medici*. Messina: G. D'Anna.

Matheron, Alexandre. 1969. *Individu et communauté chez Spinoza*. Paris: Minuit.

Matheron, Alexandre. 2011. *Études sur Spinoza et les philosophes à l'âge classique*. Paris: ENS Éditions.

Mattingly, Garrett. 1959. 'Changing attitudes towards the state during the Renaissance', in *Facets of the Renaissance: The Arensberg Lectures*, ed.

W. H. Werkmeister. Los Angeles: University of Southern California Press, pp. 25–43.

Meinecke, Friedrich. 1924. *Die Idee der Staatsräson in der neueren Geschichte.* Munich: R. Oldenburg.

Mellon, Stanley. 1958. *The Political Uses of History: A Study of Historians in the French Restoration.* Stanford, CA: Stanford University Press.

Merleau-Ponty, Maurice. 1960. *Signes.* Paris: Gallimard.

Merton, Robert K. 1938. 'Science, technology and society in seventeenth century England'. *Osiris* 4: 360–632.

Mesnard, Pierre. 1952. *L'Essor de la politique au XVIe siècle.* Paris: Vrin.

Mollat, Michel. 1956. 'Y a-t-il une économie de la Renaissance?', in *Actes du colloque sur la Renaissance organisé par la Société d'histoire moderne, Sorbonne 30 juin–1er juillet 1956.* Paris: Vrin, pp. 37–54.

Mongrédien, Georges. 1948. *La Vie quotidienne sous Louis XIV,* 2nd edn. Paris: Librairie Hachette.

Montaigne, Michel de. n.d. *Essays.* Project Gutenberg. http://www.gutenberg.org/files/3600/3600-h/3600-h.htm.

Moreau, Pierre-François. 1994. *Spinoza: l'expérience et l'éternité.* Paris: PUF.

Mornet, Daniel. 1954. *Origines intellectuelles de la Révolution française.* Paris: Armand Colin.

Moszkowska, Natalie. 1974. *Per la critica delle teorie moderne della crisi.* Turin: Musolini.

Mounin, Georges. 1952. 'Cyrano de Bergerac et Pascal', in *Le Préclassicisme français,* ed. Jean Tortel. Marseille: Cahiers du Sud, pp. 69–78.

Mousnier, Roland. 1946. *La Vénalité des offices sous Henri IV et Louis XIII.* Rouen: Éditions Maugard.

Mousnier, Roland. 1955. 'L'Opposition politique bourgeoise à la fin du siècle et au début du XVIIe: l'oeuvre de Louis Turquet de Mayerne'. *Revue historique* 213: 1–20.

Mousnier, Roland. 1958. 'Recherches sur les soulèvements populaires en France avant la Fronde'. *Revue d'histoire moderne et contemporaine* 5: 81–113.

Mousnier, Roland. 1964. *L'Assassinat d'Henri IV: le tyrannicide et l'affermissement de la monarchie absolue.* Paris: Gallimard.

Mousnier, Roland. 1965. *Histoire générale des civilisations,* vol. 4: *Les XVIe et XVIIe siècles,* 4th rev. edn. Paris: PUF.

Näf, Werner. 1935. *Staat and Staatsgedanke: Vorträge zur neueren Geschichte.* Bern.

Näf, Werner. 1949. 'Herrschaftsbeträge und Lehre vom Herrschaftsvertrag'. *Schweizerische Beiträge zur allgemeinen Geschichte* 7: 26–41.

Namer, Gérard. 1964. *L'Abbé, le Roy et ses amis: essais sur le jansénisme extrémiste.* Paris: SEVPEN.

Nef, John U. 1957. *Industry and Government in France and England, 1540–1640.* Ithaca, NY: Cornell University Press.

Nef, John U. 1958. *Cultural Foundations of Industrial Civilisation*. Cambridge: Cambridge University Press.

Negri, Antonio. 1959. *Saggi sullo storicismo tedesco: Dilthey e Meinecke*. Milan: Feltrinelli.

Negri, Antonio. 1967. 'Problemi di storia dello stato moderno: Francia, 1610–1650'. *Rivista critica di storia della filosofia* 2: 182–220.

Negri, Antonio. 1970. *Descartes politico o della ragionevole ideologia*. Milan: Feltrinelli. [2nd edn 2007, Rome: Manifestolibri.]

Negri, Antonio. 1976. *Proletari e stato*. Milan: Feltrinelli.

Negri, Antonio. 1978. 'Manifattura e ideologia', in *Manifattura, società borghese, ideologia*, ed. Pierangelo Schiera. Rome: Savelli, pp. 139–57.

Negri, Antonio. 1981. *L'anomalia selvaggia: saggio su potere e potenza in Baruch Spinoza*. Milan: Feltrinelli.

Negri, Antonio. 1998. *Spinoza*. Rome: Derive Approdi.

Negri, Antonio. 2006a. *L'anomalia selvaggia: saggio su potere e potenza in Baruch Spinoza*, 2nd edn. Rome: Derive Approdi.

Negri, Antonio. 2006b. *Political Descartes: Reason, Ideology and the Bourgeois Project*, trans. Matteo Mandarini and Alberto Toscano. London: Verso.

Negri, Antonio. 2006c. 'Potenza e ontologia tra Heidegger e Spinoza'. Speech delivered to the Spinoza-Gesellschaft, Berlin, 30 September 2006.

Negri, Antonio. 2007. 'Giorgio Agamben: The discreet taste of the dialectic', in *Giorgio Agamben: Sovereignty and Life*, ed. Matthew Calarco. Palo Alto, CA: Stanford University Press, pp. 109–25.

Negri, Antonio. 2013. *Time for Revolution*, trans. Matteo Mandarini. London: Bloomsbury Academic.

Orcibal, Jean. 1948. *Les Origines du Jansénisme*, 3 vols. Paris: Vrin.

Orcibal, Jean. 1951. *Louis XIV et les protestants*. Paris: Vrin.

Orcibal, Jean. 1957. *Port-Royal entre le miracle et l'obéissance*. Paris: Desclée de Brouwer.

Pagès, Georges. 1928. *La Monarchie d'Ancien Régime en France*. Paris: Armand Colin.

Pagès, Georges. 1949. *La Guerre de trente ans, 1618–1648*. Paris: Payot.

Pagès, Georges, with Victor-Lucien Tapié. 1948. *Naissance du Grand Siècle: La France d'Henri IV à Louis XIV (1389–1661)*. Paris: Hachette.

Palm, F. C. 1942. 'The rise of French absolutism', in *Annual Report of the American Historical Association*, vol. 3, pp. 287–96.

Pascal, Blaise. 1958. *Pensées*, with an Introduction by T. S. Eliot. New York: E. P. Dutton.

Perniola, Mario. 1998. *Philosophia sexualis: scritti su Georges Bataille*. Verona: Ombrecorte.

Picot, Gilbert. *Cardin Le Bret (1558–1655) et la doctrine de la souveraineté*. Nancy: Société d'impressions typographiques.

Pintard, René. 1943. *Le Libertinage érudit dans la première moitié du XVII siècle*, 2 vols. Paris: Boivin & Cie.

Popkin, Richard H. 1964. *The History of Scepticism from Erasmus to Descartes*. New York: Humanities Press.

Porshnev, Boris. 1963. *Les Soulèvements populaires en France de 1623 à 1648*. Paris: Flammarion.

Préclin, Edmond and Eugène Jarry. 1955–6. *Les Luttes politiques et doctrinales au XVIIe et XVIIIe siècles*. Paris: PUF.

Prestwich, Menna. 1957. 'The making of absolute monarchy, 1559–1683', in *France: Government and Society*, ed. J. M. Wallace-Hadrill and J. MacManners. London: Methuen, pp. 105–33.

Randall Jr, John Herman. 1961. *The School of Padua and the Emergence of Modern Science*. Padua: Editore Antenore.

Raumer, Kurt von. 1947. *König Heinrich IV*. Iserloh: Silva.

Raumer, Kurt von. 1953. 'Zur Problematik des werdenen Macht Staates'. *Historische Zeitschrift* 174: 71–80.

Rawls, John. 1999. *A Theory of Justice*. Oxford: Oxford University Press.

Reinhard, Marcel. 1936. *La Légende d'Henri IV*. Paris: Hachette.

Richelieu, cardinal de. 1947. *Téstament politique*, ed. Léon André. Paris: Robert Lafont.

Ricoeur, Paul. 1988. 'Le Cercle de la démonstration'. *Esprit* 2: 78–88.

Il Rinascimento: significato e limiti: atti del III convegno internazionale sul Rinascimento. 1953. Florence: Sansoni.

Rochot, Bernard. 1961. 'La preuve ontologique interprétée par M. Gueroult (Réponse aux "objections" de M. Jacques Brunschwig)'. *Revue philosophique de France et de l'étranger* 151: 125–30.

Romano, Ruggiero. 1962. 'Tra XVI e XVII secolo: una crisi economica: 1619–1622'. *Rivista storica italiana* 74: 480–531.

Rosdolsky, Roman. 1971. *Genesi e struttura del 'Capitale' di Marx*. Bari: Laterza.

Rubin, Isaac I. 1972 [1928]. *Essays on Marx's Theory of Value*. Detroit, MI: Black and Red.

Rubin, Isaac I. 1976. *Saggi sulla teoria del valore di Marx*. Milan: Feltrinelli.

Saitta, Armando. 1951. 'Un riformatore pacifista contemporaneo di Richelieu: Eméric Crucé'. *Rivista storica italiana* 63: 180–215.

Sandel, Michael. 1982. *Liberalism and the Limits of Justice*. Cambridge: Cambridge University Press.

Sapori, Armando. 1953. 'Il problema economico', in *Il Rinascimento: significato e limiti: Atti del terzo convegno internazionale*. Florence: Sansoni, pp. 107–46.

Sartre, Jean-Paul. 1947. 'La Liberté cartésienne', in Jean-Paul Sartre, *Situations*, vol. 5.1. Paris: Gallimard, pp. 314–35.

Saunders, J. L. 1955. *Justus Lipsius: The Philosophy of Renaissance Stoicism*. New York: Liberal Arts Press.

Schmidt, Alfred 1972. *Geschichte und Struktur: Fragen einer marxistischen Historik*. Munich: Hanser Verlag.

Sebba, Gregor. 1964. *Bibliographia Cartesiana: A Critical Guide to the Descartes Literature, 1800–1960*. The Hague: Martin Nijhoff.

Sestan, Ernesto. *Il secolo di Luigi XIV*. Turin: Einaudi.

Severac, Pascal. 2011. *Spinoza*. Paris: Vrin.

Sharp, Hasana. 2011. *Spinoza and the Politics of Renaturalization*. Chicago, IL: University of Chicago Press.

Skalweit, Stephan. 1951. 'Richelieus Staatsidee'. *Geschichte in Wissenschaft und Unterricht* 2: 719–30.

Skalweit, Stephan. 1957. 'Der Herrscherbild des 17. Jahrhunderts'. *Historische Zeitschrift* 184: 65–80.

Skalweit, Stephan. 1961. 'Das Zeitalter des Absolutismus als Forschungsproblem'. *Deutsche Vierteljahrschrift* 35 (2): 298–315.

Sohn-Rethel, Alfred. 1976. 'Das Geld, die bare Münze des Apriori', in *Beiträge zur Kritik des Geldes*, ed. Paul Mattick, Alfred Sohn-Rethel and Hellmut G. Haasis. Frankfurt: Suhrkamp, pp. 35–117.

Souleymann, E. V. 1941. *The Vision of World Peace in Seventeenth and Eighteenth-Century France*. New York: G. P. Putnam's Sons.

Spink, J. S. 1960. *French Free-Thought* [sic] *from Gassendi to Voltaire*. London: Athlone.

Spinoza, Benedictus de. 1928. *The Correspondence of Spinoza*, ed. with introduction and trans. A. Wolf. London: George Allen & Unwin.

Spinoza, Benedictus de. 1951. *Epistolario*, ed. A. Droetto. Turin: Einaudi.

Spinoza, Benedictus de. 1985–2016. *The Collected Works of Spinoza*, ed. and trans. Edwin Curley. Princeton, NJ: Princeton University Press.

Spinoza, Benedictus de. 1985. *The Ethics*, ed. and trans. Edwin Curley, vol. 1 of *The Collected Works of Spinoza*. Princeton, NJ: Princeton University Press.

Spinoza, Benedictus de. 1988. *Etica dimostrata con metodo geometrico*, trans. Emilia Giancotti. Roma: Editori Riuniti.

Spinoza, Benedictus de. 2002. Letter to Jarig Jelles of June 2, 1674, in idem, *Complete Works*, ed. Michael L. Morgan, trans. Samuel Shirley. Indianapolis, IN: Hackett Publishing, pp. 891–2 (= Letter 50).

Spinoza, Benedictus de. 2016a. *Tractatus politicus*, ed. and trans. Edwin Curley, vol. 2 of *The Collected Works of Spinoza*. Princeton, NJ: Princeton University Press.

Spinoza, Benedictus de. 2016b. *Tractatus theologico-politicus*, ed. and trans. Edwin Curley, vol. 2 of *The Collected Works of Spinoza*. Princeton, NJ: Princeton University Press.

Sutcliffe, F.-E. 1959. *Guez de Balzac et son temps: littérature et politique*. Paris: A. G. Nizet.

Sweezy, P. M. 1947. *La teoria dello sviluppo capitalistico*. Turin: Einaudi.

Sweezy, P. M. 1951. *The Theory of Capitalist Development*. London: Dobson.

Taylor, Charles. 1989. *The Sources of the Self: The Making of Modern Identity*. Cambridge, MA: Harvard University Press.

Tenenti, Alberto. 1962. 'Il libero pensiero francese del Seicento e la nascita dell'*homme machine*'. *Rivista storica italiana* 74: 561–70.

Tenenti, Alberto. 1963. 'Milieu XVIe siècle, début XVIIe siècle: libertinisme et hérésie'. *Annales ESC* 18 (1): 1–19.

Thalheimer, A. 1928. 'Die Klassenverhaltnisse und die Klassenkampfe in den Niederlanden zur Zeit Spinozas', in A. Thalheimer and A. Deborin, *Spinozas Stellung in der Vorgeschichte des dialektischen Malerialismus*. Vienna: Verlag für Literatur und Politik, pp. 9–40. http://www.mxks.de/files/klasse/Thalheimer.KlassenverhSpinoza.html.

Thierry, Augustin. 1856. *Essai sur l'histoire de la formation et des progrès du Tiers État*, 3rd edn. Paris: Furne et Ce.

Thompson, E. P. 1968. *The Making of the English Working Class*. London: Penguin.

Toadvine, Ted and Leonard Lawlor, eds. 2007. *The Merleau-Ponty Reader*. Evanston, IL: Northwestern University Press.

Tortel, Jean, ed. 1952. *Le Préclassicisme français*. Marseille: Cahiers du Sud.

Trevor-Roper, H. R. 1965. 'The General Crisis of the Seventeenth Century', in E. J. Hobsbawm, *Crisis in Europe, 1560–1660*. London: Routledge & Kegan Paul, pp. 59–85.

Tronti, Mario. 1966. *Operai e capitale*. Turin: Einaudi.

Tronti, Mario. 1979. *Il Politico: da Machiavelli a Cromwell*. Milan: Feltrinelli.

Unger, Roberto Mangabeira. 1983. 'The Critical Legal Studies Movement'. *Harvard Law Review* 96 (3): 561–675.

Van Gelder, Enno. 1961. *The Two Reformations in the Sixteenth Century: A Study of Religious Aspects and Consequences of Renaissance and Humanism*. The Hague: Martinus Nijhoff.

Vartanian, Aram. 1953. *Diderot and Descartes: A Study of Scientific Naturalism in the Enlightenment*. Princeton, NJ: Princeton University Press.

Vénard, Marc. 1957. *Bourgeois et paysans au XVIIe siècle: recherche sur le rôle des bourgeois parisiens dans la vie agricole au Sud de Paris au XVIIe siècle*. Paris: SEVPEN.

Vernière, Paul. 1954. *Spinoza et la pensée française avant la Révolution*. Paris: PUF.

Vicens Vives, Jaime. 1960. 'Estructura administrativa estatal en los siglos XVI y XVII', in *Congrès international des sciences historiques*, vol. 4: *Rapports*, pp. 1–24.

Vivanti, Corrado. 1963. *Lotta politica e pace religiosa: Francia fra Cinque e Seicento*. Turin: Einaudi.

Vivanti, Corrado. 1964. 'Le rivolte popolari in Francia prima della Fronda e la crisis del XVII secolo'. *Rivista storica italiana* 76: 957–81.

Wahl, Jean. 1953. *Du rôle de l'idée de l'instant dans la philosophie de Descartes*. Paris: Vrin.

Walzer, Michael. 1981. 'Philosophy and Democracy'. *Political Theory* 9: 379–99.

Weise, Georg. 1961. 'Il duplice concetto di Rinascimento', in Georg Weise, *L'ideale eroico del Rinascimento e le sue premesse umanistiche*. Naples: Edizioni Scientifiche Italiane, pp. 1–78.

Weise, Georg. 1965. *L'ideale eroico del Rinascimento: diffusione europea e tramonto*. Naples: Edizioni Scientifiche Italiane.

Wesel-Roth, Ruth. 1954. *Thomas Erastus: Beitrag zur Geschichte der reformierten Kirche und zur Lehre von der Staatssouveränität*. Lahr-Baden: Moritz Schauenberg.

Willaert, L. 1960. *Après le concile de Trente: la restauration catholique, 1648*, vol. 18 of *L'Histoire de l'Eglise*, ed. A. Fliche and V. Martin. Paris: Bloud et Gay.

Wittgenstein, Ludwig. 1958. *Philosophical Investigations: An Introduction*, trans. G. E. M. Anscombe, 2nd edn. Oxford: Basil Blackwell.

Wittgenstein, Ludwig. 2001 [1974]. *Tractatus logico-philosophicus*, trans. D. F. Pears and B. F. McGuinness. London: Routledge.

Yates, Frances A. 1947. 'Queen Elizabeth as Astraea'. *Journal of the Warburg and Courtauld Institutes* 10: 27–82.

Yates, Frances A. 1960. 'Charles Quint et l'idée d'empire', in *Fêtes et cérémonies au temps de Charles Quint*, ed. J. Jacquot. Paris: CNRS, pp. 57–97.

Yates, Frances A. 1964. *Giordano Bruno and the Hermetic Tradition*. Chicago, IL: University of Chicago Press.

Zambelli, P. 1965. 'Rinnovamento umanistico, progresso technologico e teorie filosofiche alle origini della rivoluzione scientifica'. *Studi storici* 3: 507–47.

Zapperi, R. 1974. *Per la critica del concetto di rivoluzione borghese*. Bari: De Donato.

Zourabichvili, François. 2006. 'L'enigma della moltitudine libera'. *Quaderni Materialisti* 5: 105–20.